Ain't I a Feminist?

Ain't I a Feminist?

African American Men Speak Out on Fatherhood, Friendship, Forgiveness, and Freedom

Aaronette M. White

State University of New York Press

Published by
State University of New York Press, Albany

For information, contact State University of New York Press, Albany, NY
www.sunypress.edu

Production by Ryan Morris
Marketing by Anne M. Valentine

This book was printed on acid-free, 50% recycled paper.

Library of Congress Cataloging-in-Publication Data

White, Aaronette M.
    Ain't I a feminist? : African American men speak out on fatherhood,
friendship, forgiveness, and freedom / Aaronette M. White
        p. cm.
    Includes bibliographical references and index.
    ISBN 978-0-7914-7567-6 (hardcover : alk. paper)—
    ISBN 978-0-7914-7568-3 (pbk. : alk. paper)
    1. African American men—Psychology. 2. African American men—
Attitudes. 3. Male feminists—United States. I. Title.

E185.86.W438689 2008
305.38′896073—dc22

                                                                    2007044487

10 9 8 7 6 5 4 3 2 1

CONTENTS

TABLES

PREFACE

Can Black Men Be Feminists? From Healthy Doubt to Critical Acceptance

Scholarly research is not objective; it contains value judgments grounded in the researcher's own ethical and political commitments, whether the researcher admits these inevitable biases or not. Scholars' perspectives also seep into the research process, regardless of which scientific methods and procedures are used to minimize such influences.[1] Therefore, critical social scientists have grown to consider the researcher's values and biases as an integral part of the research process and recommend that such biases be outlined and analyzed, along with the biases of those being studied.[2] Why? Because the researcher's position and the relationship between the researcher and the research participants shape how people's lives are interpreted. Thus, in addition to understanding the particular circumstances of the men I have studied in *Ain't I a Feminist*, it is equally important for me to tell you, the reader, who I am and what my relationship is to the topic and men whose lives I interpret.

Most women have been socialized to applaud the efforts of men, even if those men's efforts on behalf of women are patronizing, superficial, and short-lived. African American women, in particular, have been taught to show public, uncritical support for African American men in order to counter divide-and-conquer strategies that thwart the collective fight against racism. However, as an African American woman (currently heterosexually identified, child-free, veteran of two marriages and several other relationships) and feminist psychologist, I began this project with a healthy dose of skepticism about the sincerity of men's involvement in feminism.

My skepticism left me unprepared for the deeply moving quality of the participants' narratives. Their levels of self-disclosure, honesty about their earlier lives, and candor regarding their ongoing struggles to unlearn sexist behaviors and resist patriarchal institutions changed my attitude. I had participated in sometimes heated debates over whether any man, regardless of his actions or attitudes, could rightly be called a feminist, so the change in my own attitude unnerved me at first.

Clearly, men benefit from the power imbalance between the genders that I refer to interchangeably in this book as patriarchy, sexism, and male supremacy. When one looks at the differences between men and women in wages and career prospects; the devaluation of women's ideas and positions in a wide range of institutional settings, including leadership positions in organized religion, the political sphere, and the workplace in general; the ongoing feminization of poverty in the United States; and violence against women (rape, battering, and sexual harassment), it's obvious that men have privileges in this society that translate into disproportionate power and advantage. Such facts notwithstanding, men are also hurt and dehumanized by patriarchy, although not to the same degree as women. Several of the men presented here have been raped, beaten, and humiliated, mainly by men, but a few also by women. Others have been ostracized because of their feminist beliefs and practices. Many have felt like voices in the wilderness, in the company of both men and women.

The narratives of these men made me laugh, cry, frown, smile, scream, sigh, and (I believe) grow. After reviewing and analyzing their stories, I am convinced that some men can appropriately be called feminists because they are committed to correcting, through public *and* private actions, the imbalance of power between men and women that is built into the structures of American society. As a perspective, feminism can be accepted or rejected by anyone, male or female.[3] In my analysis, if one actively accepts that perspective in belief and practice, one is a feminist.

Perhaps my initial reluctance to call men "feminists" came from encounters in the academic world with self-proclaimed feminist men who were arrogant and intellectually abusive to women. Some use their public speaking skills, "book" knowledge of women's experiences, and access to power to show off. I have seen these men put women down during public debates and classroom discussions, where many women are still trying to find their voice. Such men have an intellectual awareness of gender issues, but lack the emotional maturity, humble disposition, and interpersonal skills characteristic of men who truly understand and respect women. Seasoned feminist men tend to be good listeners and engage in ongoing self-analysis regarding their interactions with women. By contrast, some men use the terms "antisexist," "profeminist," and "feminist" to bolster their own power and manipulate women. These men and their behavior should be confronted and challenged. Feminist men, too, must grapple with their contradictions and change their behavior when they are "called" on it. In that respect they do not differ from feminist women.

However the men in this book choose to label themselves, they are all engaged in some form of feminist activism. In my experience of feminist organizing with women and men, I have found that it matters less what people call themselves and more what they actually *do*. Nonetheless, for those who have earned the right to use the feminist label, I support them in their choice to identify themselves as such.

Feminist research that explores the lived experiences of others approaches the researched not as objects to do research on but as participants in dialogue.[4] May the dialogue continue and may you, the reader, become its next fully engaged participant.

ACKNOWLEDGMENTS

Many people supported and encouraged me throughout the process of conducting this research and writing this book. My first mentor and cofounder of the Association of Black Psychologists, Dr. Robert L. Williams, taught me to research, with confidence, the positive creative survival techniques of African Americans during my graduate school years at Washington University in St. Louis, Missouri. Thank you, "Dr. Bob."

I am extremely grateful to Dr. John L. Henderson, former president of Wilberforce University, who initially awarded me a Presidential Scholar-in-Residence Grant. My two years at Wilberforce also resulted in a Henry McBay Faculty Fellowship from the United Negro College Fund. I will never forget my humble beginnings and the faith of these two historically Black institutions that dared to envision with me the possibility of finding Black men who identified as feminists. I also thank Theresa Henderson, artist, scholar, and wife of John L. Henderson. Theresa read early drafts of the book while auditing a research course I taught at Wilberforce on content analysis. Together, John and Theresa became family and sustained me throughout the difficult early years of the project.

I deeply appreciate the administrative release time Vice-President Emeka Morah gave me when I needed to travel to conduct the interviews, and his patience when I occasionally forgot that I was serving as both administrator *and* residential scholar at Wilberforce. Dynamic Wilberforce students who served as my first group of research assistants included Monica Badgett, Rahsaan Burnley, Lolade Folarin, Monet Garrette, Tova Jordan, Carmen Mason, the Reverend Floyd Narcisse, Jenelle Thomas, Shafran Stanley, Vito Powell, and Latosha McKay.

The second phase of this research was funded by the Aldon B. Dow Creativity Center in Midland, Michigan, housed at Northwood University. A summer research fellowship provided me with room and board, a stipend, a bicycle, the camaraderie of other scholars and artists, and ongoing collegial relationships with the director of the center, Dr. Grover B. Proctor; Academic Vice-President Dr. Robert W. Serum; and the former president of Northwood University, Dr. David E. Fry. These three administrators convinced me that White, American middle-class men could also relate to the redemptive stories of Black men's struggles to redefine manhood using feminist principles. Their warmth and enthusiasm about the book renewed mine during a difficult period.

The fourth phase of this project was funded by a Du Bois Institute Fellowship at Harvard University. Heartfelt thanks to Professor Henry (Skip) Louis Gates, Jr., Professor William Julius Wilson, Dr. Florence Ladd, and feminist mentor and Professor Jane (Jenny) Mansbridge for taking a special interest in my work and professional development. Warm thanks to Dr. Jon Lief and his wife Mary Lawlor and Dr. Christina Brinkley for providing me with rent-free housing during this period.

The final phase of this project could not have been carried out without the help of research assistants at Pennsylvania State University's African American Studies and Women's Studies Departments: Hasan Amenra, Sean Bell, Kristin Lundy, Saadiqa Lundy, Gobitsa Mmereki, and Keri-Ann Tavares. I especially thank Penn State's "Sistahs Facing Mount Tenure" members (Lovalerie King, Robyn Spencer, Cassandra Veney, and Courtney Young) for supporting me during the anxiety-provoking search for a book contract, and members of the "People Who Need to Write" group for encouraging me during the final revisions of the manuscript. Professor James Stewart read earlier excerpts that were later published in scholarly journals. Roger Files, one of Penn State's computer specialists, recovered everything on my hard drive when I carelessly spilled a cup of tea on my laptop. He shared his own experiences as a nontraditional man after reading parts of the manuscript during the computer recovery process. Although I was in shock and could barely speak above a whisper, he was kind and reinforced my belief that White men who were not academics could also relate to Black men's stories.

Invited guest lectures by Professor Stephanie Shields at Penn State University, Professor Joyce Williams at Texas Women's University, and Vice-President Janice Haynie at the State University of New York (Old Westbury) helped me refine my arguments during the writing of the manuscript. Three chapters of this book are revised versions of previously published works. Chapter 4 appeared as "African American Feminist Masculinities: Personal Narratives of Redemption, Contamination, and Peak Turning Points," *Journal of Humanistic Psychology* 46(3): 255–280; chapter 6 appeared as " 'You've got a friend':

African American Men's Cross-Sex Feminist Friendships and Their Influence on Perceptions of Masculinity and Women," *Journal of Social and Personal Relationships* 23(4): 523–542; and chapter 8 appeared as "African American Feminist Fathers' Narratives of Parenting." *Journal of Black Psychology* 32(1): 43–71. All reproduced with permission from Sage Publications. Copyright © Sage Publications 2006. Haiku #99 by Kalamu ya Salaam is reprinted here with permission from the author.

Hugs and thanks to my growing inner circle of friends across several cities: "Sister Jayne," Cheryl Potgieter, Louistine Tuck, Cheryl Mason, Wendy Dunning Carter, Ann Shields, Marian Dornell, Dee Frisque, Lee Blount Jr., Enoch Page, Gary Lemons, Naomi Ward, Aishah Simmons, Sandra Morgen, Gabeba Baderoon, Aida Hurtado, and Vernis Welmon. They kept reminding me that I was brave and loved.

For being the "wind beneath my wings," I thank my parents, Earline and Aaron White; my sisters Angela, Lisa, Anitra, and Ruby; confidants Twana Cooks-Allen, John Henckmen, Dennis Heitzmann, and Alycia Chambers; and soul mates William M. Harvey and Jacqueline Lapidus. Jacqueline Lapidus read and edited all previous drafts of the book while offering feminist camaraderie and Jewish humor when I often wondered, "Whose bright idea was this?"

A profound thank you to my interviewer, colleague, and friend William Dotson; the fifty men who participated in the mail survey phase; and all twenty of the men who shared their time and life stories during the interview phase of the project. Without the efforts of all of you, the book would never have been written.

INTRODUCTION

The Patriarchal Predicament

Rural and suburban male schoolyard shooters, urban gangbangers, laid-off post office gunmen, armed men in militia groups, "bad boys" in professional sports, deadbeat dads, "endangered" Black[1] men, and angry White men have led journalists, educators, community leaders, politicians, the clergy, and social scientists to declare that boys and men in the United States are undergoing a "masculinity crisis."[2] "Men behaving badly" have been glorified in the news and on televised situation comedies; while men who have a conscience, seek nonviolent alternatives to conflict, and prioritize the needs of women and children are discounted as "girly men."[3]

Defining men's predicament as a "masculinity crisis" implies that there was once a golden time of unproblematic, stable gender relations, when men were men, women were women, and all were happy with their designated social roles. That is only a myth. In reality, we need to replace "the way we were" with facts about "the way we *never* were, and *still* are," according to some gender theorists.[4] If men seriously want to reexamine what it means to be a man in the twenty-first century, they will have to question patriarchal practices of masculinity and understand that claims to male superiority are associated with contradiction, conflict, confusion, and, in many cases, extreme anxiety.[5]

Masculinity (and its various representations) is not simply a matter of personality, requiring only that men change their personal characteristics and individually acquired social roles. Rather, masculinity also rests on *assumptions and practices of power*—particularly the *patriarchal* power of men—that interact with other systems of power.[6] In addition to patriarchy, power systems based on racial, economic, and sexual classifications reinforce dehumanizing concepts and practices of masculinity. I argue that men and women must challenge how those power systems interact in order for meaningful change to occur.

There has always been a "masculinity crisis" of sorts among most African American men due, for the most part, to the combined effects of racial and economic inequalities that have consistently limited their access to privileges bestowed upon the average White man. However, rather than address the destructive consequences of inequalities *between* men—the vicious ways that men compare themselves and compete *with each other* and the debilitating assumption that men *should* be the dominant sex—media outlets prefer to sensationalize the problems of boys and men as "the war between the sexes," blaming feminism and the growing success of girls and women.[7] Other news reports and books lead readers to believe that single Black mothers and their evil twin sisters—unsympathetic, high-achieving single professional Black women—are mostly to blame for Black men's alarming rates of physical and mental health problems, homicide, unemployment, underemployment, substance abuse, and imprisonment—despite scientific evidence to the contrary.[8] Again, blaming Black women—whether they are the mothers, lovers, or even the daughters of Black men—diverts attention from the key problem: patriarchal assumptions and practices regarding masculinity that are built into our social institutions also shape our interpersonal relationships and our identities.[9]

Though most African American men do not experience the same level of power as most White American men, patriarchy produces pecking orders across different groups of men and within different subgroups of men.[10] Each subgroup of men defines manhood in ways that conform to the economic and social possibilities of that group. However, even marginalized men (e.g., poor men of color) accept the system because they benefit from the "patriarchal dividend," which is the advantage men in general gain from the overall subordination of women, particularly the women in their subgroup.[11] This book makes clear that this explanation does not excuse African American men for abusing the meager patriarchal power they have. Mere sympathy does not encourage them to question the underlying dynamics of patriarchal power in general. A middle-class Black man usually has more opportunities to impose his will on other Black men than does a working-class one, for example, and a heterosexual Black man is more likely to be accepted than a bisexual, gay, or transgendered Black man.

This book addresses important differences *among* Black men as well as differences between men and women within and outside African American communities. Specifically, I emphasize how the contradictory experiences of power among men can lead them to question patriarchy and ultimately embrace feminism.

Despite various differences of power among African American men, most know—all too well—that it is painful, frustrating, and demoralizing to try to fulfill popular notions of manhood, which are unrealistic, unattainable, and even life-threatening. As a result, Black men have had considerable practice at revising and redefining it.[12] Although books about "the endangered Black male" and how to save him are flooding the markets, few recognize his potential for leadership. In fact, Black men's experiences place them in a unique position to take the lead during this time of gender reexamination and social awakening. Events like the Million Man March, community manhood training and Black male rite-of-passage interventions, role modeling and mentoring programs, and proposals for "Black male only" schools are seeking to challenge the popular image of Black men as violent, criminal, unemployed, illiterate, and imprisoned. These well-intentioned efforts "to save the Black male" do not go far enough in detailing how popularly accepted definitions of manhood are ultimately destructive to *all* men. Rather than creating a new understanding of "manhood," most men—including many sincere Black men—are simply reforming, reviving, and repackaging old notions. Thus, the term "masculinity crisis" becomes a rationalization for renewed efforts at maintaining men's dominant roles, particularly their sense of entitlement through personal atonement and other self-help rituals of empowerment. It is a mistake to think that African American men's issues can be resolved without addressing the institutional mechanisms that continue to undermine attempts at individual reform.

Missing from the current debate and interventions are the stories and practices of Black men who have radically redefined manhood, and who attempt to resolve their issues around masculinity through a feminist approach to relationships and social justice. *Ain't I a Feminist* is the first book to include primary research—psychological interview data—addressing these oversights and presenting actual efforts of Black men's radical search for progressive ways of being men by challenging injustices at personal and institutional levels. Unlike those whose response to feminism is defensive and antagonistic, these Black men do not view feminism as a racist plot to deny them their piece of the patriarchal pie or a social movement synonymous with emasculation.[13] Instead, they understand male domination as problematic, divisive, and self-destructive to collective action on behalf of African Americans and the good of society as a whole. Feminist Black men force us to focus on unexpected, counterintuitive forms of masculinity in their efforts to resist the pervasive, sometimes seductive, pull of patriarchy. They also demonstrate how changing these assumptions can positively affect our interpersonal relationships as well as our social institutions.

Specifically, *Ain't I a Feminist* analyzes in-depth interviews with twenty men selected from an original survey of fifty African American men across the United States who support feminism. In this book, critical theory, Black feminist perspectives, masculinities studies, and models of adult personality change are combined in a sociologically oriented psychology that illuminates the development of feminist beliefs and practices in African American men's adult lives. The activities of these men, both public and private, challenge the idea that men have to dominate women, children, and other men in order to assert their manhood. Their narratives reveal how men can redefine manhood as they make connections between the long-term negative effects of popular notions of masculinity and intersecting social inequalities based on gender, race, sexuality, and socioeconomic class. When these men translate their awareness into positive actions, they are not simply countering sexism and acting *pro*feminist—they *are* feminists.[14] Also, the fact that they are African American is crucial to the book's purpose.

An Intentional Focus on Feminist Black Men

Focusing on the lives of feminist Black men challenges several stereotypes. First, it questions the assumption that feminism is a "Whites-only" movement. Both Black women and Black men have made important contributions to feminist history. In the nineteenth century, antislavery abolitionist Frederick Douglass proclaimed, "I am a radical woman suffrage man."[15] His sentiment was shared by early twentieth century Black leaders like scholar-activist W. E. B. DuBois, Judge Robert Terrel, trade unionist A. Phillip Randolph, and other African American men who supported what is referred to as the historical first wave of feminism in the United States.[16] Thus, feminist support among Black men is not new. Although these men are popularly referred to as "race men" because of their Black civil rights advocacy, that term often obscures and diminishes vital *feminist* aspects of their activism.

True, those so-called race men supported feminism as it was narrowly defined during their particular periods of U.S. history. Like White male feminists, they supported certain legal rights for women, but did not challenge male domination in general. Now, thanks to the continued growth and influence of feminism, particularly African American feminism and the feminist expressions of other women of color, public understanding of the movement and its terminology has expanded to include the politics of race, gender, sexuality, and economics—a politics referred to as intersectional in its approach and as "intersectionality" in feminist scholarly circles.[17]

The narratives in *Ain't I a Feminist* represent a new level of awareness and action on the part of Black men today. Historically, many men have taken issue with established concepts of "a man's place" and "a woman's place."[18] The narratives in this book reveal contemporary men rejecting rigid ideas of manhood and womanhood and redefining their gender in flexible, egalitarian, and humanistic terms. Their lives show how men can discover and recover their humanity. Their narratives also counter persistent negative media images of Black men. These Black feminist men unequivocally demonstrate that men can change, despite formidable and pervasive pressures to embrace the patriarchal status quo through focused collective action in addition to individual resistance. Unlike critics who blame feminism for the so-called masculinity crisis, I suggest, on the basis of my interviews, that at least some boys and men have become better human beings *because* of feminism.[19]

Any man can identify with the emotionally, spiritually, and even physically crippling effects of popular notions of masculinity. The experiences these men recount are not entirely confined to African Americans but occur also to men in any patriarchal society, regardless of race, sexuality, or class. What is unique to this book is the radical change achieved by the narrators, despite the specific forms of harm caused by popular, stereotypical attitudes regarding African American men's behavior. Most of us can gain insights into alternative ways of being through these narratives.

Narratives as Sites for Studying Personal and Social Transformation

The narrative excerpts in *Ain't I a Feminist* provide candid, thought-provoking, and often surprising information about how men perceive change and what pivotal experiences cultivate their respect for girls and women as well as boys and men. Feminism appears here as perceptions of lived experiences that culminate in personal and social transformation. Their feminist beliefs take concrete form in everyday acts. These men have the willingness to change both themselves and the institutions in which they live and work. Anyone who wonders whether men can unlearn damaging, masculinist viewpoints and practices and assert their manhood in positive ways will be encouraged by their self-disclosures. They have a great deal to say about their experiences with male–female relationships, monogamy, violence against women, parenting, military life, organized religion, rape and childhood molestation, and sexuality politics. Like the lives of most human beings undergoing change, the change process is rarely smooth, uniform, or free from contradiction and backlash. In fact, it is routinely messy. The men's life stories reflect this "messiness" and have not been sanitized or glamorized. Nor have they been pathologized.[20]

Because their versions of masculinity have largely gone unnoticed by scholars and the public, I have privileged the subjects' voices by including large segments of interview text in each chapter. However, my own voice as a feminist activist, psychologist, and African American woman analyzing the text also comes through clearly (see Appendix A and B for recruitment procedures, interview topics, and data analytic procedures). In addition, I make an argument for, and provide an example of, critical theoretical assumptions and a transformative agenda for the field of Black feminist masculinities studies.

This book describes an evolving, collective life story of individual African American men's varying relationships to privilege, which complicate their experiences of subordination as they deepen their commitment to feminism. Each chapter links institutional and individual factors that shape the diversity of Black men's behavior, as well as their sense of agency when they consciously engage in feminist forms of masculinity as creative resistance. Chapter 1 describes the theoretical framework that shapes the research and introduces the reader to Black feminist masculinities studies. The second chapter offers introductory biographical sketches of the twenty feminist men whose lives constitute the core of the book's research. Chapter 3 highlights Black men's conflicting experiences of power and powerlessness across various contexts, showing how specific, contradictory social interactions with women and men increase their chances of coming to challenge patriarchal masculinity norms. The fourth chapter provides detailed information on the pivotal events, situations, and experiences that led them to accept feminism as a guide in their lives. Chapter 5 discusses the significance of romantic relationships with feminist women in the lives of those men—the majority—who are heterosexual. The sixth chapter addresses the impact of platonic friendships with feminist women. Chapter 7 addresses the relationship among sexism, homophobia, and heterosexism and how it affects feminist Black men's friendships with other men. The eighth chapter analyzes the men's parenting styles and practices. Chapter 9 assesses feminist men's political consciousness and its expression in their public behavior, arguing that individual resistance alone is not enough. As this chapter demonstrates, their ongoing feminist development can be equally frustrating and exhilarating. The conclusion discusses the broader implications of the study's findings for socializing boys and reeducating men, in the interest of their humanity and to encourage and foster profound social change. A multi-pronged approach is recommended that goes beyond creating material opportunities for individual African American boys and men; it aims to undermine the interlocking institutional effects of patriarchy, racial discrimination, and market-driven economic policies.

I do not claim that the men in this book represent a cross section of African American men. On the contrary, the participants were deliberately chosen because they are *atypical* in their efforts to reshape manhood through a feminist lens. Furthermore, their efforts are characterized by an unusually high level of education—a bias that is addressed in detail in the conclusion. My hope is that the reader can envision how, despite such biases, men can engage in collaborative efforts with women that actually go beyond definitions of gender and outline models of personhood that are applicable to all, so as to reshape our expectations, interpersonal relationships, and institutions.

CHAPTER 1

Critical Black Feminist Intersections

Framing the Issues

An intersection is a place or the point where two or more things meet, cross, or overlap.[1] The word "intersection" pictures precisely how I conceived of this project. Only by crossing between disciplines, allowing various theoretical perspectives to overlap, and acknowledging how multiple social constructions meet at both individual and institutional levels can the lives of feminist Black men, and the complexities surrounding their concrete practices of manhood, be understood.

The notion of intersections or "intersectionality" is also one of the central themes of Black feminist theory. Articulated early on in a statement by the Combahee River Collective, a Black feminist Boston-based group, intersectionality emphasizes how multiple and simultaneous forms of oppression in society interlock, work together, and transform one another in people's lives.[2] Today, feminist scholars in sociology, psychology, political science, anthropology, critical legal studies, philosophy, history, and a host of interdisciplinary specialties use the intersectional model of oppression or "intersectionality" to conceptualize their work.[3] In the social sciences, the model emphasizes particularly that "no social group is homogeneous, people must be located in terms of social structures that capture the power relations implied by those structures, and there are unique, nonadditive effects of identifying with more than one social group."[4]

In addition to the intersectional model, I combine (a) social, personality, and political psychological perspectives and (b) interdisciplinary models from critical social theory, sociology, African American studies, and masculinities studies to contribute to a burgeoning area I introduce as Black feminist masculinities studies.

Critical Psychological Perspectives and Assumptions about Knowledge

Critical social theory grapples with central questions "facing groups of people placed in specific political, social, and historic contexts characterized by injustice."[5] What makes critical social theory "critical" is its commitment to justice.[6] Thus, a critical social psychologist like me asks, how can psychology be used to facilitate social justice?[7]

Critical psychology is an umbrella term that describes a broad number of politically radical responses to and differences from mainstream psychology. Although critical psychology comes in different forms (e.g., feminist, Marxist, antiracist, Afrocentric, and queer), all forms pay particular attention to oppressed and vulnerable individuals and groups and tend to be interdisciplinary in approach.[8] Critical psychologists use our research not only to document social injustices but also to promote social change. We intentionally carry out projects in which research and political practices overlap. We also try to ensure that people who are involved in social change have access to our research findings, and that we have some access to their perspectives.

If the goal of critical social psychologists is to create scholarship that transforms society, we must identify processes that explain change and successful attempts at creating equality. Thus, during the planning stages of this project on feminist Black men, the burning question was: what can be learned about feminist Black men's definitions and practices of manhood that would challenge institutional inequities, while contributing to the viability of African American communities and the construction of a humane and just society?

Mainstream psychology often views scientific knowledge as an accumulation of objective facts, based on an ongoing quest for a universal truth devoid of personal and political interests or biases. Critical psychologists, however, view all scientific knowledge as infused with political interests, and the field of psychology as a value-laden enterprise heavily influenced by the biases of the elite classes.[9] As critical psychologists, our aim is not to find an alleged "universal truth"; rather, it is to study multiple perspectives, granting legitimacy to some often ignored by mainstream psychology.[10]

Bias is unavoidable. Our values shape "the questions we ask, the methodologies we use, and the interpretations we generate."[11] Thus, critical psychologists accept that some form of bias is part of being human. High-quality research requires recognizing our beliefs and assumptions at the start of the research project, challenging them throughout the research process, and reexamining them as part of the research design.[12] To accomplish this task, we must make concerted efforts to remain open to the views of all participants in the research. Instead of trying to forget, deny, or ignore our biases, prejudices, or expectations, we attempt to discover their limitations.[13] I would add that we should also acknowledge the strengths of such biases, particularly when they serve the interest of social justice. That is what makes us "engaged scholars."

Examining our biases also pushes us to examine the power imbalances that we, as psychologists, bring to the research environment itself; it exposes our work to a level of scrutiny that mainstream psychology often avoids.[14] Throughout every phase of our projects we must ask, can we put aside what we think we know in order to make room for the unexpected, the counterintuitive, and whatever else we have yet to learn? This attempt at openness encouraged me to search across disciplines, theoretical frameworks, and research methods for insights that could illuminate the lives of feminist Black men.

Multidisciplinary Intersections: Theoretical Influences

The theoretical framework of this research is designed to underscore that what happens to the individual is not merely the result of individual processes. That is, social structures or institutions shape individuals, and individuals simultaneously shape institutions through their social interactions. Therefore, my concern is with how societal institutions shape individual choices and how human agency creates, sustains, modifies, and outright resists prevailing norms and institutions. Both dimensions are important; however, a particular concern is with how individuals choose acts that resist societal institutions and norms and interpret their lives on the basis of such acts.

Gender, in this research, is interpreted as a social structure and a socially constructed category of identity that is embedded in the individual, interactional, and institutional dimensions of our society.[15] Social constructionists argue that gender is determined not by one's biological sex but by various institutions within a society that restrict each sex to characteristics and activities defined as feminine and masculine. However, societal institutions shape an individual's gender identity only to the degree that an individual conforms to societal values. An individual may also resist and negotiate the gender norms of a society, depending on existing alternatives; thus, one's gender identity can change and is not fixed, but is dynamic—a means of becoming–often characterized by ambiguity, contradictions, and frustration.[16] Race, sexuality, and socioeconomic class are also interpreted as social structures, as well as socially constructed categories of identity, in this research. Also, the present study is influenced by narrative psychological perspectives on identity changes during adulthood, Black feminist critical social theory, and feminist masculinities studies.

Narrative Models of Adult Personality Change

Psychologist Dan McAdam's life-story model of adult identity change serves as part of the conceptual and methodological framework for this project; thus, life history interviews with feminist Black men were conducted, and the resulting narratives analyzed by content and themes.[17] McAdam conceives of *identity* as an "evolving story that integrates a reconstructed past, perceived present, and anticipated future."[18] Each individual creates and revises his or her life story throughout adulthood "as the changing person and the person's changing world negotiate niches, places, opportunities, and positions within which the person can live meaningfully."[19] In this model, each life story contains different features, some of which appear to remain relatively stable over the adult years while others do not. Life stories typically include turning points, pivotal or nuclear episodes, and key scenes (symbolic high or low points).[20] These scenes symbolize the way the individual perceives certain life changes or feels that he or she has remained more or less the same person through changing circumstances. Thus, "adults adopt a narrative perspective of their lives, consciously marking their important personality changes throughout the life span."[21]

Contemporary research on identity narratives suggests that the stories that make up these narratives are often fragmented and full of contradiction in ways that do not provide clear, coherent, or immediately meaningful text. The "self," rather than being unified and coherent, is actually "multifaceted, composed of parts sometimes highly interdependent and sometimes not, some conflicting and some reinforcing."[22] A person's various identities compete for expression, may be distant or close in salience, or may share meanings such that behavior reflecting one identity will reflect the other.[23] Many identity narratives include abrupt discontinuities that defy fixed sequences or clear developmental stages. Relational models of identity processes that have emerged within sociology and psychology underscore how intertwined with social, cultural, and historical factors the processes of identity are.[24] In this way the new theories depart from earlier identity models that stressed *intra*personal factors such as inner conflicts and their resolutions (like those described by Erikson's identity stages: trust vs. mistrust, autonomy vs. shame, and so forth).[25] Insisting that every narrative identity is multiple, fragmentary, and unfinished, the new theories shift our attention from assessing personality variables to studying "how historical events, interpersonal relationships, and the life narrative itself are purposeful social co-constructions by both those who experience these events and those to whom they tell their stories."[26] Such telling, which includes the interaction between the interviewee and interviewer, constitutes a performance of sorts. In so performing, "we express, display, make claims for who we are and who we would like to be in the stories we tell."[27]

I see the life narratives I have gathered from the men in this book as their subjective evaluations of events. I do not regard their stories as facts, per se, but as the result of a process by which people selectively construct, retrieve, and change their narratives to fit their own self-concepts.[28] Centrally, these narratives represent what each man believes is important in his life, and illustrate how these beliefs and perceptions affect his behavior.

If narratives do not depict actual (and accurate) facts, why are they important? Life narratives are worthy of study—with all of their reconstructions and potential biases—because they tell us how people make sense of their lives. No narrator is ever capable of specifying all of the multiple factors responsible for certain changes in his or her life. However, most people can usually recall the events leading to an important change, the methods they used in an attempt to effect that change, the difficulties they have had with these attempts, and the strategies they used to maintain the change they have effected.[29] People's "beliefs and attributions regarding specific changes are related to actual, successful changes in their lives as well as their inability to effect certain changes."[30] Whether a change involves beliefs, attitudes, or behaviors, the psychology of individual change is a complex process involving many motivational, cognitive, emotional, and interpersonal factors that act in confluence and facilitate or inhibit change.[31]

In analyzing these men's narratives, I also explore how certain institutional factors facilitate or inhibit the development of a feminist Black masculinity. Adult personality change has been described, in particular, as nonlinear, gradual, subtle, and often frustrating.[32] I ask, what are the individual, interpersonal, and institutional factors tied to the various turning points, peak experiences, or frustrating life crises that shape each man's feminist masculinity? How does he grapple with his own personal contradictions without becoming too discouraged? What individual and institutional factors continue to create difficulty for each man as he attempts to maintain a feminist Black perspective amid a world of contradictory attitudes or behaviors?

Black Feminist Critical Theory

As a guiding frame for my study, I also adopt Patricia Hill Collins's conception of Black feminist thought as critical social theory. Black feminist critical theory represents a dynamic, oppositional system of ideas that responds to actual social conditions that are always changing.[33]

Black feminism is frequently misunderstood. It may help to note what it is not. Adding the adjective "Black" to the term feminism does not mean that it is White feminism donned in blackface, for Black women only or Black people only. Rather, there is more than one kind of feminism because culture, class, sexuality, and a host of other experiential factors shape feminist perspectives. Thus, Black feminist thought, as used here, does not assume an essence of Blackness; instead, it understands "Black" as a construct that reflects the intersection of a variety of institutional power relations. Black feminist thought has historically emphasized the intersection of race, class, and gender, highlighting how African American women *and* other social groups are positioned within unjust power relations.[34] Black feminist thought also adds complexity to more traditional approaches to social phenomena that focus only on race, class, or gender, by broadening our understanding of how mechanisms of institutional power mesh with personal expressions of power.[35]

Black feminism comes in different strains, although the strains are more alike than different.[36] Yet, with few exceptions, anyone can apply the principles and practices of Black feminist thought.[37] My own use of Black feminist thought to analyze the lives of Black men demonstrates its versatility in addressing pressing issues in African American communities. Even though this study emphasizes Black men who are thriving, it indirectly problematizes the "plight of the Black male" and asks in what ways a Black feminist perspective can interrogate popular "endangered Black male" discourse and contribute favorably to related public policy initiatives. My goal is to deconstruct "endangered Black male" discourse by portraying not only the damage caused by systemic injustices but also the healthy and powerful sense of agency that some Black men display in their daily lives through feminist reconstructions of masculinity. Deconstructing "endangered Black male" discourse using "Black feminist male" discourse allows me to delineate individual and institutional forces that allow Black men to resist and negotiate patriarchal masculinity norms. Addressing these various discourses and practices requires using overlapping concepts in what is currently referred to as masculinities studies.[38]

Black Feminist Masculinities Studies

This book introduces an area of study that empirically assesses the lives of Black men who are sociopolitical actors. As such, these men continually reconstruct their lives by actively engaging feminist perspectives in their practices of manhood. Their evolving life stories reveal multiple concepts of masculinity traceable to the multiple influences of power and powerlessness that scholars in the predominantly White field of masculinities studies often investigate.

Feminist Masculinities Studies. The academic area of masculinities studies is "a significant outgrowth of feminist studies and is strongly influenced by queer studies."[39] Investigators in this field agree that "masculinity is not monolithic, not one static thing, but the confluence of multiple processes and relationships with variable results for differing individuals, groups, institutions, and societies."[40] Therefore, it is currently beneficial to discuss the different kinds of masculinities, rather than a single masculinity. Scholars in this area also investigate masculinity as a system of power relations *among men* as well as a system of power relations *between women and men.*[41] The belief in universal, unchanging, and "traditional" gender identities suggests that social change is not possible between men and women; therefore, one goal of scholars in masculinities studies is to unveil the masquerade of masculinity as "natural" and biologically determined. What is perceived as masculine or manly is socially constructed and affected by historical, cultural, and political processes.[42]

Feminist masculinities studies, the discipline, examines in particular "how male power and privilege are constituted and represented, explores the effects of men's masculinity on women and on diverse men, and seeks to foster more egalitarian forms of manhood."[43] Individual studies examine "who has a stake in retaining masculinity as a coherent category, restricting that category to men, and valorizing it as both a goal of individuals and a necessary component of society."[44] Some feminists suggest that masculinity can be restructured so that it is not based on men's dominance over women.[45] Others believe that the very concept must be abolished through a "feminist degendering movement" that focuses not so much on binary concepts of sex, gender, and sexuality that emphasize who is male and female, a man or a woman, or even gay or straight, but on "what does it mean to be human" and "what is personhood?"[46] Despite these differences, most researchers in this area would agree that it is in men's own best interests to support feminism because most men are themselves harmed in their efforts to attain the ideal characteristics of "manhood" in patriarchal, heterosexist, racialized, and market-driven societies. Revealing how traditionally dominant ideas and practices of masculinity do in fact harm men is therefore a necessary goal of feminist masculinities studies.[47]

African American Men's Creative Agency. While most of the published social sciences literature on Black men and boys mentions the harmful impact of systemic racism and economic inequalities on their lives, research accounts using "endangered Black male" discourse often represent Black men and youth as merely pawns, victims, and victimizers.[48] Paradoxically, Black men are viewed as *endangered*, yet remain stereotyped in U.S. society as the most *dangerous*. The creative and active sense of agency many Black men possess is often overlooked for the sensationalized image of Black men as violent, criminal, jobless, and reactionary. I will not attempt an exhaustive review of that literature. Rather, my intent is to counter its narrow focus by examining the combined systemic effects of race, class, gender, and sexuality on Black men in ways that also encourage the documentation of Black feminist male discourse and practices. I introduce and refer to such documentation as Black feminist masculinities studies.

Although the devastating effects of racism and economic disparities must indeed be documented, social science must also point out the damaging effects of sexism and patriarchal values on the lives of Black men and boys. Patriarchal values underlie Black men's ideas about manhood and undermine progressive ways of coping with racial, economic, and other systemic injustices. I envision Black feminist masculinities studies as a discipline describing complex stories, not only of the enduring effects of systemic oppression on Black men but also of their ongoing creative resistance and resilience, despite systemic barriers. An emerging trend among scholars who study Black masculinities involves acknowledging the impact of dominant notions of White, heterosexual masculinity on Black men and Black men's agency in creating alternative masculinities.[49]

My specific interest, however, is in alternative Black masculinities that are explicitly *feminist* and which recognize the limitations of reforming masculinity without dismantling patriarchy. Rather than refashioning and repackaging patriarchy for African American men, I argue that Black feminist masculinities studies must analyze the experiences of Black men under patriarchy in order to challenge patriarchy's assumptions and practices for *all* men. In addition, the emerging discipline of Black feminist masculinities studies must examine the history of African American men's resistance to patriarchal values and practices, and its continuity in contemporary times, from both humanities and social sciences perspectives.

Historical and Contemporary Perspectives. African American men have supported each historical "wave" of feminism, and scholars have meticulously documented that stance.[50] However, no published social science studies describe how African American men develop a feminist outlook in ways that encourage institutional change. The few published studies on profeminist men in general provide demographic information about White American men who join profeminist organizations, childhood and adult factors that shaped the feminist development of White British men in antisexist self-help groups, and White left-wing academics in the United States who use a gendered analysis in their scholarship.[51]

Most of what we know about feminist Black men comes from their published creative writings, which shed some light on how Black men negotiate feminist masculinity in their lives. A few autobiographical accounts of Black men's development of antisexist consciousness provide details about what a budding feminist Black man experiences as he tries to unlearn sexism, and how a seasoned feminist Black man tries to expand his feminist analyses and practices over time.[52] Some feminist Black men's writings also make important contributions to Black feminist theory, history, pedagogy, and literary criticism.[53] Their writings criticize heterosexist forms of gender oppression and offer insights on how Black men might resist these destructive forces at individual and collective levels. Feminist Black men's writings also detail their activist efforts in such areas as discrimination against Black women in higher education,[54] the recruitment of Black men within the predominantly White profeminist men's movement,[55] Black men's coalitions with Black feminists,[56] rape prevention in African American communities,[57] and AIDS awareness and discrimination against gay, lesbian, bisexual, and transgendered sexualities.[58] In particular, "out" Black feminist gay and bisexual men have taken the lead in exposing and challenging the underlying assumptions of stereotypical, heterosexist, and destructive notions of Black masculinity in their writings.[59] Scholars in Black feminist masculinities studies can build on this literature in important, innovative ways.

We can analyze the writings of feminist Black men historically and contribute research on the lives of contemporary feminist Black men, demonstrating (a) the complexity and situational variability of Black men's identities; (b) how multiple social systems work together to create Black gendered identities; (c) which social contexts encourage feminist Black men's identities to emerge and under what circumstances; and (d) how Black men's varying relationships to privilege complicate the experience of their subordination, conformity, and resistance within interlocking systems of oppression. Black feminist masculinities studies should inform *as well as* transform our understanding of Black men, suggesting that pessimism regarding the plight of Black men is not entirely appropriate.

Social policies aimed at creating opportunities for disadvantaged African American men certainly help to alleviate some of the destructive patterns of violence and high-risk behaviors that are associated with some Black men's failure to thrive. However, without challenging the underlying patriarchal assumptions of our raced-gendered, market-driven system, African American men may increasingly displace their fears about themselves and their masculinity into contempt for Black women, resentment toward disproportionately privileged White men, and disdain for other subordinated men (e.g., other men of color, sexually diverse men, and differently abled men). Ignoring patriarchy in the analysis of the plight of Black men creates glaring omissions in the literature, which keeps researchers, policy makers, and community workers revisiting the problem without creating effective, long-term solutions. The intersectional emphasis of this book and its use of African American men's evolving life stories demonstrate how men perceive change, then actually change themselves and institutions as a result of their perceptions.

The Present Study

Life stories suggest that gender behaviors fluctuate over time, that identities are not completely stable, and that narrative methodology is good at exposing the fragility, contradiction, and context-bound aspects of the human experience; surveys and laboratory studies often miss these non-linear human phenomena.[60] Therefore, in each chapter that follows, I analyze life narratives of feminist Black men, gathered from face-to-face interviews with them, to discover what contexts at the individual, inter-actional, and institutional level increase the chances that Black men will use feminist perspectives to develop alternative ways of interacting with women, children, and other men. Although the majority of the men in the study are heterosexual, I also examine gay, bisexual, and transgendered feminist Black masculinities to find out how sexuality and gender identity in various social contexts facilitate or inhibit feminist identity development and practices.

The conclusion links theoretically explained observations from each chapter to practical applications. What can feminist Black men's narratives teach us about how to raise boys? How do we recognize feminist Black masculinities and support the different versions of it when we see them, in the interest of broad social change? What are the public policy implications of their feminist activism? Using a critical Black feminist lens that captures the intersectional aspects of Black men's resistance narratives, I disentangle such questions and their intersecting answers without presuming there is one right answer for all men in all places at the same time.

CHAPTER 2

Biographical Sketches

The Sons of Sojourner Truth

Sojourner Truth's "Ain't I a Woman" speech was a response to jeers from White men, who often yelled during her antislavery public speeches, "We don't believe you're really a woman!" Those insults also came from some White women's rights activists, who felt it was beneath them to listen to a Black woman speak publicly about the rights of Black women to vote and to be free.[1] Isabella Baumfree, as she was called before she took the name Sojourner Truth, through her famous "Ain't I a Woman" speech shared her personal "truth" about slavery and challenged White men, White women, and Black men to beware of exclusionary practices in the name of social justice regarding Black women's right to vote. I consider feminist Black men her sons, continuing her legacy. Just as Sojourner Truth argued that she was a *woman*, even though she was not White, I argue that each man in this study is a *feminist*, although he is not female. Most important, Sojourner refused to prioritize race over gender when she stated in one of her speeches:

> There is a great stir about colored men getting their rights, but not a word about colored women; and if colored men get their rights, and not colored women theirs, you see the colored men will be masters over the women, and it will be just as bad.[2]

Sojourner Truth aptly understood that most Black men and White women of her day were insensitive to the plight of Black women, who also desperately needed the right to vote. "An acute observer, Truth recognized the patriarchal insistence of black male abolitionists to assert their right to vote over women of either race and the separate resolve of white women suffragists to assert their right to vote over black people of either sex,"[3] notes African American feminist political scientist Evelyn Simien.

The struggle for the Fifteenth Amendment, and thus for the right of Black men to vote, highlights the ongoing plight of Black women as a group situated at the center of at least two distinct, yet related, social movements, the Black civil rights movement and the women's rights movement.[4] While Truth opposed the passage of the Fifteenth Amendment, another public figure, Frances E. W. Harper, insisted that women of both races must take a step back and wait their turn so as not to jeopardize the political fate of black men. Simien compares the struggles of earlier Black feminists like Sojourner Truth and womanists like Frances E. W. Harper with the contemporary struggles of Black women activists:

> Then, as now, black feminist theorists argued that the hierarchy of interests within the black community assigns priority to race over gender. For this reason, today some black women (like Harper) subordinate issues of vital concern to them as women to protect black men (like [Frederick] Douglass) from racism and others (like Truth), when issues of race and gender collide, refuse to rank interlocking systems of oppression to protect their own interests as individuals who face twin barriers simultaneously. By refusing to prioritize race over gender, Truth gave birth to a radically different vision and sowed the seeds for contemporary black feminism today.[5]

The men in this book adopt Sojourner Truth's intersectional outlook on race and gender.

All twenty were interviewed after taking part in an earlier, extensive mail survey that included fifty self-identified profeminist Black men.[6] In the biographical sketches that follow, they recognize the need for multi-dimensional approaches to social justice and an expanded notion of group consciousness and Black identity.

During the time of the interviews (1996–2001) the men ranged in age from 23 to 58, most had a college education, and would be considered "middle class" because of their combined educational level and income. Ten were legally married, two were cohabiting with their partners, five were partnered but not living together, and three were single. Fourteen of the twenty men were the primary caretakers of children. Thirteen described themselves as heterosexual, three as bisexual, three as gay, and one as transgendered (female-to-male transsexual).

Although I refer to all as feminist, eight of the men actually prefer to be described that way; nine tend to prefer "profeminist," and three prefer the term "antisexist." Two of them also use the terms "womanist" and "feminist" interchangeably. Although all participants are U.S. citizens and are generally comfortable being referred to as African American, one man (Carlos) also describes himself as "Black Latino," another (Cudjoe) as "Black Indian," and one other (Rex) as "African West Indian." Most of them wanted me to use their real names. However, my concern about violating the confidentiality of the other people mentioned in their life stories led me to create first-name pseudonyms for everyone. Each man is presented alphabetically by his pseudonym in the following sections. Table 2.1 provides a quick glance at the participants' general characteristics. Readers will meet each man again throughout the book in ways that highlight both his similarities to and differences from the others.

The Communalist

Abdul is a counselor and community educator for a nonprofit organization that offers intervention programs for men who batter women. Born in 1946, he was 50 years of age at the time of the interview. He holds a master's degree in counseling psychology and is a member of a local activist group that addresses domestic violence in African American communities. He is from a working-class family background and grew up in a small town in North Carolina. Abdul has diverse life experiences that include previous involvement with the Nation of Islam, Rastafarian philosophy, and natural food cooperatives. He has practiced polygamy and experienced communal living arrangements in cities on the East and West coasts, the Midwest, and the South. Currently he is in a monogamous marriage and actively responsible for ten children from previous polygamous unions. At first glance, I incorrectly assumed that his rather light complexion meant he probably had one Black parent and one White parent (he later described both his parents as Black and said his mother's skin was extremely fair). Dressed casually in a track suit, relaxed, and with his water bottle at his side, he recounted:

I really didn't connect with my own sexist influences and behavior until around seven or eight years ago. I was only able to see my sexist stuff when my mind started to open up. I believe women have always said things to me about my behavior and their difficult experiences with me, but because of my indoctrination and socialization, like most men, I just never really heard them! I mean, I've always been one of those men who had the answer before the woman even asked the question! I just figured I knew what she was thinking before she even opened her mouth. So, basically, I was at a place where I didn't have an ear for whatever a

Table 2.1. Interview Participants

Pseudonym	Age	Sexual Identity	Preferred Descriptor(s)	Education	Occupation Status	Relationship
Abdul	50	Heterosexual	Profeminist	Master's degree	Instructor and trainer, batterer intervention program	Married
Alan	44	Bisexual	Feminist Womanist	Ph.D.	English professor	Married
Bruce	47	Heterosexual	Profeminist Womanist	Master's degree	Project coordinator, batterer intervention	Married
Cabral	49	Heterosexual	Feminist	Associate's degree	Poet	Partnered, living together
Carlos	23	Heterosexual	Feminist	Master's student	———	Partnered, living apart
Chad	37	Heterosexual	Feminist Profeminist Antisexist	Bachelor's degree	Director, youth educational program	Partnered, living apart
Cudjoe	29	Heterosexual	Feminist Profeminist Antisexist	Doctoral student in joint Ph.D/J.D. program; J.D.	———	Partnered living apart
David	33	Heterosexual	Profeminist Antisexist	Ph.D.	Literature professor	Married
Donny	42	Gay	Profeminist	Bachelor's degree	Restaurant owner/ workshop facilitator	Partnered living apart
Eddie	36	Heterosexual	Antisexist	Bachelor's degree	Urban planner	Married
Edmund	46	Heterosexual	Profeminist	Master's degree	Writer, director of theater guild	Married
Jake	51	Heterosexual	Antisexist	Some college	Program director, human rights organization	Married

Table 2.1. Interview Participants (*Continued*)

Pseudonym	Age	Sexual Identity	Preferred Descriptor(s)	Education	Occupation Status	Relationship
Malcolm	23	Gay	Antisexist	College student	Youth trainer & workshop facilitator	Single
Paul	58	Heterosexual	Profeminist Antisexist	Some graduate & professional training	Entrepreneur, tax accountant	Divorced Single
Ralph	41	Heterosexual	Profeminist Antisexist	Ph.D.	Social scientist	Married
Rex	36	Gay	Profeminist	Master's degree	Social worker and administrator, batterer intervention	Single
Solomon	46	Heterosexual Transgendered	Feminist Antisexist	Ph.D.	Anthropology professor	Partnered living together
Soyinka	49	Heterosexual	Profeminist	Doctoral student	College Instructor	Partnered, living apart
Toussaint	44	Queer/Bisexual	Feminist	Doctorate Theology	Priest professor of religion	Poly- amorous marriage
Victor	38	Fluid	Feminist Profeminist Antisexist	Law degree	Entrepreneur, former prosecutor and law professor	Married

woman had to say....When I spend time trying to judge, challenge, confront, and deny a woman's reality I never have to deal with my role in her pain and anguish. I never have to deal with how I have been socialized to ignore her reality and overly promote mine.

The Pentecostal Professor

Alan is an associate professor of English who specializes in gender studies and feminist theory at a private university. He was born in 1953 and was 44 years old at the time of the interview. He is from a working-class background, grew up in a small city in Arkansas, and earned his doctorate at an East Coast university. He is married, with two children. Alan refers to himself as a Black male feminist and challenges both secular and nonsecular beliefs about gender and sexuality. He recently acknowledged his call to preach in the Pentecostal faith as practiced by the Church of God in Christ. At least six feet tall, with an athletic physique and smooth dark complexion, Alan's warm sense of humor offset his otherwise formal interpersonal style. Early in the interview, Alan discussed his views regarding the various terms used to describe men who support feminism:

I want to make a distinction regarding how I use the words "antisexist," "profeminist," and "feminist" when referring to men. The term "antisexist" does not make a strong, clear statement about one's support of feminism; it simply states that one is against sexism, as opposed to what one is for. In my mind, feminism is more than just antisexism. So, when someone says I am an antisexist man, rather than saying I am a profeminist or feminist man, the question for me becomes, how much traditional manhood is he willing to give up to take on what feminism means? The term "profeminist" indicates that one is not a feminist but an advocate of feminism, and sidesteps the issue of whether men can be feminists. I think the most radical position a man can take is to declare himself a feminist man. I never call myself an antisexist man. I occasionally call myself a profeminist man, but most often I say that I am a feminist Black man because I believe that the radical gesture is what's going to move the feminist agenda forward. Of course, I want to always give men the opportunity to come to feminism however they choose. The important point is that they learn to embrace feminism. I'm never going to say they have to say they are feminists and that they can't call themselves the other terms. But, when a Black man proclaims himself a feminist, he boldly challenges every Black male stereotype!

The Defector

Bruce has a master's degree in community counseling and is project coordinator of a mentoring program for men who batter women. He also volunteers as coordinator of African American outreach for an AIDS awareness organization. Bruce was born in 1949, grew up in Georgia, and was 47 at the time of the interview. He was involved in two violent marriages before his current marriage of almost ten years. He currently resides in Georgia and has six children from previous relationships. Wearing a flannel shirt and denim overalls that blended well with his ebony skin, and with a warm, casual, down-to-earth interpersonal style, Bruce boldly admitted:

When you become antisexist, you are perceived by others as a defector. Men don't trust you, and a lot of women don't trust you either.

Nobody really trusts a defector. You're not one of the boys anymore. You have broken rank with other men by stressing the importance of women and their reality. It's often a lonely, scary, and uncertain path, so many men revert back to their previous ways or find new ways to abuse power. I don't know many men who are willing to defect from sexism, but, I have learned that this is the right thing to do for women as well as for myself. What I find so interesting about becoming antisexist is how you start out so full of yourself and end up so "unfull" of yourself and humble—if you continue to grow.

The Poet

Cabral is a performance artist, cultural critic, music producer, journalist, essayist, and advertising executive. However, his most developed and comfortable voice is as a poet. He was born in 1947 and was 49 at the time of the interview. He grew up in a middle-class family in Louisiana and became both writer and civil rights activist in junior high school. His early sociopolitical involvement evolved into active participation in the Black arts movement and the Pan African liberation struggle. He was a founding member of a collective in Louisiana that ran an independent school, a food co-op, bookstore, and publishing company. Cabral writes on a variety of topics emphasizing "art for life" as opposed to "art for art's sake." His most popular book includes essays on sexism that are read widely by Black women's groups across the country. This self-described "word singer" has five adult children from a previous marriage and currently lives with his partner, Zawadi, in a committed, stable relationship. Over six feet tall with a velvety dark complexion, dressed in casual slacks, a Black Arts T-shirt, and wire-framed eyeglasses, Cabral came to the interview with a briefcase full of papers. These papers included his writings; throughout the interview, Cabral would shuffle through his many papers and supplement answers to the interview questions with his poems and a few of his short stories. His commitment to ongoing self-analysis came out at the start of the interview:

I definitely see myself as profeminist, but I don't see myself as non-sexist because I don't think anybody can grow up in this society and not be sexist. It's a struggle, so....I have elements of that just as everyone has elements of it. I may struggle with it more than some other men, and I may struggle with it less than some other men. The elements within me may be more deeply seated than some others and less deeply entrenched than others, but it's in me. So, there's no way that I can accept being described as "nonsexist." I can be and have described myself as a profeminist in the sense of defining feminism—to use a real compressed shorthand—as self-determination for women and the power to enforce and activate that self-determination. Because I advocate and work from that assumption, I consider myself feminist....I wrote this haiku that explains my approach to social justice:

> *everything is the*
> *way things are simply because*
> *we've not changed them yet.*

The Profeminist Organizer

Carlos has been a social activist since high school. He was working on his master's degree in environmental science at a university in Ohio during the time of the interview. He identifies himself as a Black Latino from a working-class background, whose parents are from the Dominican Republic. He was born in the United States in 1973, grew up in New York, and was 23 years old when interviewed. Before moving to Ohio to attend graduate school, Carlos attended an historically Black men's college in the Southeast, where he cofounded a profeminist Black men's organization. Because of my lack of exposure to Black Latinos and the diversity within the Latino community, I incorrectly assumed Carlos was *only* Latino, not Black, and thought he might have misunderstood the requirements for participating in the study. Tall, with deep brown eyes and light honey complexion, Carlos removed all doubts I had when he confidently stated:

I'm from the Bronx and grew up in a Latino neighborhood that was like an extended family. I identify myself as Black, which isn't common in the Latino community. In the Dominican Republic people identify themselves as Black, but in the USA, if you say "Black," people think "African American." So, many Black Latinos don't identify as Black in the USA because...there is a desire is to preserve the Latino cultural identity as well. I started to identify myself strongly as Black in high school. Most of my friends were African American and a lot of the people I knew outside of high school were African American. African Americans were the main people struggling against racism in New York, and as an activist, I gravitated toward them. However, it is frustrating because I have always had to struggle with the way people separate Latinos and Blacks when dealing with racial issues.

I also grew up used to being broke. My mother and I were on welfare for a while and had to use food stamps....I certainly don't think that being poor makes you feminist, because plenty of men are broke and are the most sexist people out there! However, growing up poor in my neighborhood shaped my interest in grassroots activism, and activist experiences helped me appreciate other people's experiences of oppression. As an activist, I learned that a lot of different people catch hell in a lot of different ways. I learned early on that I can't really expect other people to take my experiences of injustice seriously if I'm not taking their experiences of injustice seriously.

The Men's Movement Critic

Chad is a supervisor in a nonprofit organization for youth development services in Georgia. He was born in 1959, grew up in New York within a middle-class household, and was age 37 at the time of the interview. He has a master's degree in political science and has taught political science courses in a university setting. Chad has been a volunteer for at least two profeminist men's organizations: one in the Southeast that works with men who batter women, and another in the Northeast that works with men to prevent rape. Chad has never been married, but is currently dating. Slight in stature, chestnut-brown complexion, wearing glasses, and with a polite unassuming manner, Chad reflected on his years of experience in the profeminist men's movement:

I have seen a lot of self-righteousness among men doing antisexist work, and I just personally find it very unattractive. I also think it is very counterproductive to spend a lot of time talking to each other in men's groups and feeling self-righteous about what we do when there are so many men out there who are not doing these things who we really need to be talking to! I've been fortunate enough to be thrust into a situation that allows me to realize how much work there is to do on so many different levels when it comes to teaching men to be antisexist.... It can be frustrating to think that "where we are as antisexist men" is where every man needs to be, and that we somehow have to figure out how to get them there. Strategically, we have to assess what is the kind of change we can reasonably hope for in certain situations of gender abuse and oppression. In academia, one of the most important issues may be getting students to understand that gender is a socially constructed category; however, on the streets, getting young people to understand "No, it is not okay to smack this woman just because you feel like it or because she dissed you" is often the reality. Leaving the academic environment has forced me not to lose sight of the very basic challenges of gender issues "next door," versus the challenges discussed and eloquently theorized about in academia.

The Multiculturalist

Cudjoe, 29, was born in Oklahoma and describes himself as "a Black Indian of mixed heritage" because his mother is Native American

(Seminole) and his father is African American. Cudjoe grew up in pre-dominantly White, middle-class neighborhoods in Oklahoma and is currently enrolled in a joint J.D./Ph.D. program. He recently finished the law-school portion of his degree program and is completing his studies in political science for the Ph.D. After getting his bachelor's degree and before starting his graduate studies, he taught social studies at a private eastern boarding school. Early in his graduate school years, he worked as an editorial assistant for a feminist journal editor. He has never been married, but is currently dating. Cudjoe has a smooth caramel complexion and is of average height and weight. His youthful energy and fast-talking pace kept the interview intense and highly spirited. What's more, his personal adventures "on the road to feminism" and his hilarious storytelling style kept us both in stitches. With some coaxing, he described his fascination with the writings of White American feminist Naomi Wolf:

I was driving somewhere and I picked up a book on tape by popular feminist writer Naomi Wolf. I heard her speak when she was on the college lecture circuit promoting her book The Beauty Myth. *She was very popular on many college campuses, so when I saw her next book,* Fire with Fire, *on tape before starting my long drive to wherever I was going, I picked it up to take with me. I really got excited listening to this book because her voice was on the tape and what she said about the pressures on women and other gender issues in everyday language were convincing and made so much sense to me. By the time I went back to graduate school, I felt kind of embarrassed to admit how much her books had influenced me, because academics feel like her work is too oriented toward popular culture, and thus too "lowbrow" for serious scholars. But, I still love reading Naomi Wolf books and sometimes "we gotta take it where we can get it" because I wouldn't be as interested in gender and women's studies if I had only been exposed to the books of those "abstract, academic, high-theory" feminists!*

The Black Studies Professor

David is an Assistant Professor of English and African American studies at a southeastern university. He was born in 1964 and was 33 years old at the time of the interview. He was raised in a middle-class family in North Carolina where both of his parents were university professors, attended a private liberal arts college in Ohio, and obtained his doctoral degree at an Ivy League university. He is married to an African American feminist who is also a college professor. Extremely articulate and well mannered, David is dark-complex-

ioned and muscular and was one of the few sports enthusiasts among
the participants:

*I have to be very honest about how the opinions I am expressing are
ones that I have grown into over time. I was very homophobic, not just
during my adolescent years, but when I was in college. I was pursuing
this narrow Black nationalist agenda that included the political line that
homosexuality was antithetical to our agenda as Black people. In college,
I was guilty of challenging men's masculinity by inferring that they
might be gay.... Through personal experiences, reading, and largely,
through my feminist wife, I have grown to expand the parameters of my
social justice framework. If I can understand and be critical of racism,
then I also have to understand and be critical of sexism and homophobia.
This understanding also includes examining the ways in which I exercise
privilege as a Black man when it comes to gender and sexual orientation.*

The Restaurateur

Donny completed his bachelor's degree at a private midwestern university. He later became co-owner of a semivegetarian restaurant in
Missouri that specializes in macrobiotic cuisine. He was born in 1955,
grew up in Washington, D.C. in a working-class family, and was 42 at
the time of the interview. Donny has conducted workshops and programs for Planned Parenthood, the National Organization for Men
Against Sexism (NOMAS), Rape and Violence End Now (RAVEN),
and the United Nation's Conference on Women in Beijing, China. His
workshops address issues regarding racism, sexism, and homopho-
bia/heterosexism. Now he facilitates local support groups for men and is
the primary caretaker of one child. Tall, with a sandy complexion, some-
what thick build, and an attractive smile, Donny's gentle strength and
spiritual warmth were almost palpable.

*I've had some women say, "See that thing you're doing" or "See that
way that you're acting, that's what we mean by sexist" and I'm like,
okay, I can hear that without getting too defensive. I know I haven't
heard all of it yet, but, I'm open to instruction and to information.... I
have a person who I consider to be my "femtor"—like "mentor" without
the "men" prefix. I also have what I call a "sistren" of women friends in
my life who are willing to inform me about gender issues, so, I've been
lucky in that way. I like offering women a chance to be around a man
intimately, warmly, tenderly, yet nonsexually. And I don't let women
criticize men unfairly, either. I try to help my women friends understand
that whatever it is that they're mad about or feeling is connected to a
larger system as well as that particular individual.*

The Pan-Africanist

Eddie has his bachelor's degree and works as an urban planner in a cor-
porate setting in Missouri. He was born in 1960, grew up in Maryland in
a middle-class setting, and was 36 years old when he was interviewed.
He is currently married, with two adopted children. Eddie has spent
approximately fifteen years in a Pan-African socialist revolutionary
organization working on a variety of social justice issues. He and his
wife are currently making arrangements to move their family to a West
African country because of their political beliefs and organizational networks abroad. Of average height and weight, with bronze-colored skin,
Eddie is analytical, soft-spoken, and seemingly unflappable. His mild-
mannered interpersonal style is an interesting contrast to his extremely
revolutionary beliefs and political practices. In a low yet direct voice,
Eddie recalled:

*My relationship with my wife and being able to communicate with
her about the horrible things that happen to women have certainly
shaped me. Through her social work activities I have met lots of women
who were in abusive situations with men, so it is not an option for me to
be oblivious to the conditions of oppression that Black women face. My
wife has come home totally stressed out because she's dealing with some
inhumane situation where a woman has been burned by her partner and
left for dead, or a woman has been thrown out of the house with only the
clothes on her back. I have also been a member of a revolutionary organization where I have been pushed by sisters and some brothers to think
more deeply about gender issues and how they affect our community.*

The Performance Artist

Edmund is a writer, performance artist, and entrepreneur, cocreator of
an African American theatrical company in Georgia. He was born in
1950 and was age 46 at the time of the interview. Edmund grew up in a
Black middle-class family in the Northeast. He received his bachelor's
degree from a southeastern university where he specialized in urban
planning. Edmund's writing is influenced by the politics of the Black
arts movement. His creative work examines racism, sexism, class
exploitation, homophobia, and other social ills that plague African
American communities. He has received various awards for his dramatic
solo performances, which are often autobiographical. He has also written a novel that addresses the competing forces of racism and sexism in
the African American community. He is married to a Black feminist
writer whom he credits for having a tremendous impact on his antisexist

consciousness and development. He has two adult children from a previous marriage and one stepdaughter. Cocoa brown, with thick hair in long dreadlocks and a well-groomed beard, impeccably dressed in a two-piece suit and tie, Edmund's physical presence, dry humor, and broadcast voice stand out in a crowd.

I think women should have the freedom to be left alone and to live and act in ways that are of their own choosing. My consciousness insists that any rights, acts, or choices of men should be the same rights, acts, and choices available to women. Any attempt to limit the choices of women by men is patently wrong. I think once you understand that the place of a man in the world is no more exalted than the place of a frog, then, you have the humility necessary to challenge sexism and the special treatment that men receive.

The Conscientious Objector

Jake coordinates international programs for a Pennsylvania nonprofit organization that promotes peace education, human rights, and social justice. He was born in 1945 and was 51 years old at the time of the interview. He was raised in a working-class family in Pennsylvania. His activism began in high school and was significantly shaped by the civil rights movement. He became a field secretary for the Student Nonviolent Coordinating Committee (SNCC) during the 1960s and credits this organization for shaping his political worldview. Jake was a conscientious objector during the Vietnam War and served two and a half years in prison for his refusal to be drafted. He speaks publicly on various topics, such as the crisis in former Yugoslavia, the abolition of nuclear weapons, African American involvement in U.S. foreign policy, and domestic and international issues regarding rape. He is currently married and has a son and a daughter from two previous relationships. Light brown, with a thick build and equally thick beard, Jake emphatically stated:

Men have to take responsibility to educate their kids and other men about sexism in the same way that White people have to take responsibility to educate their kids and other White people about racism. We must demand that our sons and other men accept the responsibility to avoid hurting another human being. Being involved in a variety of social movements expanded my consciousness; in fact, these involvements were fundamental to my antisexist consciousness. I wasn't always open to being enlightened. Many women were kicking my ass along the way and challenging me on various issues. It wasn't like I was just sitting back and saying, "Oh, I think I'll be antisexist!"

The Youth Organizer

Malcolm was 23 years of age at the time of the interview and attending an historically Black college in the Southeast. He was born in 1974 and grew up in a working-class extended family in a small Alabama town. Malcolm has extensive experience working with nonprofit community agencies that address youth empowerment and grassroots organizations that use direct action forms of protest. He is also a member of a Black men's antisexist organization and served as a co-organizer of its national conference addressing the implications of being Black, male, and feminist. He conducts workshops that train youth to challenge racism, sexism, and homophobia. When his oldest sister died, he became a single parent to his niece and nephew. Malcolm is currently majoring in psychology and plans to become a community psychologist. Lean, with medium-length dreadlocks, a milk-chocolate complexion, and a hearty laugh, Malcolm confided:

It's been my experience when talking about issues of sexism and oppression, especially in organizations where people have a "social justice-oriented consciousness," that it is so easy to intellectualize these problems. So, instead of just talking about theory and ideology, we train youth to engage in personal acts and personal relationships that break out of that "think-tank mode" where we analyze things to death!

The Tax Accountant

Paul, an entrepreneur in Missouri, was the oldest participant in the study. He was born in 1938 and was 58 at the time of the interview. He grew up in a lower-middle-class family and received undergraduate and graduate degrees from Missouri universities. Paul has been active in organizations such as the League of Women Voters, the YMCA, the local support network of the United Nations, the National Association for the Advancement of Colored People (NAACP), and the Congress for Racial Equality (CORE). He is active in community forums that address local electoral politics, homelessness, and adult education. He has also been active in the nuclear freeze movement. Paul studied to become a Baptist minister but was never ordained, given his insistence that the denomination ordain women. Paul blends his spiritual ministry into his businesses practices and community service. He has one adult son from a previous marriage. Paul's smooth, clean-shaven dark skin, his closely cropped Afro, and his formal interpersonal style are characteristic of his generation. He was dressed fastidiously in a navy blue suit with a white shirt and matching tie for the interview.

The League of Women Voters and my involvement with the labor movement exposed me to feminist thinking. Reading feminist literature and writings about the suffrage movement by Frederick Douglass and W.E.B. DuBois have had a tremendous impact on me. I have actively supported a variety of female political candidates. Many of the people who I respect and think represent the model for politicians are female. Even today, I still have a crush on the former representative from New York, Shirley Chisolm. I've supported programs she proposed, and I must admit—it goes beyond politics—I just like that woman! I admire and have also been influenced by Congresspersons like Maxine Waters of California and Barbara Jordan of Texas. I liked Clinton's former Secretary of Energy, Hazel O'Leary. Even though the political insiders attempted to demoralize her; she was too outstanding for them! In politics, beyond a doubt, with the exception of Ron Brown and a few others, Black women have had the greatest influence on me. What affects Black women affects me. If we could view situations where women or any human being suffers, as being a situation where we all suffer, we could uplift this society.

The Social Scientist

Ralph, a social scientist, works for a federal agency in the Southeast. Before that, he taught at an East Coast university. He has his doctorate, is married to a Black feminist university professor, and has two children. Born in 1956, Ralph was 41 at the time of the interview. He grew up in a working-class family in Georgia. Neatly dressed and of average height and weight, Ralph, an expressive and gifted orator, exuded intellectual sophistication and a passionate interest in the lives of Black men throughout the interview. He was one of the few heterosexual men who boldly affirmed how close friendships with gay men contributed to his development of a comprehensive, feminist understanding of manhood:

My relationships with men who are gay have been really liberating for me. To befriend men who are openly gay is to take a chance and raises all kinds of questions about me, my masculinity, and has even opened me up to attacks by others. However, in these relationships, I've come to understand how the patriarchal system keeps men in check by getting men to appear one-dimensional.... Women and men must be kept in their places for the system to work. This realization has been powerful in helping me to understand this gender stuff.

The Social Worker

Rex was born in 1960 and grew up in the West Indies. He came to the United States in 1980 and ultimately earned a master's degree in social work. At the time of the interview he was 36 years old and working as both a counselor in private practice and a social worker in a nonprofit organization for men who batter women. He is from a low-income working-class background, gay, and single. Rex is an active member of a Black gay men's support group that regularly discusses sexual orientation, race, and gender issues. His slender frame, light West Indian accent, pleasant disposition, silky dark complexion, and bright smile made him easily approachable. When asked about how he became involved in feminist activism, Rex responded:

My experiences as a Black gay man have been at the heart of the antisexist work that I do.... One of the messages that men get growing up is that the worst thing in the world for a man is to be gay, and to be gay is interpreted as being like a woman. People think, "Oh, you're gay so you must want to be a woman" or "You're a fag because you are acting like a woman." To come to grips with being gay has meant, for me, coming to grips with the negative attitudes that men have about women and to realize that there is nothing awful about being like a woman! I mean, tell me, what is so awful about a man being like a woman? So, addressing these woman-hating attitudes is at the heart of my work with men.

The Anthropologist

Solomon is a female-to-male (FTM) transsexual who has undergone various medical treatments (hormone injections and reconstructive surgery) to make his physical body congruent with his male gender identity. Solomon saw himself as male from an early age and felt trapped inside a female body. Medical treatments have enabled him to attain some measure of wholeness. Solomon was born in 1951 and was 46 at the time of the interview. He grew up in the Midwest in a working-class family, attended private midwestern universities, and eventually obtained a doctorate in anthropology. He currently researches the various cultural implications of racism, affiliated with anthropology and women's studies programs at a university on the East Coast. Solomon's deep voice, beige skin, closely cropped salt-and-pepper Afro, short beard, and broad chest would rarely lead anyone to question his masculinity. However, the complexities of his past and present life mirror the complexities of individual and institutionalized beliefs about race, gender, sexuality, and freedom. In a blunt, matter-of-fact speaking style, Solomon discussed his gender identity:

As my awareness of racism evolved, my awareness of sexism and other "isms grew. I didn't really experience the oppression I endured as "female" oppression because I didn't identify myself as a female, plus, I *was preoccupied with learning about and responding to the practice of racism. However, I was born in a female body, so I was also exposed to some of the ways that women suffer. As my understanding of the practice of sexism grew, I realized that the emphasis on only two genders, rigid gender roles, heterosexuality, and other practices of sexist, gender oppression deny me my male gender identity, which is labeled by the medical community as transsexual. According to the medical community, I am a female-to-male transsexual. In the lesbian, gay, and bisexual community, I am referred to as transgendered. My experiences as a transsexual have prepared me to accept that many people will not recognize me as a man. So, I have to be clear within myself about who I am, regardless of the confusion of others.*

The Labor Unionist

Soyinka is working toward his Ph.D. in political science, with a specialty in Africana women's studies and African American studies, at a university in Georgia. He was born in 1947 and was 49 at the time of the interview. He grew up in a working-class family in a small Ohio city. He is a part-time professor, a writer, and an avid social activist whose teaching interests include labor studies, women's studies, and African American studies. He is also a member of a Black labor union, a board member of an organization that works with men who batter women, a participant in an African American support group that addresses violence against Black women, and an advisor for a student organization that challenges men to confront sexism on Black college campuses. Tall, muscular, with a clean-shaven head, a goatee, and a walnut brown complexion, Soyinka's physical stature alone demands respect. The sincerity in his voice, his anguish about his past, and the tears he shed throughout the interview were constant reminders that all things are possible.

I grew up in a family where I saw a lot of violence meted out by my father to my mother. I hated how my father treated my mother. But I had to learn that if you're not actively involved in unlearning behavior that you hate, you may find yourself repeating what you hate. I know what I'm talking about because I became a batterer just like my father. I owe a lot to my ex-wife because she showed me pretty dramatically that being a batterer was not the thing for me to be. She shot me. If that doesn't get your attention, nothing will.

The Priest

Toussaint is a priest, social activist, and "out" bisexual man on the faculty of a Unitarian seminary in northern California, where he grew up in a Black upper-middle-class family. He was born in 1952 and was 44 years old at the time of the interview. Toussaint attended private boarding schools from junior high to high school and received his undergraduate degree from an historically women's college in New York. He obtained his master's degree from an Eastern Orthodox seminary in New York and his doctorate from a theological school in Switzerland. For eleven years, he was on the Divinity School faculty at an historically Black university. Toussaint teaches courses that analyze religion and popular culture from race, gender, and queer theoretical perspectives. His participation in an AIDS awareness organization, an independent political party, and antisexist men's groups and conferences in the United States and Europe are only a few examples of his fervent and unswerving social advocacy. For over twenty years, Toussaint has been in a stable, yet open, marriage with a multiracial, bisexual woman who is a feminist theologian. Toussaint has one child with his marriage partner and one adopted son, who is now an adult. Statuesque, with a golden-brown complexion and extremely long reddish blonde and dark brown hair in dreadlocks, Toussaint turned the heads of both men and women when I picked him up from the airport because of his multiple facial piercings (ears, eyebrows, and nose) and athletic physique. His fluency in French, formal educational experiences, fluid sexuality, polyamorous lifestyle, and radically feminist parenting practices made him a particularly interesting person to interview. Early in the process, Toussaint flatly stated:

Anything that Black men don't want sisters to do they write off as a "White woman's issue" without ever asking sisters, "What do you think about this situation?" In my work, I ask, how do we rectify a particular situation so that everybody has equal access to everything? How do we get men to see that they are also hurt by sexism and that many of them do self-destructive things because they believe, "We're men, that's what men do." So, until men—let's just say Black men—until Black men acknowledge our privilege and power and are willing to let it go for something even better, then we're not really seriously engaged in a struggle for justice and equal access.

The Advocate

Victor was born in 1959 and was age 37 at the time of the interview. He grew up in New Jersey in a lower-middle-class family. During his years at a private Ohio liberal arts college, Victor triple-majored in government, women's studies, and African studies. He also immersed himself in student activism and taught self-defense courses for Ohio Women

Against Rape. He eventually became a prosecutor for the district attorney's office in New York and worked in both the homicide and sex
crime bureaus. Later, he became a law professor at a northeastern university, where he taught critical race and gender studies. He is currently
an entrepreneur. Victor is a survivor of childhood sexual abuse. This
trauma, in part, shaped his early ability to empathize with marginalized
persons. Victor is currently married, with one child. Tall, clean-shaven,
with almond-brown skin, Victor was warm and personable. Even
though he found the childhood section of the interview particularly difficult, he persevered and answered every question thoroughly. After
reflecting on some of the most painful experiences of his childhood and
adult life, Victor proposed the following:

*We have to teach our children that their potential or their ability to
think highly of themselves is not based on this box or that box. I have a
real objection to rigid identity norms and gendered boxes because I've
suffered from them. So, I think the ideal characteristics for a man would
be no different than the ideal characteristics for anybody. There are so
many ways to be a good person. Maleness, manhood, masculinity have all
of these tightly wrapped boxes around them! You've got all of these
"thou shalts" and "thou shalt nots." Feminism has taught me that I
should find the road that gets me from wherever I am to whoever I am.
In other words, I grow; therefore, I am.*

Summary

This descriptive chapter offers a foundation for understanding the
diverse profiles of feminist Black men. Subsequent chapters demonstrate
similarities across the various profiles, despite their differences. In the
next chapter, feminist Black men describe the various ways in which a
confluence of individual, interpersonal, and institutional factors shape
Black men's collusion with patriarchy. Their examples portray the pressures they and other Black men experience to conform to patriarchal
norms, as well as the consequences they face for their nonconformity.

CHAPTER 3

Pawns and Patriarchs

Challenging Assumptions About Power

One obvious question this book explores is whether African American men can be feminists. This chapter asks a related question: Can African American men really be patriarchs in a society that devalues them? If so, in what ways do they practice patriarchal power, and how do feminist Black men interpret and resist those influences?

Most African Americans would acknowledge that *some* Black men do indeed display patriarchal attitudes and behavior. Many also insist that such patriarchal ways do not qualify as "real" patriarchy because White men exercise power on a grander scale, including control of the nation's major institutions.[1] In this chapter I argue that African American men *do* enjoy patriarchal privileges, particularly within African American institutions and communities. Fortunately, feminist Black men's narratives in this study lend support to empirical findings demonstrating a Black feminist consciousness related to, yet distinct from, feminist consciousness and Black consciousness.[2] That distinction is characterized by four themes based on national survey data.

> The first theme, intersectionality, suggests that interlocking oppressions circumscribe the lives of black women through day-to-day encounters with race and gender oppression....The second theme emphasizes the struggle to eliminate patriarchy in all aspects of black life. It is the acceptance of the belief that gender inequality exists within the black community and beyond. The third theme maintains that feminism benefits the black community by challenging patriarchy

31

as an institutionalized oppressive structure and advocating the building of coalitions to further the cause of equality and justice for
women. The fourth theme suggests that...individual life chances are
inextricably tied to the group and that collective action is a necessary
form of resistance.[3]

In short, the four themes underscore: (a) intersectionality, (b) gender
inequality in and outside Black communities, (c) the benefits of Black
feminism in and outside Black communities, and (d) a fate linked with
that of Black women. The following sections present feminist Black
men's narratives that support these important themes. The narratives
show clearly that patriarchy exists within African American communities and that some Black men courageously name it, claim it, and resist it.

The Patriarchal Dividend and African American Men

Patriarchy, as a social system, includes varying degrees of privilege and
powerlessness among men, resulting in contradictory experiences for
them; that is, it exists as social systems of men's power over women,
plus hierarchies of power (pecking orders) among different groups of
men and different displays of masculinity. Specifically, each subgroup
of men, depending on race, class, sexual orientation, and other factors,
defines manhood in ways that conform to the economic and social possibilities of that group.[4] The isolation and the alienation that these hierarchies create among men are key in preserving patriarchy because they
increase the probability that men will end up colluding with the system
in order to experience *any* sense of power and control.[5] Thus, many
men are complicit with the system. Even though the ideal forms of
dominant masculinity are beyond the capabilities of most, they benefit
from the "patriarchal dividend," that is, the advantage men in general
gain from the overall subordination of women.[6] Meanwhile, other men
are marginalized because of their varying degrees of nonconformity to
the dominant White, heterosexual, wealthy male ideal.[7] Many men also
end up colluding under tremendous pressure to conform and out of fear
of the consequences if they do not. Thus, while White men, on the average, have more power than Black men, some Black men have more
power than others. Aspects of the patriarchal dividend from which
Black men benefit—specifically, Black men's power over African
American women who share their socioeconomic class background and
over certain subgroups of other African American men—are often
ignored in the popular press and minimized by most scholars studying
Black men.

The "endangered Black male" perspective, which rests on an analysis of racism and economic impoverishment, omits a critique of patriarchy and does not fully explain Black men's varying degrees of power *inside* African American communities. Focusing solely on the power of the average White man versus that of the average Black man inadvertently excuses Black men for abusing the meager power they have and does not encourage them to question its underlying dynamics. As we will see, the cost to women and children is high, but the cost to Black men and African American communities as a whole is also significant.

In the narrative selections that follow, feminist Black men reveal how patriarchal institutions and expectations are powerful in Black religious institutions, predominantly Black workplaces, the Black family, and even within predominantly Black social movement organizations. Their narratives also show that patriarchal norms can be questioned and challenged when the contradictions become overwhelming and the cost of conforming becomes greater than the cost of resisting.

The purpose of this chapter is *not* to single out Black men as more patriarchal than other men—in fact, national surveys suggest the opposite.[8] Nor is my purpose to minimize the unique hardships that Black men endure, or the historical and ongoing resistance of Black feminist women in mainstream feminist and Black liberation movements. Rather, my intent is to demonstrate how the degrees of patriarchal privilege among Black men serve as a microcosm of other hierarchies of power among different subgroups of men, so as to reinforce the White-dominated, patriarchal capitalist system. Their collusion inadvertently compounds Black men's suffering because whatever patriarchal dividend they derive from the subordination of Black women (and women in general) is a trade-off for their own subordination to White men. That dynamic is evident in African American religious institutions and related faith communities.

Patriarchal Underpinnings of African American Religious Institutions

Powerful men have long used religious institutions and texts to justify slavery, segregation, and other exclusionary practices.[9] The refusal of predominantly White, male-led religious institutions to view Black men as equal leaders in their organizational structures led many Black men to found their own denominations, sects, and spiritual groupings, such as the African Methodist Episcopal Church and the Church of God in Christ; others left the Christian churches altogether and made commitments to religious institutions such as the Nation of Islam.[10] Black men have reinterpreted religious texts as justifying their active presence as leaders in religious institutions, challenging the practice of segregation and the use of scripture to legitimate racial discrimination.[11] However, Black men protesting racism have often embraced the sexism and hetero-sexism found within those same texts and institutions.[12] Narratives from Alan, Paul, and Toussaint help us understand how Black men reap the benefits of the patriarchal dividend through gender-based hierarchies within Black religious institutions, and how feminist Black men interpret and resist such practices.

Alan, a 44-year-old professor of English literature and a Pentecostal minister, describes his understanding of what is perceived as manly and powerful in the Church of God in Christ:

In traditional Christian patriarchal culture, God is always male; and in traditional Christian patriarchal White supremacist culture, God is always a White male. So, my struggle has been—over the course of my life—to remove the Whiteness from God's image, then—over the course of my feminist life—remove the maleness from God's image. I believe that God is pure Spirit, thus, God has no gender. This belief goes fundamentally against what is practiced in the Church of God in Christ. My beliefs have gotten me into trouble in my current church and in other churches.

In the Church of God in Christ, women cannot be ministers. They cannot be pastors. They cannot be preachers. Women can be teachers and are often called "missionaries." Missionaries can give messages, but not sermons—only ministers can give sermons. Women cannot give their messages in the pulpit where the male ministers sit. Only men are allowed in the pulpit. Women can teach other women how to act with men, appreci-ate men, understand the particular pressures that men who are serving God are under, and how to be servants to 'the master.' The 'master' here on earth is your husband, the man who is in a position of authority in the church, or the other brethren in the church.

The image of God that Alan was taught as a child included a com-bined politics of race and gender that legitimated established social inequalities. The Church of God in Christ, as an institution, supports the patriarchal concept of God so as to legitimize its patriarchal policies and guidelines regarding leadership roles. However, Alan exercises a sense of agency by consciously resisting his church's patriarchal religious ideol-ogy. Later in the interview he acknowledged his "call to preach a Black womanist theology that confronts racism, sexism, classism, and hetero-sexism in the Pentecostal faith." Citing the writings of womanist theolo-gians such as Delores Williams,[13] Jacqueline Grant,[14] and Katie Cannon[15] that shaped his own theology, Alan challenges the notion that the male

body is naturally designed for leadership and that the subordination of
Black women by Black men is somehow the "natural order of things."
In addition, he denounces the unhealthy competition it creates among
Black men in the church.

*There is this false notion that a male is supposed to be imbibed with a
kind of power and authority because of his penis, in other words, phallic
power. Well, I just really abhor the notion that I have been given a leadership position simply because biologically I was born with something
between my legs! What an odd rationale for a leadership qualification.
When you think about it, the penis isn't even erect all of the time, in fact,
most of the time it is in a flaccid state, so how can it represent power?
Nonetheless, for many men, particularly in the Pentecostal faith, the
pulpit comes to symbolize phallic/male power. They don't want to remain
out there in the congregation. They want to end up behind that pulpit in
the supreme position of power.*

Alan's personal calling as a minister is accepted, even though he uses
the pulpit to challenge patriarchal interpretations of the Bible. However,
Paul, a 58-year-old tax accountant and a former Baptist minister-in-
training, was denied ordination by Black ministers representing the
National Baptist Convention because of his position regarding the rights
of women.

*In my attempt to become an ordained Baptist minister, I was told
that I had to agree that I would not permit a female to preach from the
pulpit. My teachers referred me to a scripture in the book of Titus as proof
that women should not be ordained. Well, I did not interpret the scripture the way they interpreted it, and they decided not to ordain me. I
don't see how gender affects the ability of a person to preach the gospel
and to serve in the role of authority.*

For the most part, Black men have monopolized the ministry as a
profession and are unable to see the injustices of their own practices,
even though they parallel the injustices of the racist churches against
which they rebelled.[16] Many Baptist and Pentecostal churches still do
not ordain women, although exceptions exist.[17] As womanist theologian
Jacqueline Grant puts it, "Although Black women are often referred to
as the 'backbone' of the church, it should not always be taken as a com-
pliment; when men use the term they may really mean that women are in
the background and should be kept there."[18] Black women are often perceived as "powerful" support workers, yet support workers nonetheless.
They are consistently given responsibilities in the kitchen and on committees (particularly women's auxiliaries), while men are granted positions on the decision-making boards and other policy-oriented
leadership positions; these political maneuvers help to keep women "in

their place" in the denomination as well as the local congregations—in the pews but out of the pulpit.[19]

When Paul was asked to explain why he still attends church and how he grapples with the disconnect between his individual beliefs and those of the National Baptist Convention, he quietly stated:

We cannot deny that the Black church has been a vehicle whereby Black women have been able to assume certain positions of authority not available in the broader White community that provide them with confidence and a strong self-esteem. Most of the leadership within the Black church is female leadership, even though the pulpit is often reserved for males. If it were not for the women, various programs and events in the church would end! Of course, during these programs, pompous males in the pulpit jump out there and spread their wings, but when it comes to actually preparing the program, doing the behind-the-scenes work, and ensuring that things are done successfully, most churches depend upon women. I enjoy being in the company of these women and a 'thorn in the side' of the male leadership.... Also, I grew to realize that I did not need to be ordained to serve, and today I view my ministry as outside the walls of organized religion and its ornate structures. I integrate my ministry into my business and volunteer work. No man, no institution, and no one's refusal to ordain me, can deny me that sacred calling.

Both Alan and Paul exemplify how institutional structures shape individual choices and social interactions, as well as how individual human agency can disrupt the status quo. Although their interpretations of religious institutions were similar when compared to the responses of the other men, their choice to remain active in religious institutions was exceptional. Only five (25%) out of the twenty feminist Black men interviewed reported regularly attending church or other religious services. Those five gravitated toward Christian churches or religious services that were also nontraditional in rituals and doctrine, and politically progressive. Seven of the men did not espouse a clear concept of God (35%) describing themselves in agnostic and atheist terminology (e.g., dialectical materialist, religious skeptic, and nonbeliever). The remaining eight (40%) had clear God-concepts, but did not support institutionalized religion or attend religious services because of the harsh patriarchal and homophobic attitudes they associated with these institutions. African American religious institutions have lost considerable credibility as effective vehicles of Black liberation among this group.[20]

Toussaint, a 44-year-old Eastern Orthodox-trained priest and professor, embodies another mode of defying institutional regulations and cultural expectations while remaining intertwined with religion.

I practice Eastern Orthodox Christianity, the Yoruba religion, and some Cherokee spirituality. Even though I practice these various religions, I am a dissident voice within them.... For example, in the Yoruba religion there are people who say that women cannot hold certain religious positions. In Cherokee spirituality there are people who believe women shouldn't drum at certain rituals. In the Eastern Orthodox tradition there are people who feel that women should not be ordained. I do not support these positions. I am also a dissident voice within broader Black religious communities. For instance, I wholeheartedly support the ordination of women. It's an important issue for me after eleven years of teaching at the Divinity School of an historically Black university where folks still said, "The ordination of women is not in 'The Word of God' and that is not a Black woman's issue."

The fact that these issues are relevant today indicate that Black ministers definitely have power, although in varying degrees, and use it as a subgroup of men in a White male-dominated society. Even most Black women prefer male ministers and are suspicious of women leaders, particularly female pastors.[21] Recent studies suggest that Black women who are most active in the church are least supportive of the notion that "Black churches or places of worship should allow more African American women to become members of the clergy" and also unsupportive of the idea that "African American women should share equally in the political leadership of the African American community."[22] Feminist Black men recognize this patriarchal dividend and challenge other Black men (and Black women) to resist its lure.

Patriarchal Dynamics in Work Settings

Black men and women have fought against unjust treatment as second-class citizens collectively; therefore, it is equally unjust for Black men to ask Black women to learn how to be second-class citizens a second time.[23] Because feminist Black men can see how the combined effects of racism and sexism affect Black communities, they also recognize the combined benefits of Black feminism for the entire Black community, not just Black women. Also, because they see their fate as Black men as linked to the fate of Black women, they are often willing to support Black women's interests, even when pressured by other Black men to rank race issues as more important than gender issues. That pressure is especially grueling for feminist Black men when everyday politics pit Black men and women against one another. Toussaint recalls the patriarchal dynamics at the prestigious, historically Black university where he taught.

I worked as a professor at the Divinity School of a predominantly Black university for eleven years. Initially, I thought the predominantly Black male faculty members were sensitive enough to know that they needed to recruit Black women faculty. I was wrong. Even the women who were already on faculty were undercut and sabotaged—unless they posed no threat to the men. I saw some very underhanded, nasty things happen to Black women faculty and students. I saw how the brilliant women students were given second-class status if some "boy preacher" came along. Students who were men were clearly favored. A Black male faculty member badgered one Black woman colleague of mine so badly that she resigned. She just said, "I can't work in an environment like this."

I've been on search committees for recruiting new faculty and have heard important things mentioned about women candidates that were glossed over and petty things that were highlighted about the women that were never mentioned about the men candidates. Administrators and senior faculty would say, "We have equality for women here" or "There are women on our faculty, even womanist theologians," and I would just find those comments to be very patronizing. Basically, at that Divinity School, Black men reproduced along the lines of gender what White people are guilty of reproducing along the lines of race when they talk about affirmative action but aren't really committed to the principles of affirmative action.

In my teaching experience at this Divinity School, men were not encouraged to go into religious education. It was perceived as a field for women. Interestingly enough, a woman chaired the religious education department—and precisely because a woman chaired that department it became the "Ha! Ha!" Department! In other words, students and faculty would say, "Who takes that department really seriously?"... When there was a search for a dean of the Divinity School, there was no aggressive search to get women candidates.... Black male faculty often treated Black women faculty like "nice window dressing." It was such an unhealthy environment. Working there really exposed me to some really upsetting experiences about Black men—particularly men who were involved in the broader civil rights movement and who professed the significance of spirituality in that movement. I just could not believe how they used their power in such harmful ways.

When Black men collude with, rather than challenge, patriarchal assumptions and practices, African American communities suffer collectively because Black men are often fighting Black women instead of the systemic injustices that contribute to the powerlessness of them both.[24]

Many Black men aid and abet a system that leaves them only crumbs. However, the narratives of the feminist Black men in my study suggest that when Black men truly see their fate as linked to that of Black women, they move from sympathy to genuine empathy. In this context, empathy is like the African proverb "I am because we are" and a process of "putting yourself in the place of others, orienting to objects in their world as they would, not only as you would."[25]

Victor, a 38-year-old former prosecutor and law professor, described his empathy for Black women seeking employment at certain Black law firms.

I have African American friends who have law firms that won't hire Black women or who put glass ceilings in front of Black women. These are Black law firms with Black male law partners, so, their sexism restricts their access to talent....Some would rather cut their own throats to stop sisters from achieving, but when they do that, they are cutting the throats of Black people in general. Her throat, my throat, your throat.

Malcolm, a 23-year-old college student and outreach worker, described working in a predominantly Black nonprofit organization that had national status.

The brothers who are associated with community agencies are often considered "the national leaders," "the figureheads," and the "spokespersons," but the majority of the people who I see physically doing the outreach, the case management, attending the rallies, maintaining the organization's records are Black women. I haven't seen many men do any of the hands-on work. These work experiences have helped me to see how sexism operates at a subtle level even in social justice-oriented Black community agencies. It's enough to make you cry, and I have cried.

The pressures to conform are tremendous, and the refusal to join in creating something akin to an "old boys' network" has its own negative consequences for Black men who break ranks with other Black men in support of Black women. Toussaint eventually resigned from his faculty position at the historically Black university and became a professor at a West Coast educational institution. Victor left the practice of law and became an entrepreneur. Malcolm continues to work in nonprofit community organizations, but may apply to graduate school in order to gain additional credentials for addressing what he refers to as "the demoralizing" intersectional politics of community agencies. Most problematic for Malcolm has been the patriarchal practices of African American men who represent organizations linked to the civil rights movement. The collusion of Black men with patriarchy in social justice movements—both sectarian and nonsectarian—is especially disheartening.

Social Movements: Civil Rights, Black Power, a Million Men, and the Promises They Keep

Far from being unified, Black social movements are diverse and have had complicated influences on concepts of race, gender, class, sexuality, and nationality. I have chosen here to highlight how feminist Black men have responded to and incorporated Black feminist themes into their analysis and practices as activists across various social movements. My aim is not to characterize these movements as fundamentally or exceptionally sexist. Rather, my purpose is to demonstrate the patriarchal dividends that Black men obtain through the institutional dynamics of certain social movement organizations and to show how feminist Black men respond individually. Edmund, Cabral, Jake, Solomon, Soyinka, Abdul, and Donny recount, in their narratives, how their experiences in social movements during the 1960s raised their consciousness about Black patriarchal practices.

Edmund, a 46-year-old performance artist, says male power dynamics in the Black Power movement deterred him from joining any particular group during the 1960s and early 1970s.

The artistic wing of the Black Power movement known as the Black arts movement influenced my writing. But the sexism within the Black arts movement was blatant. Literary anthologies were published that only included a few women, yet there were many women who were writers in the movement. Many of the men who were popular within the Black arts movement didn't view women artists as participants of equal status. Around that same time, Black political leaders like Stokely Carmichael were pushing the idea that the only position for a Black woman in the Black Power movement was prone! I liked the political ideology of the Black Muslims, but I couldn't bring myself to join them because in addition to the fact that I liked pork, I did not believe that women were subordinate to men.

Scholars of the Black arts movement note how "a paternalistic, often homophobic, masculinism was a powerful strain within the Black arts and Black Power movements as it was in many of the ideologies and social lives of post-World War II bohemias and countercultures."[26] However, it was not the only strain. Cabral, a 49-year-old poet in this study, cofounded a Black activist organization affiliated with the Black arts movement during the early 1970s. His organization struggled with race, gender, and sexuality issues in ways that led to the adoption of Black feminist perspectives.[27] I quote him in detail to illustrate the dynamic relationship between individuals and institutions, such that, as institutions can affect individuals, individuals can affect institutions.

In the beginning, we were what I would call classic Black national-ists. Even though we thought we were being progressive, our position on "the woman question" was suspect. Also, there was a strain of homopho-bia in the collective. I know some people say that both sexism and homo-phobia were part of the times, but there is no need to hide from the truth. On these accounts, our collective was initially backwards. Within the next five to six years, we wrote poems and essays that tackled homophobia and sexism, demonstrating that through self-criticism—regardless of where we started from—we kept developing. I took the lead on pushing gender issues and wrote a collection of essays in support of the struggle to smash sexism and develop women....The essays reflected our collective's most thorough, ongoing critique of sexism. By then we were presenting lesbians at our annual Black women's conferences....I remember one panel dis-cussion that included a sister who was openly lesbian. Some people thought, "You have lost your mind, what are you all doing with a lesbian on the panel, blah blah blah." I told them they better wake up! If you don't believe that gays and lesbians have been discriminated against, ask the insurance companies, ask the medical providers, ask about state inher-itance rights, ask why marriage is restricted to heterosexuals. Homo-phobia is the problem, not the sexuality.

Cabral's narrative attests to the fact that patriarchal norms can be questioned and challenged. However, some feminist Black men succumb to patriarchal pressures and to homophobic taunting that questions their masculinity. Like feminist women, they grapple with the possibility of being ostracized by their peers. All the men in the study admitted the different ways they themselves benefited from the "patriarchal divi-dend," particularly before being exposed to feminist points of view.

Jake, a 51-year-old human rights advocate and conscientious objec-tor during the Vietnam War, gives one example of how patriarchal assumptions and practices played out in civil rights organizations like the Student Nonviolent Coordinating Committee (SNCC).

I became a field secretary in SNCC. The men were mainly chosen for these leadership positions, but when a woman was chosen, we kind of made her "an honorary male" as if to say that a real woman couldn't be so talented. I was guilty of that. A woman I dated was considered an "honorary male" because she played roles that men played in the civil rights movement.

Jake's awareness of his own sexist practices in SNCC came later in life, thanks to increasing social interactions with feminists in his work environments. Yet social movement organizations often played a pivotal role—despite their patriarchal practices—by providing a context for men to interact with feminist women face-to-face. The role of feminist friendships, which proved to be important for all feminist Black men in the study, is discussed in the next chapter.

Like Jake, Solomon, a 46-year-old anthropologist and the only transgendered man in the study, was active in the civil rights and Black power movements. He was closeted in some social movement organizations but not in others, so he vacillated between conformity and nonconformity regarding his transgendered identity even more than his feminist identity. Solomon waxed indignant about the experiences of Bayard Rustin, a Black gay civil rights activist who planned the logistics of the groundbreaking March on Washington in 1963 but was not publicly acknowledged at the time by Adam Clayton Powell, Martin Luther King, and other organizers who held homophobic and dogmatic ideas about what was "manly" and "upright."[28]

I think that when Bayard Rustin agreed to organize the March on Washington, he should have made it clear to Martin Luther King and everybody else that "If I do this and you get to benefit from my services, then it's not going to just be a civil rights movement for 'racially' oppressed people; it's going to be a civil rights movement for ALL [his emphasis] oppressed people, including lesbian, gay, bisexual, and transgendered people."

Some of us agree to stay in the closet in order to preserve certain privileges and to experience certain opportunities. I don't blame Bayard Rustin for compromising that way, but the March on Washington wouldn't have happened if he hadn't organized it. The March on Washington has meant so much in improving the quality of Black life in this country, but it never would have happened had it not been for his personal commitment and organizational skills, and HE WAS A BLACK GAY MAN [his emphasis]. Do I think that we should pretend that Bayard Rustin wasn't gay? No, I think that's foolish.

Toussaint, the priest, also refers to himself as a "queer-identified bisexual man." He boldly stated his concerns about "hetero-patriarchy" (heterosexism and patriarchy) in African American social movements:

The presence of Black queers throughout the Black liberation movement should be acknowledged. If we're not all liberated together, we're not liberated. The assumption that everybody in the Black liberation movement is straight is ridiculous. How do we acknowledge the diversity within the Black community, and when we are all there with all of our pieces, isn't the liberation is all the sweeter?

Deeply embedded race, gender, class, and sexuality factors interact at individual and institutional levels in ways that shape opportunities for some Black men and constraints for others. Both Toussaint and Solomon are "out" about their gender and sexual identities. Being middle class, highly educated and working in liberal educational environments created enabling contexts that helped them resist the debilitating sexual politics of certain Black social movements and the lack of tolerance regarding representations of Black manhood. Most of the feminist Black men who became activists during the 1960s developed the empathy, confidence, and oppositional consciousness that characterize the following passage by Solomon.

Should we continue to pretend that James Baldwin wasn't gay, when he was obviously a "flaming queen"? No. Should we continue to pretend that Langston Hughes, Alain Locke, Countee Cullen, and so many others were heterosexual when we have proof that they weren't? Hell no! Why are we willing to erase the sexuality of people who have become prominent cultural donors to Black culture and society in general? We have been able to produce brilliant Black people who are not only suffering racial oppression, but also gender oppression and sexuality oppression, yet still manage to raise our culture to a high level! How have we been able to produce such brilliance given multiple experiences of oppression? We never get to ask or debate that question because we're so busy pretending that all of these people weren't gay or that they had no sexuality . . . Aw, come on! We need to get off of that![29]

The legacy of the March on Washington appeared clear to Solomon and other participants who were adolescent activists during that time. However, the legacy of the Million Man March (October 16, 1995) was less clear to the men in this study, and their responses to it were varied. When one internalizes a Black feminist perspective and is faced with a sociopolitical issue where race interests and gender interests collide, an intersectional analysis should lead one to reject ranking one (race) over the other (gender) in favor of treating both interests simultaneously.[30] However, even Black men who are cognizant of the particular predicament of Black women, as persons who experience both racism and sexism, tend to prioritize race issues over gender issues and argue that Black women should do the same (likewise, liberal White feminist women often expect Black women to rank gender issues over race issues when the interests of both collide).[31] Highly publicized examples when race and gender issues collided for African Americans included Anita Hill's testimony against Supreme Court nominee Clarence Thomas at his confirmation hearings and boxer Mike Tyson's trial for rape. The Million Man March shows how feminist Black men tend to respond to these dilemmas.

The Million Man March energized major groups within Black communities across the nation. However, the solutions it promoted for African American problems (such as self-help, atonement, and men taking control of the situation) "reflected a severely limited political vision rooted in deeply patriarchal assumptions and knee-jerk nationalism" according to some feminist Black men scholars.[32] Clearly, not all Black men who supported and attended the march agreed with every aspect of organizer Louis Farrakhan's message. In fact, some feminist Black men went there to protest the rhetoric, as well as to create critical dialogue with the Black men attending the march about other ways of defining the problems within Black communities.[33] Only three (15%) of the men interviewed here attended or said they supported the march.

The Atlanta Committee for Black Liberation sent Farrakhan and other Black men and women a position paper that critiqued the strengths and weaknesses of the march, yet urged Black people to support it.[34] One participant in this study, Soyinka, a 49-year-old labor unionist and part-time college instructor, served on the committee that wrote the paper. He gives this summary of the document's intersectional analysis:

Our position paper outlined that after "careful analysis of the platform proposed by the Nation of Islam and its National Representative, Minister Louis Farrakhan, as stated in speeches, interviews, and essays published in the Final Call newspaper" we were disturbed by: (1) the "strong patriarchal thrust of the Million Man March"; (2) "the lack of a thorough political and economic solution in addition to the spiritual call put forth"; (3) "the chilling similarity in tone to the conservative, right-wing, Christian White males"; and, (4) the "ultimate reliance on divine intervention" which suggests that it primarily is sufficient to "solve the crises plaguing the Black Nation."[35]

In addition, the committee stated unequivocally that the Million Man March should be supported because "it is a reflection our people's desire for solutions," the concept of the march dramatizes "the conditions of our people" and plans for "concerted action to achieve peace, justice, basic human rights, and self-determination," it is a righteous call for "Black women and men to reconcile differences with one another," it is a call for "reconciliation" along with the call for "Black men to become involved with their families and to find solutions to crises plaguing our communities," and it is a call for "unity of the Black Nation."[36]

Although most participants in this study supported the position paper's critique, their decisions on whether or not to attend the march varied. Alan commented:

I am no longer going to align myself with Black men who are marching and talking about "We need our rights as men."...That is not empowerment from a holistic perspective. Black liberation and empowerment can no longer mean "empowerment for the Black man first."

Empowerment, for me, does not mean going somewhere with my broth-ers and hugging them on national TV and thinking that we are really moving forward by simply saying, "We're sorry for not being real men who are the heads of their households." I am not trying to undercut the very real spiritual connections among Black men who went to the Million Man March, however, I did not attend the march. I saw the tears of many Black men and they were real tears — but we need more than a "feel-good-get-together." We need a critical consciousness that takes into consideration a comprehensive liberating perspective. Black feminism can help us attain that consciousness and can serve as an excellent road map as we redefine the terms of our manhood, and it can transform our rela-tionships with women as well as with each other.

Toussaint agreed and added:

I decided not to participate in the Million Man March. I put a mes-sage on my answering machine at the time that said if we are opposed to White supremacy, to heterosexism, and so forth, we have to oppose them consistently. We cannot say that as men of color we can have male privi-lege sometimes and in other situations we don't have to have it. If the sis-ters had been invited to the march, that would have been a totally different event for me. But, I saw this kind of "Black nationalist men's thing" being reinforced that was like a Black version of that patriarchal Christian group of men called the "Promise Keepers."

Abdul, a 50-year-old counselor at a nonprofit agency dealing with men who batter, also thought Farrakhan's solutions bore a striking resemblance to those proposed by Christian groups such as the Promise Keepers.[37] He did not attend the march.

There's this huge movement called the "Promise Keepers" and that movement really upsets me! The men in the movement are talking about how men need to go back into the home and accept the tradi-tional roles of maleness based on biblical scripture that says the man is in charge. If you got 50,000 men coming together in a stadium, why not talk about how those men can be different in a relationship and not be abusive? Why don't we talk about the hurt and the pain that we've created for others and begin to take responsibility for that? As opposed to figuring out only how to "heal our wounds" we need to pri-marily look at how we've created so many wounds in others! It really concerns me that at this stage of the game, we're still trying to figure out how to take care of men. We've been so responsible for the pain and the suffering of so many women, yet all we can talk about is how men have been hurt!

Donny, a 42-year-old restaurant owner and seasoned gay rights activist, was the only feminist Black man who did not critique the march to the same degree as the others. He attended the march and narrated the personal impact it had on his family.

Yes, many of these movements are sexist and patriarchal and regressive in many ways, but the fact that they are growing demonstrates to me how desperate men are for some sort of deeper connection with other men. The void and the hurt that men experience due to their isolation are at an all-time high. I had an incredible experience at the Million Man March. Being there with my grandfather, father, my brothers, and my nephews—four generations of us plus friends and strangers—was a profound experience for me. There was the incredible sort of contradiction that so many Black men were standing in a place together being gentle and sweet and thoughtful and loving and showing our magnanimity and concern. That one gathering was so healing. I'll never forget it. I'll never underestimate the influence of that moment.

We should expect diversity among feminist Black men, given different levels of exposure and the fact that there are many ways to be a feminist. However, when African American social movements depict the central problems of African Americans as "race-related" and cast Black men as the primary victims of these problems, they obscure the problems of Black women and minimize how Black women and Black men together can solve such problems. They also construct Black women as figures who have suffered less than Black men and ought to stand behind their men because Black men's problems are alleged to be more urgent.[38] Furthermore, these male-centered approaches reduce Black women's problems to mere consequences of Black men's problems, as a rationale for putting the problems of Black men first, claiming that strategy will simultaneously solve the problems of Black women.[39] Such views reproduce and legitimize a patriarchal political agenda for African American communities and ignore problems, such as rape and other forms of violence outside and inside the home, that affect African American communities as a whole.

The Black Family: "The Master's Tools Will Never Dismantle the Master's House"[40]

Adversely affected by race and gender oppression, Black women also make up a disproportionately high percentage of the working poor and underclass in the United States. Thus, as a result of the combined effects of multiple systemic injustices, Black women's experiences encompass the reality of Black men (racism), White women and women of color (sexism), and the poor across race and culture (classism), stretching beyond but also including the realities of Black communities. By emphasizing the simultaneous effects of various systemic oppressions, I challenge those "save the Black family" campaigns that promote a conservative, middle-class politics of respectability.[41] Such politics inadvertently contribute to the patriarchal dividend of Black men.

Specifically, policy makers, Black religious leaders, and social scientists guided by a "politics of respectability" choose to point to a decrease in the numbers of Black women marrying, the increase in female-headed households, and the increasing visibility of same-sex unions in Black communities. Black feminists discussing the Black family prefer to focus on institutional forces that keep marriage a patriarchal, heterosexist institution; economic and workplace policies that deprive female-headed households of the multiple resources needed to raise healthy children; and ways to increase a Black woman's economic independence regardless of her marital status, sexuality, and number of children.[42]

Religious institutions like Black churches and the Nation of Islam have been impressive and phenomenal supporters of the family. In particular, the Nation of Islam has done an admirable job of rescuing drug abusers and imprisoned Black men, encouraging them to return to and support their families. However, the models of the Black family that they support are limited, given the heterosexist and patriarchal assumptions that underlie their middle-class politics of respectability.[43] Likewise, certain Black nationalist groups have placed the Black family at the center of their programs, yet the Afrocentric, complimentary models they popularize often reflect precolonial, patriarchal African societies rather than the precolonial egalitarian ones that have also been documented by scholars.[44]

Many African American women have tolerated the patriarchal and heterosexist models of the Black family advocated by these institutions because they "offer protection from the harsh realities of poverty, racism, and street violence"; in addition, these institutions "call upon Black men to assume responsibility for their families, offer an incisive analysis of racism, affirm African and African American cultural styles, and acknowledge the burdens that Black women often carry single-handedly in their homes."[45] However, they simultaneously promote patriarchal ideology and practices at the expense of gender equity and Black mothers' autonomy. Thus, patriarchy's ills remain unacknowledged and intact.

Missing from this focus on the "Black family," "marriage," and "two-headed households" is the fact that such options are not always the best or the safest for many Black women, given alarming rates of family violence. Some Black men experience the "patriarchal dividend" within their families, particularly through the threat and actual use of violence. Scholars have extensively documented the association of violence with patriarchal concepts and practices of masculinity.[46] Black men and other subordinated groups of men are aware that they do not possess the power and privileges that society has taught them "real men" should possess. As a result, they often feel frustrated and alienated by their inability to live up to mainstream notions of masculinity, such as becoming the head of a household, a father, and a breadwinner. Rather than question these popular and dominant notions of "manhood," some men express their alienation and frustration by blaming, beating, raping, or emotionally abusing the women and children in their lives.[47] The feminist Black men in my study discussed the degree to which those dynamics played out in their families.

A participant was identified as coming from a violent family if he described his home as including "domestic violence," "frequent or ongoing physical fights among parents," or "frequent physical abuse of one parent." Six of the twenty men interviewed—Bruce, Soyinka, Alan, Donny, Toussaint, and Solomon—described a regular, almost predictable pattern of violence that occurred in their homes. All six came from two-parent homes in which their parents were married and their fathers were working as well as the primary breadwinners. Soyinka and Bruce described themselves as former batterers. Bruce is a 47-year-old project coordinator at an agency that develops intervention programs for men who batter women.

My father had two separate families. I didn't know about his other family until I was in high school. I had two younger half-brothers and a younger half-sister. I knew them on a casual basis, but never really bonded with them.... The hatred my parents had for each other toward the end of the marriage was obvious. My mother was a very plain speaker and would just say, "I hate your guts, you son-of-a-bitch."

Even though my mother could not articulate what was happening to her in a sophisticated way, I was always exposed to the plight of women through observing her experiences. My father used to violently attack my mother. I never thought that I would end up doing the same thing to the women in my life, but I did.... I was a blood donor, coached football in the neighborhood, was part of the neighborhood cleanup campaign, but at home I was a domestic terrorist.

Men, primarily, teach boys and men to be violent. Regardless of how badly a father treats his child or the child's mother, he also teaches, by example, a shameless way of being in the world; his actions say to the boy, "You, too, can behave as I do when you become a man."[48] Too often, "what fathers pass on to their children is their own unacknowledged pain, and in instances of violence, a male sense of entitlement to inflict pain on others."[49] The percentage of men in prison has something to teach us about the ways in which men are taught to handle pain, anger, and conflict. Men make up close to 93% of the prison population, leading some men to quip that the largest men's gathering in the United States is San Quentin.[50] There are more college-aged Black men in prison than in school, nearly half of all prison inmates in the United States are African American males—even though they constitute only 6% of the total national population, and one of every fourteen adult Black males is locked up on any given day.[51] Criminologists have found that men actively use crime in a variety of situations to make statements about their status as men; however, men also use crime as a breadwinning strategy when other economic resources are unavailable.[52] As a result, prisons as institutions perpetuate subordinated forms of masculinity that thrive on dominance, violence, and other predatory behaviors.

Soyinka (labor unionist) recalls in detail how his father's violent conception of Black masculinity pushed away the very people whom he most loved and needed.

I often say I come from a "fractured home," as opposed to a broken home, because my Dad was often "absent without leave." He had a number of extramarital affairs that my mother, sister and I knew about. Women would call our house. We didn't know their names, but we knew their voices. My father used to beat my mother, and I hated how he treated her.

I never knew of a time when my father worked only one job. He was the first Black bus driver in our town. He was also a janitor and typed bulletins for the church and theses and dissertations for students on the side. Later in life, he was a social worker and a probation officer....My father constantly talked about racism and had a profound hatred for segregation....I guess the anger he held inside was let out at home on my mother, my sister, and me.

He was very active in the African Methodist Episcopal Church and directed the church choirs. One day we had just come home from church. I was about 12 years old. I remember hearing my father hit my mother. I ran from my room and saw my mother's beads all over the floor. My father had apparently grabbed or karate chopped her around the throat and my mother was trying to catch her breath. She saw me and told me to run next door to get help....I was very fearful of my father until I got taller and one time I tried to kill him. I was about 17 or 18 years old and he was beating my mom and I was just fed up with it. My mother stepped in between us....I would describe my parents' marriage as stormy and unfulfilled for most of the twenty-five years they were together. When they weren't arguing, they weren't speaking. Mother cried a lot and said that if it weren't for us kids, she would leave

him....When it became apparent to the family that my father had
cancer, he finally reconciled with my mother. During that year or so, I
actually saw them communicate. He died without the two of us being
able to resolve certain things....To this day, I have only a few positive,
strong friendships with men.

The idea that men should be the sole breadwinners in families, that
it is acceptable for men to violate the integrity of a marriage with extramarital affairs ("he's just being a man"), and that men and their needs
are more important than women are assumptions and practices that
foster gender inequities and destroy families. Soyinka's father's acceptance of these popular beliefs—reinforced by his experiences of racial
and economic inequalities—impaired his ability to communicate effectively with his wife and children. He cut himself off from genuine intimacy, even as he tried to assert himself "as a man" by battering and
terrorizing family members.

Although Soyinka's father was keenly aware of racism and economic injustice, he probably died unaware that his assumptions about
manhood also disempowered him and the rest of his family. Soyinka was
adversely affected by his father's violence emotionally and physically
and has spent years trying to recover from the trauma. Although children can be remarkably flexible, they are still fragile beings, and the
trauma they experience in childhood can have lifelong effects.[53] Anger
toward his father and inappropriate distance from him created later difficulties for Soyinka in determining appropriate boundaries with women
and establishing trust with men.

Alan's experiences, which made him unable to see himself as lovable
and worthy, led him to beat up on himself emotionally. Alan (Pentecostal professor) recalls:

My father is no longer living; in fact, he died from cancer just a
couple of months ago. He worked for the city's sewer system for the
greater part of his life. Within the framework of what a Black man could
do in that company, he climbed through the ranks and became an assis-
tant superintendent. He perceived working with his hands as a symbol of
"manliness." He would say, "Real men aren't afraid to get their hands
dirty!" My father also talked about the ways that he was insulted on the
job, given the countless racist comments and attitudes that he had to
endure. The issue of respect was very important to him.

My father was happiest when he was outside of the home and drink-
ing with his friends. Even though my father was in the home, I was
always aware of my father being away. For example, he would work
during the week until five o'clock in the evening, but would always come
home late at night. On the weekends he would come home Friday

evening, then head back out until Saturday night. He would come home Sunday morning to change clothes, then go out again until Sunday night. So my father lived in the home with us, but his "present absence"—the contradiction of my father being there technically, but not there otherwise—best describes how my father was in the home. When he was physically in the home, he was there in very loud and horrific ways often physically abusing my mother.

Alan's father, like Soyinka's, was overwhelmed by his own victimization in the world and resorted to rage and violence to pump up his sense of superiority in the home. Years of minimizing their pain and denying their need for help probably contributed to their ill health. Men's willingness to downplay weakness and pain is so great that it has been called a factor in shortening their life span because they often do not take care of themselves.[54] Men wait longer to acknowledge that they are sick, take longer to get help, and once they get treatment do not comply with it as well as women.[55] Substance abuse and other addictions are common but ineffective ways that many men cope with the debilitating contradictions and the varying degrees of power and powerlessness they experience as men. Their inability to acknowledge their own human frailties plays violently on the frailties of others perceived as weak.

Donny (restaurant owner) also grew up with a violent father who neglected his health and worked more than one job to make ends meet. Donny bonded with his mother against his father's alcoholism and physical abuse. Like Bruce, Soyinka, and Alan, he also felt protective of his mother at an early age.

My father worked for the federal housing administration as a full-time office worker and drove a taxicab in the evening and on weekends. He was overworked, addicted to alcohol, and didn't take care of himself. Caring for his family was very important to him—that's why he was so overworked.... Until about ten years ago, my father's drinking was in the way of him having close relationships with anybody. He was violent, he was abusive, he was mean when he was drunk, and he was drunk most of the time.... My mother had to be the peacemaker, super responsible, and supportive of him in the best way she could. She took her wedding vows seriously and was never going to leave my father. So, that relationship was really harsh for her.... My mother and I received most of my father's abuse, so we have a special "battered bond."

Bruce, Soyinka, Alan, and Donny all came from working-class homes in which their fathers were economically responsible and married to their mothers. However, behind closed doors, these outward signs of "respectability," which policy makers push for in welfare reform, were mere illusions and undermined the psychological well-being of family members, including the fathers. Toussaint confided how violent family dynamics play out in an upper-middle-class outwardly "respectable" Black family.

Like most Black upper-middle-class families during the 1950s, my parents basically tried to model themselves after White middle and upper-middle-class nuclear families. I was sent away to a boarding school at a certain point and grew up taking piano, violin, and voice lessons.... I think my father felt—like a lot of brothers I know—that he had bitten off more than he could chew in terms of all that he was trying to do...he had a child, he was married, he was finishing college, and he was work-ing. So, there was tension, sometimes pretty intense tension.

Every six months or so on Friday nights they would get into it and there would be this big explosion. I remember the trigger of one of these really tense scenes. Some people had come from my father's office to our house one evening. My mother had been sick with the flu, but she had to get up and serve them their little cocktails and snacks. Afterwards, she told my father, "I was sick, why did you ask me to serve your friends, you could have done that!" They exchanged words and a fight broke out. Once, I saw my father with his hands around my mother's neck during a blowup.... I just feel really sorry for my mother that she didn't feel like she could leave my father. We were in private schools and if they had divorced at that time, my father probably would have made sure she was destitute, to punish her. I am just so grateful that she didn't get killed. They divorced many years later when I was in graduate school.

Toussaint's narrative demonstrates how, regardless of class, the sense of power Black men experience fluctuates. I found that, as a result of such pressures, boys in single-parent homes with their mothers or grandmothers were often better off emotionally than boys in two-parent, violent homes.

Carlos, a 23-year-old Black Latino, cofounder of a Black profeminist men's organization and graduate student in environmental studies, discusses his relationship with his mother.

My parents were never married. They weren't involved with each other from the time that I was born. I have no brothers or sisters. Growing up, I saw my father on the weekends. During my early years he would come by my mother's house. When I was in high school I would go to see him on the weekends. For a while, my mother and I were on wel-fare and got food stamps. So, I know what it means to be broke.

My father is so quiet! Even today, when I see him not much is said. When I visit him, we just sit there. These days I hardly ever go back to New York, so, I don't see him that often. After sitting there for a while and nobody's really saying anything and nothing is on television, I leave....

My mother and I are cool! We both like to travel. I speak to my mother about once a week. We talk and joke with each other. She'll call me or I'll call her—but, usually she calls me. I identify more with my mother because she likes to live the adventurous life. She's 61 years old and just loves New York. She came to Ohio to visit me at this university and said that Ohio was too slow for her. Like her, I'm open-minded and am eclectic in my approach to life. My mother attended community college and is a teacher's aide for autistic children in the Bronx. My mother is really independent and counters many stereotypes about women, particularly Latina women.

Frequent phone conversations and a recent visit to his campus suggest that Carlos's mother is actively involved in his life. Her high energy, travels, and broad interests indicate a zest for life that one rarely hears or reads about when single parents are discussed in the media.

Boys who show the worst psychological adjustment are not always those without fathers but, often, those with abusive or neglectful fathers. Scientific studies demonstrate that a father can have a meaningful presence in a child's life whether he is in the home or not.[56] The fathers of Bruce, Soyinka, Alan, and Donny were emotionally unavailable and, when physically present, violent tyrants. The problem in Carlos's relationship with his father is not that his father did not live with him or marry Carlos's mother, but that he was shut down and taciturn. Carlos takes what he can from this example, accepting that his father is someone he may never really know.

Current research suggests that the key factor in a boy's healthy relationship to his father is affection, not some essential, yet vague, role modeling of a particular concept of masculinity.[57] The idea that boys need a stable masculine identity assumes that women in general, and mothers in particular, cannot raise boys without robbing them of their masculinity. The rationale is that it takes other men—fathers and designated mentors—to loosen the "apron strings" that mothers tie around their sons' identities. Despite years of research, not a shred of evidence has been found to substantiate this popular patriarchal fairy tale.[58] In fact, nothing consistently proves the theory that boys without fathers *automatically* develop impaired masculinity.[59] These boys are, however, at risk for a drop in socioeconomic status because of gender inequities regarding employment and division of household labor.

Malcolm is a 23-year-old youth outreach worker and undergraduate student. Being raised primarily by his grandmother and spending summers with his godparents exposed him to experiences that neither his mother or father could provide, together or separately.

My family is from a very small town in Alabama, and my parents were very young—I think ages 17 and 18—when they had my sister and me. They got divorced almost a year after I was born. So, they were married and divorced relatively young. When my mother became pregnant with my older sister, I think that was an unintended pregnancy. So, the marriage happened as a result of that. They tried to do the right thing, but it was a mistake. They just were not compatible. My parents have a hostile relationship to this very day.

After the divorce, my mother cooked, cleaned, and went to work in order to provide for us financially. She eventually got her GED, then went to a vocational school where she received her associate's degree. Today, she's an administrator for a social service agency. She's very independent and has always felt that she could do for her own. My grandmother was also around when I was growing up and was another constant support for me. I would live with my mother for a brief period, then I would live with my grandmother. As I got older, like from age 16 to 18, I lived primarily with my grandmother. With my grandmother and her friends, I got a chance to travel and meet different people who did a variety of things in life. My grades improved over time, and by junior high I happened to be labeled "the smartest boy."...My grandmother made sure that I was exposed to different things.

One of the most significant relationships that I have is with my godparents, Daisy and Mark. They are like surrogate parents. I met them at a camp for youth that my grandmother took me to one summer. Daisy and Mark are civil rights attorneys and cofounders of an organization that trains youth for community political involvement. I became active in their organization and spent a great deal of time in their home. They value education, both graduated from Harvard Law School, and both have strong ideas about family and community service. They exposed me to Black political leaders in the country like Jesse Jackson, Congresswoman Maxine Waters, Congressman John Lewis—the entire gambit of people.

Malcolm realizes that his parents did not have the resources, the help, or the insight to give him the experiences his grandmother and godparents were able to provide. I am not, however, suggesting that single-parent homes are idyllic. Carlos's and Malcolm's mothers had the emotional resources, but not the economic resources that many two-parent homes offer.

Rex, a 36-year-old social worker and administrator, spent his formative years in the Caribbean. He, too, felt the financial pinch that children of single mothers often experience. He describes how he grew close to his mother over time and the powerful influence her resourcefulness had on him.

My father wasn't married to my mother and spent a lot of time away, and actually went off and married another woman. So, he wasn't around much. My mother raised nine kids, seven boys and two girls. All of us shared the same father except the youngest one. My mother worked in the home taking care of the children and, simultaneously, worked hard labor in the sugar-cane fields. I'm from the Caribbean, and the major income for my country is the sugar cane. Most people worked in the sugar-cane field and that's what my mother did, along with her work at home caring for people's children. My mother, because she was a single parent most of the time, did everything in the home that would be considered "women's" and "men's" work.

As Rex's narrative continues, we learn that not only Black women end up as victims of Black men's violence; other Black men do also. Rex's narrative becomes more emotional as he tells how his older brother inflicted a brutal concept of masculinity on his romantic partners as well as his younger siblings.

My brother used to beat his girlfriends in front of us. There were a number of other men who beat their girlfriends, so it was very common. I was a teenager and I remember feeling very sick, very sick of it, very sick—it was very troubling for me and scary because he used to beat me, too. Knowing how painful those beatings were made me feel that, as a man, I didn't want to repeat that brutality in my life....I was horrified, absolutely horrified by the physical abuse that my brother inflicted on me.... I'm also really fighting for my own life and taking care of myself by doing the antisexist work that I do with men who batter.

Empathy is a feeling of being "with" another person; Rex empathizes with victims of batterers because he, too, has been battered. Sometimes it takes generations before boys can experience recovery from dominant, destructive notions of manhood exhibited by their fathers, brothers, and peers. When individual boys manage to do that in the course of becoming men, it benefits their communities, as Rex's story shows, because they are in a healthier position to serve and pass on legacies of human connection and wholeness. Rex's work with men who batter offers the men a chance to heal and offers him a healthy alternative to becoming a batterer himself. Although empirical evidence suggests that agencies like his are better at prevention and outreach than at intervening with men who already batter, these organizations and the men on their staffs demonstrate how individuals can create new institutions and model alternative ways of being men through such institutions.[60]

Not all fathers of the men in my study used violence in the home to establish their patriarchal sense of entitlement and power. Eight of the twenty men came from relatively peaceful two-parent homes.[61] I am not suggesting that their parents never fought or that they were never emotionally abusive; their parents are characterized here as nonviolent because they did not often use physical force to address problems. In addition, most of these feminist Black men said they were close to both their mothers and fathers. All of them indicated that their conversations with their mothers, in particular, created intimacy and empathy in ways that heightened their awareness of the disproportionate sacrifices Black women make for the family, compared to men. The patriarchal dividend their fathers reaped was noticeable, making their fathers patriarchs by virtue of the sense of entitlement they exhibited in various family dynamics. In other words, no man in the study came from a home in which the father identified as a feminist or significantly and consistently behaved in ways that could be considered overwhelmingly feminist.

Solomon (the anthropologist) was the only participant in my study whose mother was the primary perpetrator of violence in the marital relationship.

My father is still living and was the son of a sharecropper in Mississippi.... My father had numerous jobs. He scrubbed floors at a major corporation, he spray painted cars at a car shop, he stripped paper for a local newspaper company, and he eventually qualified for a job at the electric company reading meters. He finally qualified as Assistant Control Tower Operator at the electric company.

He has never been a mean or gruff person. However, I felt that he shouldn't have taken my mother's abuse. Whenever they would have a fight, she would throw things at him. He was rarely violent with her. He may have hit her back just before she got sick, but, for the most part, he accepted the abuse. There's no question that I identified with my Dad and empathized with him more. I saw my father as the real underdog in the relationship.

By recognizing that women do sometimes abuse male partners, I do not want to detract from the importance of male-to-female violence in terms of its prevalence and cost to society. Family violence is primarily a crime against women. In general, women simply do not inspire fear in men as men do in women; moreover, women are much more likely to be injured, and injured severely, in family violence situations.[62] Nonetheless, we have to acknowledge that women are sometimes perpetrators of violence in the home, and feminist scholars are beginning to study these women.

Although the research in this area is scant, emerging studies suggest that women who batter, like men who batter, are a heterogeneous population. Surveys that report an increase of violence among women as perpetrators must be placed in their proper context; human behavior does not develop in a social vacuum but is situated within a sociohistorical and cultural context of meanings and relationships.[63] For instance, verbal and physical abuse may be the last resort of a woman who feels powerless otherwise. Women shout, hit, and throw things to let men know they will not be dominated or humiliated without a fight, literally.

A woman who fights back against her partner's violence or who initiates violence in a relationship violates society's notion of acceptable feminine behavior. Note, however, that men who do not fight back or who fight back unsuccessfully also violate society's cultural conception of masculinity; they are also viewed as not deserving sympathy and protection under the law.

Women who initiate and escalate violence outside of situations of self-defense may end up reinforcing the patriarchal idea that women are out of control and deserve to be beaten. Solomon explains how he perceived the patriarchal dynamics that shaped his two-parent home:

My mother was a "housewife," but she was an unusual housewife for a Black woman because she had completed two years of courses at a business college. My mother was industrious and was not satisfied with just "keeping house." She had six children and grew tired of sitting at home. So, she eventually sold Avon products and became a self-proclaimed missionary. She had a social network of friends in the church and used her Avon work as an avenue for conducting her missionary work. Avon products would get her in the door. The next thing you know, my mother would be trying to save somebody or giving somebody spiritual counseling for their problems.

My mother was depressed a lot when she was at home. Her depression had a lot to do with the fact she had six children and lived a poorer lifestyle after she married my father. Fights with my father often involved the different ideas they had about what women and men are expected to do in a marriage. My mother was considered a northern urban girl and my Dad was considered a southern rural boy. My mother saw my father as "country" and saw his ideas about women as backward. So, she rejected his "backwardness," particularly his complaints about how she didn't respond to him like southern women relate to him. Basically, he was never "man enough" for her and she was never "woman enough" for him. My parents' stayed together for about thirty-eight years before my mother died, but I wish they had gotten a divorce.

*Before my mother became ill, they started having such horrific fights that
I feared that they might kill each other.*

Solomon's narrative illustrates how patriarchal norms and practices
are prisons for men and women. Neither parent's cultural expectations
of the other were met, leaving both with resentments and uneven, embit-
tered responses to their circumstances. Solomon learned to empathize
with men who did not fit hegemonic notions of masculinity, whether by
choice or circumstance. Moreover, he saw how even with patriarchal
privilege, Black men can remain terribly dissatisfied. Solomon's father's
internalization of patriarchal masculinity continues to complicate their
relationship, even though his father has made some effort to accept
Solomon's transgendered identity.

*At first, my father never talked to me about being a man, because he
still saw me as his daughter. I told my parents when I was 18 that I saw
myself as a man with a female body, but they never could deal with the
information. As I grew older, and as I continued to maintain that my
identity was male, my father couldn't deny it anymore. Today, we can
talk about it. Today, he accepts me as his oldest child and his oldest son,
but it still hurts him to acknowledge it. In some ways, he probably feels
guilty about who I am because of the sexual abuse that happened in our
family. He fondled my sisters and me at one point when we were growing up. In some other ways, he probably doesn't feel guilty about it and
just assumes that my male identity is my personal sin or my confusion. If
he could make it go away, he would—but it won't go away, so, he deals
with it.*

Current research suggests men, like Solomon's father, are likely to
seek out sexual contact with children for a variety of different reasons: to
experience power and control, to seek sexual gratification, and possibly
to obtain intimacy and affection.[64] Feminist psychologists familiar with
child sexual abuse admit that male socialization and issues of power and
control are not enough to explain father–daughter sexual abuse in childhood; they realize that a comprehensive explanation requires understanding the cultural (institutional) and social (interactive) factors as well
as psychological (individual) factors involved.. Understanding why
Solomon's father sexually abused his daughters is beyond the scope of
this study, but a feminist perspective[65] on child sexual abuse is helpful
here because it challenges the conventional idea that Solomon's mother
was somehow "to blame" for Solomon's father's actions.

Mothers of incest victims are commonly blamed for (a) failing to
play their maternal and wifely roles by nurturing and protecting their
children and their husbands; (b) failing to meet the sexual needs of their
husbands and so "forcing" their husbands to seek gratification from

their daughters; and (c) denying the incident and failing to throw the father out, even though he "may also be physically and sexually abusing the mother."[66]

Because incest occurs within a family system that has incorporated the values and standards of traditional patriarchal society, it is important to understand fathers' sexual abuse of daughters as an outgrowth of patriarchy, even though other circumstances may also be relevant. Solomon's father committed the sexual abuse, not the mother. Even though Solomon empathizes with his father, the father, like many sex offenders, expresses little or no remorse for what he did to his daughters.[67] According to feminist sociologist Anne Cossins, sexual offending against children is the way some men alleviate their own experiences of powerlessness and establish their masculinity and power.[68] Sexuality is central to the construction of masculinity, the site at which masculinity and power are established. Offenders sexually abuse children in circumstances where there are real or perceived challenges to their masculine power, such as direct experience of impotence or a lack of power as a man in other arenas of life.[69] Cossins argues that socially and economically powerful men use child sexual abuse to maintain their experience of power, such that "women, other men and children may become the victims of some men's need to stay on top" and that "marginalized men who are less privileged sexually offend in order to resist the oppression they face" due to their subordination.[70] Thus, marginalized men like Solomon's father, both suffer and become implicated in the suffering of others in their families.

Summary

African American essayist and novelist James Baldwin wrote in *The Price of the Ticket*, "Not only was I not born to be a slave: I was not born to hope to become the equal of the slave-master."[71] Black men's acceptance of patriarchal values and practices within religious institutions, social movements, work settings, and the family alienate Black men from Black women and each other in ways that hurt African American communities. The emotional and physical abuse that accompanies such alienation means that Black men cut their own throats and hamper their advancement by mimicking aspects of power relations that reinforce the strength of racism, sexism, heterosexism, and economic exploitation as systems that interlock and feed off each other.

The narratives of the men in this study emphasize that the collective power of men relies on the ways in which different subgroups of men internalize, individualize, and come to embody and reproduce existing structural inequalities, patriarchal institutions, and abstract notions of power. The privileges associated with that power, often referred to as the "patriarchal dividend," give men a reason to oppose feminism. Yet Black men have paid a high price for their meager advantage, considering the costs to themselves, women, and the community as a whole. Thus, it is important to talk specifically about the costs of patriarchy to men if they are ever going to understand the benefits of feminism.

Acknowledging those costs allows feminists to point out men's stake in creating social change. As bell hooks argues, "As long as men are brainwashed to equate violent abuse of women with privilege, they will have no understanding of the damage done to themselves, or the damage they do to others, and no motivation to change."[72] Instead of "privileged behavior," the disturbed behavior that characterizes men's practice of perverted power relations should be described as a lack of self-control, emotionally crippling, unacknowledged male depression, predatory forms of stress relief, necrophilic acts, and other symptoms of distress.[73] If Black men refuse to acknowledge, critically and systematically, how they wield power in destructive ways as men, their social justice efforts on behalf of African American communities in general will fall short.

However, Black men's contradictory experiences of power can motivate them to embrace feminist principles and serve as key incidents that trigger change. The next chapter demonstrates how institutional and individual dynamics can mesh, creating a Black feminist consciousness.

CHAPTER 4

Turning Points

The Need and Willingness to Change

My approach to analyzing life narratives views identity as an evolving life story and—to a certain degree—a product of the imagination, but life stories are not imagined out of thin air.[1] Instead, a complex relationship exists between what "actually happens" in a person's life and how that person chooses to remember and understand it.[2] How do Black men who are feminist activists describe the key life events that led them to accept feminism as a useful formulation of principles that now guide their lives? In this chapter, I analyze the key events in each man's life, referred to here as "turning points," that shaped his feminist commitment and development. Institutional factors, social interactions, and individual personalities were involved, but this chapter focuses primarily on the social interactions and emotions that nourished the development of Black men's feminist identities.

Narrative Accounts of Perceived Life Transitions

Different cultures provide different frameworks for how to tell a story about life.[3] People use fairly common storytelling techniques for making sense of transitions in their lives. For instance, religious stories about redemption and falling from grace drawn from Christianity, Islam, and even Buddhism shape and eventually appear, in varying degrees, in people's life stories.[4] Furthermore, they choose to make changes in their lives—or they make changes in the way they perceive their lives—in response to external events and their interpretations of such events.[5]

Two storytelling patterns, which personality psychologists refer to as "redemption" and "contamination" stories, are frequently used to explain transitions in people's lives. A *redemption* narrative sequence occurs when the story moves from an emotionally negative or bad scene to an emotionally positive or good outcome; a *contamination* narrative sequence is characterized by an emotionally positive or good experience in the story that is spoiled, ruined, sullied, or contaminated by an emotionally negative or bad outcome.[6] Redemption sequences often convey a progressive understanding of the self as growing, moving forward, making progress over time. In sharp contrast, contamination sequences tend to express decline or stagnation in the plot as characters fall backward, lose ground, fall from grace, or circle over the same ground again.[7]

I looked for redemption (a positive experience following a negative experience) and contamination (a negative experience following a positive experience) in the narratives of feminist Black men in order to understand the kinds of experiences that either deepened or, possibly, detracted from their commitment to feminism. In their life stories I also noted narrative sequences in which a positive experience related to feminism or feminists followed another positive experience. I refer to these as *peak* narrative sequences.[8] After categorizing aspects of the men's stories that exhibited these three types of narrative patterns, I found that redemption and peak experiences were more frequent than contamination ones. Feminist Black men provided a total of forty-three redemption, twenty-three peak, and seven contamination narrative patterns in their life stories. In fact, redemption accounts significantly outnumbered both peak and contamination sequences. Furthermore, in accordance with previous research, many of the men described more than one turning point regarding their feminist development. Table 4.1 provides condensed examples of the three narrative patterns for all twenty participants. The following sections offer a select group of participants' narratives that exemplify the central features of redemption, peak, and contamination themes.

Narrative Accounts of Redemption

Redemption sequences in life narratives include key events that lead people to reevaluate whether their attitudes and behaviors are congruent with their overall self-perception.[9] Often the attitudes and behaviors that individuals wish to change are incongruent with how they would like to view themselves. When social interactions lead to a reevaluation, atti-

Table 4.1 Redemptive (R), Peak (P), and Contaminative (C) Turning Points: Condensed Examples

Interviewee	R	P	C	Description
Soyinka	√			Unhappy, violent marriage led to being shot by wife → stopped physically battering women and reevaluated how to treat women
		√		Pessimism regarding chances of having a happy romantic relationship → took a women's studies course and declared women's studies a specialty in graduate school while simultaneously developing a network of close feminist friends
		√		Disappointment with outcome of a relationship with a womanist → sought help from an organization that worked with men who batter and was granted an opportunity to heal and serve on its board of directors
			√	Became an advisor for an undergraduate feminist Black men's organization → greater insights into sexist effects and practices of hip-hop culture
Carlos	√			Frustration and disagreements with fellow activists during high school → developed empathy for a range of oppressed groups
			√	Curiosity about feminism and a popular undergraduate women's studies course → registered for course and developed insight into private sexist practices by the end of the course
	√			Painful awareness of inability to grapple with the emotional effects of oppression → engaged in reevaluation counseling with other men and increased his sense of wholeness and well-being as well as his effectiveness as an activist
	√			Discontent from disagreement with feminist partner about his lack of public feminist behavior and sadness as a result of being ostracized by men in Black student empowerment group → cofounded a feminist Black male student organization
Donny			√	Excited about participation in Black gay rights movement and learning about the women's movement and lesbian politics → painful experience while taking a women's studies course in college

Table 4.1 Redemptive (R), Peak (P), and Contaminative (C) Turning Points: Condensed Examples (Continued)

Interviewee	Turning Point Type			Description
	R	P	C	
Donny (Con't)	√			Grappled with ongoing challenges as a member of a predominantly feminist and lesbian restaurant collective → awareness about how he is both a victim and an oppressor in society
	√			Became aware of his need and the need for other Black men to heal while participating in an informal counseling support network → volunteered as a facilitator in an organization that provides a forum for Black men to discuss and heal from various experiences of oppression
	√			Anguish while trying to stop a stranger raping a woman → became a workshop facilitator for a local men's antirape group
Victor	√			Trauma from being sexually abused by Cub Scout leader → developed the ability to empathize with "outsiders" and others who are oppressed
	√			Grappled with prejudices about wealthy Black people and other diverse groups at an activist-oriented liberal arts college → development of close relationships with his peers
		√		Attended an activist-oriented liberal arts college that allows students to design own major → specialized in women's studies as part of undergraduate major in government studies
		√		Attended activist-oriented liberal arts college with strong Black student and lesbian, gay, bisexual, and transgendered organizations → served as liaison for Black Student Caucus for the LGBT group and the liaison for the LGBT group for the Black Student Caucus
	√			Disillusionment with criminal justice system while working as a prosecuting attorney in Homicide and Sex Crimes Units → became advocate for women and eventually became a law professor teaching critical race and feminist courses
	√			Disappointment about not being mentored by Black male law professors → was the only man invited to a Black women's law professors group and was moved by their personal life stories

Table 4.1 Redemptive (R), Peak (P), and Contaminative (C) Turning Points: Condensed Examples (Continued)

Interviewee	Turning Point Description	Type R	P	C
Victor (Con't)	Anguish while supporting feminist partner during a sexual harassment lawsuit → reinforced his commitment to Black feminist activism after leaving academic world	✓		
Abdul	Wife agreed to a polygamous relationship and allowed him to have a second wife → unable to find fulfillment in unconventional arrangement when wife invited a second husband to the union			✓
	Attended conference on gender relationships → took graduate school internship, then current job with feminist nonprofit agency that works with men who batter			✓
Alan	Ostracized by heterosexual male peers during college → developed profound friendships with bisexual and gay men and a fluid understanding of gender	✓		
	Took a women's studies course during graduate studies → achieved insight into his past as a physically abused child and his mother's past as a physically abused wife		✓	
	Chose a Black feminist dissertation topic → wrote dissertation under the tutelage of a well-known Black feminist who became his mentor and friend			✓
	Married a feminist-oriented wife who exposed his sexist contradictions → developed humility, self-acceptance, and openness to other men who are struggling with sexist contradictions	✓		
	Disappointment about denial of promotion and tenure to a Black feminist lesbian colleague → became committed public activist for Black feminist issues in the university	✓		
	Painful memories witnessing and experiencing father's violence → called to teach and preach a womanist ministry in a university setting and in church settings	✓		
Solomon	Painful experiences grappling with the unsympathetic reaction of others to his transgendered identity → became strong advocate for challenging binary perceptions of gender	✓		

Table 4.1 Redemptive (R), Peak (P), and Contaminative (C) Turning Points: Condensed Examples (Continued)

Interviewee	R	P	C	Description
Solomon (Con't)			√	Identified strongly with father and other men and modeled behaviors after them → experienced the emotional, and sexual abuse of male power while in a female body
	√			Dated and lived with feminist or feminist-oriented women who had been sexually abused by men → became strong advocate for gender equity within the civil rights and Black Power movements
	√			Experience of homelessness → invited to live and work in a feminist bookstore, which facilitated his participation in the feminist movement
	√			Endured painful surgery and engaged in prolonged hormone treatments → increased physical self-esteem, inner and outer harmony between body and gender identity, and sense of well-being
			√	Excitement about new body and joining a female-to-male transsexual group → disappointment with macho, sexist behaviors of members and their inability to challenge unhealthy forms of masculinity
Toussaint	√			Unhappy experiences at an all-men's university → attended a predominantly women's college and developed a network of close women friends on the cutting edge of gender and sexuality issues
		√		Attended graduate school in Switzerland → participated in a gay and bisexual feminist group during years overseas
	√			Discontentment regarding heterosexist, patriarchal, and racist teachings within organized religion → became radical priest and activist in the academy and in oppressed communities
		√		Married a bisexual feminist woman and theologian → both "came out" to each other and agreed to have a polyamorous partnership encompassing their sexualities
		√		Became the biological parent of an infant → deepened his commitment to fighting gender discrimination and decided to raise child genderless

Table 4.1 *Redemptive (R), Peak (P), and Contaminative (C) Turning Points: Condensed Examples (Continued)*

Interviewee	Turning Point Type			Description
	R	P	C	
Cudjoe			√	Took a women's studies course at college → established rewarding and close relationships with feminist women
		√		Discontent with aversive, sexist behavior of male students while an instructor at a boarding school → mentored two female students running for student government
			√	Took gender studies courses and worked at a gender institute during graduate school/law school → established rewarding and close friendships with feminist mentors and other women
Bruce	√			Painful and regretted experiences involving violence against women → volunteered at feminist nonprofit agency that works with men who batter and returned to graduate school to specialize in community counseling
	√			Discontent regarding ongoing tendencies toward emotionally abusive behavior with current wife → engaged in couples counseling with an antisexist therapist and grew emotionally
Eddie	√			Discontent with global and local injustices → joined a socialist, pan-African organization that supports women's rights
		√		Married a woman with revolutionary ideas about race, gender, class → developed deep friendships with wife's friends and deepened understanding of the plight of Black women
Edmund	√			Disappointed and shocked by content of feminist partner's private journals → developed antisexist views and became open to personal growth and change
			√	Cocreated theater company with feminist partner that addresses race, gender, and class issues in African American communities → eventually married feminist partner and became grateful for her influence in his life
David			√	Attended activist-oriented liberal arts college with strong humanities program → took a women's studies course by a Black male feminist and enjoyed other courses that emphasized equity in human relationships

Table 4.1 Redemptive (R), Peak (P), and Contaminative (C) Turning Points: Condensed Examples *(Continued)*

Interviewee	R	P	C	Turning Point Description
David (Con't)	√			Frustration over challenges faced while dating a feminist → eventually married feminist and deepened his appreciation for social justice, particularly the struggles of women
Jake		√		Met strong, interesting Black women in SNCC during Black Power movement → disappointed and ashamed of his sexually opportunistic behavior with women during decline of Black Power movement and emergence of women's movement
			√	Developed close relationship with daughter despite divorce → won confidence of lesbian feminist daughter who "came out" to him, deepening their relationship
			√	Divorced one feminist woman due to differences of opinion regarding celibacy in marriage → married another feminist woman and deepened his commitment to feminist principles
Rex	√			Trained as undergraduate and graduate residence advisor and supervisor, taking required workshops on race, gender, class, sexuality issues → "came out" as a Black gay man and supported feminist gay student organizations
	√			Mentored by a feminist woman during graduate school → deepened his commitment to social work, women, and feminist issues
	√			Discontent with rigid definitions of masculinity and experiences of heterosexism → joined Black gay and lesbian organizations during graduate school
			√	Worked at a feminist organization that rehabilitates men who batter → mentored by a feminist woman in the workplace, developed a lifelong friendship with her, and deepened his commitment to feminism
Ralph	√			Disappointment with lack of expressivity among men and rigid attitudes regarding manliness → befriended Black gay and bisexual men (students and faculty) at a men's college as well as other men who expressed masculinity in alternative ways

Table 4.1 Redemptive (R), Peak (P), and Contaminative (C) Turning Points: Condensed Examples (Continued)

Interviewee	R	P	C	Turning Point Description
Ralph (Con't)	√			Mentored by a White, antiracist, antisexist, and Marxist male professor during graduate school → deepened his commitment to feminism and its relationship to other social justice issues
		√		Discontentment with the lack of diversity in university setting → participated in scholarly activism that supported transformation of the academy into a more diverse environment regarding race and gender
			√	Discomfort with challenges inherent in egalitarian marriage with feminist woman → grew individually as a man within the partnership, deepening his understanding of equity in heterosexual relationships
Malcolm	√			Granted the opportunity to go to summer camp for youth during high school → mentored by camp's founders, an African American couple who were activist lawyers
	√			Discontent with direction of a newly founded Black male feminist organization → challenged the organization to raise funds, became grant writer, and received grants to sponsor community and university programs on gender issues in Black communities
			√	Participated in coed rites-of-passage organization for Black college students that emphasized community service and human values congruent with feminist values → deepened his commitment to race, gender, class, and sexuality issues of social justice and community service
Paul	√			Unhappiness with the lack of equity among male and female high school friends → took a stand in support of young women on two separate occasions as a teenager
	√			Disappointment with male leadership among politicians → joined the League of Women Voters in order to support potential women politicians
	√			Denied formal ordination as a Baptist minister for disagreeing with the church's refusal to ordain women → developed an informal Christian ministry by volunteering in homeless shelters for women and engaging in community activism to empower the disenfranchised

Table 4.1 Redemptive (R), Peak (P), and Contaminative (C) Turning Points: Condensed Examples (Continued)

Interviewee	R	P	C	Turning Point Description
Cabral	√			Discontent with lack of registered voters → became a high school activist engaging in voter registration and developed a respect for the working class and unemployed, especially Black women
		√		Became aware of the exploitation of women internationally through friendship with Korean sex worker → vowed to never buy sex again and developed into an activist focusing on global racial, gender, and class issues
			√	Cofounded an activist-oriented collective that eventually addressed race, class, gender, and sexuality issues → experienced decline of the Black power movement while his marriage ended in divorce
Chad	√			Exposed to political theory and institutional power dynamics in undergraduate political science courses → specialized in political science in graduate school and became committed to feminist politics
		√		Discontentment witnessing women he cared about "get the short end of the stick" due to sexism → volunteered with organizations working with men who rape and batter
	√			Disillusionment with the "ivory tower" isolation of academic life → sought employment with a youth development agency, got in touch with the everyday problems of young people, and found an opportunity to help shape their lives
			√	Volunteered in profeminist men's organizations → disappointment with self-righteous attitudes of some of adherents

tudes and behaviors that are not consistent with one's identity create unpleasant feelings and thoughts and motivate the person to change. Thus, the interaction crystallizes a certain amount of discontent in a way that people find difficult to ignore.[10]

Most of the profound turning points in the redemption sequences suggest that deep emotional pain accompanies the men's discontent and serves as an important motivator for change. In Soyinka's story, for example, the combination of discontent with both physical and emotional pain motivates a man to change his sexist behavior as well as his perceptions of interpersonal relationships.

Soyinka's story. Soyinka (labor unionist) is a 49-year-old man who used to batter women. His story is neither typical nor average. That a former batterer has chosen to specialize in labor movements and Africana women's studies is unique. Nevertheless, others like him with a family background and personal history of violence toward women have developed a feminist consciousness, redefined manhood, and redeemed themselves in the eyes of significant others. Here is how he described his awakening:

I owe a lot to my ex-wife because she showed me pretty dramatically that being a batterer was not the thing to be. She shot me. If that didn't get my attention, nothing would.

When I got married, I was about 34 years old. It was my first marriage, and I had brought quite a bit of baggage into it. I was raised in a home where I saw a lot of abuse. My wife had come from an abusive home as well. We were economically strapped. I was working and trying to complete graduate school. Times were real tough for us. One day my wife called me at work and asked me to come home to fix a flat tire. I was very upset that I had to leave work and told her so when I got home. Her response was that I "wasn't a real man" and that I "didn't take care of business." Her words started messing with my head; so I took my open hand and slapped her in the face several times. It was in the first year of our marriage.

Then, I went inside the house, got a gun, and said, "I ought to pistol whip you, but I'm not going to do that this time." I put the gun inside the house, and then went back outside to fix the car. The next thing I knew, my wife had found the gun and was standing in the doorway with it. I thought, "I'm going to take this gun away from her." As I stepped toward her, the gun went off. I had been shot. The bullet barely missed my spleen. I really did not understand how to relate to a woman in a way that was not controlling or abusive. Only after being shot did I start questioning the way I physically treated women.

Being shot "jump-started" my antisexist consciousness, but I still had a lot of problems I needed to work through, so change came slowly. I didn't physically abuse women after being shot, but I kept trying to control them in other ways by insisting on my point of view, withholding affection, using "the silent treatment" and other subtle and not so subtle threats. I'm extremely grateful now that my ex-wife was a poor shot because I've been given an opportunity to make some major changes in my life.

Although a bullet wound "jump-started" Soyinka's feminist consciousness, that wound was not enough to create a firm feminist commitment. Nor—as we saw in chapter 3—was his reaction to his father beating his mother, or his empathy for his mother. However, Soyinka's motivation to change, coupled with healthy feminist information about *how* to change, led him to modify his practices of manhood step by step, day by day. This is not a straightforward process. His redemption narrative—with its inevitable twists, turns, and outright dead ends—is characteristic of the gradual, nonlinear process of developing feminist consciousness. Ultimately, during an eight- to ten-year period, Soyinka experienced a series of turning points that, taken together, facilitated his firm commitment to feminism.

Soyinka's complete interview suggested that feminism did not have much impact on him in college; he was preoccupied with racial issues during the Black Power movement, then racial and class issues through Marxist and Pan-African political circles. In contrast to his awareness and activism around race and class, Soyinka's feminist beliefs and practices developed more than a decade later. During his mid-thirties, the demands of being a new husband and instant father of two stepsons, financial stress, and the mental stress of the first year of graduate school allowed the emotional baggage he had buried since childhood to resurface. He became violent with his wife, until she shot him. His physical wounds triggered a process that enhanced his readiness to rethink his personal relationships. This major life crisis helped Soyinka realize that he needed to stop *physically* abusing women.

Subsequently, dating a self-identified womanist[11] in graduate school helped him see how he needed to stop *emotionally* abusing women and trying to control them. Soyinka's daily practices and emotions lagged behind his intellectual understanding of feminism. Soyinka hit another low point in his life when the relationship with the womanist ended abruptly. That rejection opened him up to the possibility of change at another level. Soyinka stated:

During the time that we were going through this interpersonal struggle, we were intellectually united around the fact that the interpersonal abuse of power was not appropriate in the world that we wanted to build for Black people. My struggles with our relationship forced me to take what was intellectually "in my head" and actually apply it, practice it, use it. Applying it was extremely difficult. The relationship didn't last long, but I have to give her credit, give her "her due props" because she really had a profound impact on my life. She was the first sister I ever knew who called herself a womanist.

Through personal tragedy and loss, Soyinka thus became increasingly open to relating differently to women.

Two other major events occurred during his graduate studies that led him to reconsider popular assumptions and practices of masculinity: enrolling in a feminist theory course and seeking help from an organization that worked with abusive men. Soyinka took a feminist course to understand women, particularly Black women and the relevance of feminist perspectives in their lives. The course went beyond the feminist rhetoric and slogans that Soyinka had heard in the Black Power movement, yet seldom saw applied. Through readings, class discussion, and interactions with an actual Black feminist instructor and other Black women, Soyinka had multiple opportunities to engage deeply in feminist thought and to develop authentic relationships with feminist women. This redemptive experience led Soyinka to declare a subspecialty in women's studies as part of his doctoral program in political science and labor studies. Following up on a suggestion from a woman friend, he also contacted an agency that counseled male batterers. Here, Soyinka found the tools for his emotional recovery. He was exposed to feminist literature about battered women and spoke with counselors about his experiences with physical and emotional abuse—as an adult perpetrator, but also as a childhood victim.

Acknowledging that Soyinka was victimized does not excuse him for his adult actions, nor does it minimize the gravity of the pain he has caused women. It simply reminds us that a person can be both oppressor and oppressed, victim and perpetrator, and that either/or categories often blur the complexities of human experience. What separates Soyinka from men who do not seek help at this stage is a redemptive account of a perceived life transition that includes the combined *effects* of his emotional pain, *acceptance* that he was part of the problem (instead of solely blaming women and remaining in denial about the role he played in causing pain), *awareness* that help was available, and *willingness* to seek out and accept help.

This cluster of experiences led to a powerful rehumanizing process in Soyinka's life. Although at one point his life appeared to be falling apart, actually it was coming together, and his humanity was being restored. A recent, apparently peak episode in Soyinka's narrative is his current role as advisor to an antisexist Black men's student organization. Although peak experiences—a positive experience followed by other positive experiences—will be discussed in detail in the next section, a preliminary example demonstrates how various life experiences work together to strengthen a man's perception of or actual change in his identity.

Being in a space with only men in the Black antisexist student organization is particularly good because those brothers are much younger than I am. So it's an opportunity for me to mentor, and at the same time be mentored by them. They come to the question of sexism and issues surrounding homophobia based on their experiences within the hip-hop context. In some instances their experiences are significantly different from mine. Not terribly different, but the immediate influences on their lives are different and some of the issues that they're dealing with are ones that I don't have to deal with in the same way. It's been a real challenge, but a positive and compassionate challenge for which I'm thankful.

Interview data suggest that multiple turning points are common over the course of each man's life. The degree to which pain is experienced varies, along with the situation. The most profound redemption narrative sequences typically involve deep pain and discontentment. Edmund's redemption narrative exemplifies another level of pain and discontentment.

Edmund's story. Edmund, a 46-year-old writer and performance artist, begged his wife, Ruby, to let him read her private journals. She had kept journals about her life for many years, and Edmund was curious as to what she had written in them. Ruby finally gave him permission to read them, but stipulated that he must not question or mention what she had written, unless she had previously brought the topic up in their conversations. He agreed to her stipulation.

I read every journal that she had. I knew about a lot of events that she had written about and could not believe how we interpreted the same events so differently! Every single thing in her journal that I read countered my perspective about the issue or event. Not once was my perspective supported by what she had written. I thought to myself, "Damn, if I'm wrong about the things that I felt certain about concerning women, I must be wrong about everything else when it comes to women!" When I finished reading her journals I told her, "I don't want to talk to you about your journal, but I definitely want to talk to you about how wrong I have been about women." Reading my wife's journals made me understand just how complete the sexist training had been in my life... but simply knowing that I am sexist is not enough; I have to correct my sexist ways....The most fundamentally incorrect information that I had about women was the presumption that I didn't have any incorrect information! I felt like I knew women better than they knew themselves....Ruby helped me a lot, but I also wanted to be correct, so that helped. You can plant a seed, but in order for growth you have to plant it on fertile ground.

Until Edmund read his wife's private writings about events that she and he interpreted differently, he saw himself as someone who "knew women better than they knew themselves." This illusion was shattered, not by just one example but "every single thing in her journal." The sheer number of instances was difficult to ignore. At this point, his discontent with "how complete the sexist training had been in his life" crystallized. His motivation to change and the beginning of his redemptive efforts appear in the statement, "I want to talk to you about how wrong I have been about women."

Humility is indispensable in the redemptive phase of the change process because, with it, one becomes teachable. In other words, it's hard to learn something if one feels one already has all the answers. Being teachable facilitates a certain openness in budding feminist men that allows them to redeem themselves and, simultaneously, convinces others that they *can* be redeemed. Edmund expressed this openness, and his willingness to change, by saying that Ruby's suggestions would be "planted on fertile ground." Eventually, he redeemed himself by changing specific sexist behaviors. Subsequently, he cocreated a theater company with Ruby that addresses feminist themes relevant to African American communities.

Victor's story. In another redemption narrative, Victor, a former prosecutor and law professor, experienced a major turning point when, to maintain his integrity as a feminist man, he had to reevaluate his ideas about what being a lawyer meant to him.

When I worked for the district attorney's office, I got to see the worst of everyday sexist and racist abuse....I heard the racist and sexist comments that Black women had to put up with by judges, police officers, court clerks, and lawyers. I saw how certain judges would make women recreate rape scenes in unnecessary detail....I really saw how this society has a hatred for women at certain levels. Working in the Sex Crimes Unit just confirmed to me how devalued women are....The courts would tell women who were physically abused that we would protect them by giving them a restraining order, an order of protection. But, I had to start telling women, "It's just a piece of paper, you need to do some of these other things." I kept a list of safe houses for women who were battered and needed shelter. I felt that I had to do something in addition to what the courts did because the courts were simply giving women a piece of paper and the judge was letting the male abuser out of jail....The entire experience as a prosecutor was a confirmation for me that things have to radically change in this society.

Victor's narrative helps put key social interactions into proper perspective within the change process. These key interactions may serve only to dramatize a person's dissatisfaction, rather than being the principal source of it.[12] A single incident is rarely the cause of the life change; rather a person's doubts and dissatisfaction reach the critical point after a particular incident. Each person's key incident crystallizes an already growing level of discontent.[13] Victor's narrative is replete with incidents in court that contributed to his growing discontent. His narrative suggests that he transformed a bad situation into a positive one, and thus redeemed himself, by fighting "the system" and providing women victims with information regarding feminist resources.

Table 4.1 summarizes other redemption narrative accounts that include different levels of pain, in addition to discontent, across the men's experiences. In each case, a negative situation was transformed into a positive one. Specifically, the range of all participants' experiences included being ostracized by male friends (Alan), witnessing a rape of a woman (Donny), being sexually abused by a Cub Scout leader (Victor), feeling sad about sexism endured by women friends in work settings (Chad), being homeless (Solomon), not fitting in at an all-men's university (Toussaint), perpetrating violence against women (Bruce), enduring injustices at a university (Ralph), being challenged by a feminist partner (Soyinka, Carlos), going through a divorce (Jake), experiencing heterosexism and homophobia (Rex), experiencing frustration in trying to reorganize the priorities of a Black empowerment organization (Carlos), being denied ordination as a minister (Paul), being disappointed with political male leadership (Malcolm), becoming aware of the pervasiveness of men's violence against women (Eddie), becoming aware of the global exploitation of sex workers (Cabral), discovering the dearth of registered voters among poor working-class Black women (Cabral), and experiencing general disillusionment with societal institutions and structures (Victor). Positive (redemptive) situations included getting therapy or counseling, changing life philosophy regarding violence, specializing in women's studies, serving community organizations, developing better relationships, preaching, teaching, mentoring, "coming out" as gay or bisexual, and social activism.

Positive experiences following negative experiences may take many years to manifest themselves. Nonetheless, feminist Black men's narrative accounts overwhelmingly support previous research, which suggests that a narrative identity celebrating redemption often provides a solid platform from which to launch generative projects—projects that demonstrate a concern for and commitment to the well-being of later generations.[14] Thus, perceiving one's own life in terms of redemption sequences may offer hope that suffering and hard work today will yield positive dividends for the future. That hope may sustain private efforts such as raising one's own child to be antisexist and public efforts like committing oneself to feminist teaching in the academy and womanist preaching in the church.

Narrative Accounts of Peak and Contamination Experiences

If redemption is to occur, there must first be pain. Sometimes, however, there is pain and no redemption. Typically, a contamination sequence in a narrative describes a positive experience that turns negative. The negative experience ruins, spoils, sullies, or contaminates the positive experience that precedes it. Although redemption sequences sustain hope, contamination sequences suggest despair, hopelessness, or a fall from grace.[15]

Consistent with previous research on highly generative adults, feminist Black men reported more redemption sequences than contamination sequences in their interviews. Nonetheless, it is not uncommon for one explicit contamination sequence to appear in an account, particularly in the narratives of midlife adults. Previous research on narrative accounts suggests that even when the redemption theme is so pervasive in a narrative that it serves as something like a creed, contamination incidents can appear in it that run counter to the story's dominant, redemptive events.[16]

In this study, seven contamination events were reported; five men narrated one contamination event each and one man described two (see Table 4.1). Although these contamination experiences are clearly in the minority compared to redemption and peak narrative sequences, they are poignant and powerful. These experiences might have weakened each man's commitment to feminism if his life had not included other, profoundly redemptive or peak sequences that somehow outweighed the effects of the contamination experience.

Donny, a gay rights activist and co-owner of a semivegetarian restaurant, said:

I took my first class on feminism in college. It was a horrible experience. I took the Philosophy of Feminism because it looked interesting. I didn't know it was taught by a White radical lesbian feminist separatist who thought men shouldn't be alive—and certainly not in her class-room. She couldn't ban men from enrolling in the class because of the university policy. She couldn't put me out, but she was so abusive....I hung in there. . . . It was a very hurtful, experience, very hurtful, hateful politics, and just plain hurtful.

How many men like Donny has the feminist movement lost who have not had sufficiently positive redemptive or peak experiences—in women's studies courses or other feminist-related external events—to counter the negative effects of a contamination account? Fortunately, Donny reevaluated the significance of feminist *courses* rather than the significance of feminist *principles* to his life.

In another example of a contamination experience, Abdul's polyga-mous relationship with Nia and Rosa falls apart when Nia (his first wife) exercises her right to take an additional male partner. What had previ-ously been a happy tale to tell became a nightmare for Abdul, and accepting Nia's new man was a "bitter pill to swallow." Later, he chose not to attribute any redeeming value in his life to the additional man's role in their polygamous union. Abdul recounted:

Nia felt she needed more than I was giving her and wanted another man, Joshua, to become a part of our family. She was really excited about him. He was into yoga and music and started meeting some of her needs that I wasn't meeting. I had always said that if more than one partner was okay for a man, it should also be okay for the woman. I believed it in my mind, but I had hoped that I wouldn't be tested on it....Nia was my first partner in life, my primary partner, and I loved Nia, so I invited Joshua to be a part of our family....Having to do that really, really, got to me in a very hard way. I remember sitting up at night crying. I remember even one time sitting by the railroad tracks and thinking when the next train comes I'm going to end my life right here. Joshua being in our lives just messed me up! I saw Joshua as a person who would never take care of Nia and the children. Rosa and I finally had a child together and Nia and Joshua had a child together....Joshua eventually showed his true feathers and flew away....and our polygamous household fell apart. At this point in my life, I've worked through a lot of my pain, especially the pain that I caused to Nia, Rosa, and the children from those unions. I've accepted and resolved most of my pain, but at the same time I can acknowledge Rosa's and Nia's pain and be as supportive of them and our children as possible. However, I no longer live in their homes, and I have no intention of going back to those relationships.

Abdul later reevaluated the significance of polygamy to his life and is currently monogamous.[17] His narrative does not describe his polyga-mous relationship in redemptive terms, and he admitted "polygamy is definitely out of the question....I know, for me, polygamous relationships didn't work....Monogamous relationships probably work best in the United States because there are already so many opportunities for men to really use women in this country." Abdul accepts his responsibilities to his children and his former partners as they continue to sort through the difficulties of managing blended families. Later, when Abdul described his relationship with his current, legal wife, he mentioned his growing awareness of the redemptive value of the difficulties experienced in this *monogamous* relationship, rather than seeing the polygamous one as redemptive.

Jake, a human rights advocate, included another variation of a contamination experience that has left him feeling particularly embarrassed and contrite.

The period when I left SNCC [Student Nonviolent Coordinating Committee]and the simultaneous emergence of the women's movement had a significant impact on me. I started noticing the shallowness of my antisexist perspectives....I had a number of double standards that I applied to various women. I treated women differently depending on how they looked, how assertive they were, and how intelligent I perceived them to be. At one point, I was extremely paternalistic toward working-class Black women and elevated White women and light-skinned Black women at the expense of dark-skinned Black women....I had to admit—and it is almost the most painful lesson that I've ever lived through—that my definition of beauty was based on European standards....I simply could not face how I—-who thought I was on the political cutting edge—could have somehow internalized a certain level of sexual opportunism when it came to how I may have exploited certain groups and classes of women.... My current relationship has forced me to really look at all of my contradictions. My current wife and I have known each other since college. We've always been intellectually compatible. However, it took me a while to face up to my opportunism even with her, such that I tended to emphasize more of our sexual compatibility rather than our intellectual compatibility.

In the next narrative sequence, Cabral, the poet, describes a crisis in his life that even his Black, feminist, socialist politics could not prevent him from experiencing.

Our collective believed that confrontation of contradictions among Black people was healthy as long as the contradictions were debated without resorting to violence among ourselves. We had an active organization whose total goal was to turn words and ideals into revolutionary deeds. We had an ironclad rule that we made all decisions by consensus. We actively studied political theory and developed position papers that delineated a methodology for both giving and taking criticism. We were much more than just talk—we were action—and that action inspired me to write like I had never written before. But, when the Black Power movement zigged toward electoral politics, I zagged. By the mid-1980s, piece by piece, the foundation and inspiration for my artistic work crumbled and I was forced to reexamine everything. I left the collective and other organizations that I was involved in, but what was most emotionally wounding to me was that I also left my marriage. The breakup of my marriage hurt me precisely because my "ideology" couldn't save it, nor could my deep respect for women and commitment to antisexist struggle.

Cabral experienced a period of disillusionment, isolation, and grief over the practice of his art, politics, and marriage. As he questioned the significance of his earlier commitments, he slowly retreated from his previous lifestyle, returned to his childhood home where he shared a house with his widowed father, and desperately recorded his agonizing life transition in a book of essays and poetry that a popular African American press published.

In another example, Chad, a former academic now directing youth groups, offered a contamination narrative that implicated other feminist men and left him doubtful of the degree to which some of them had actually changed their behavior.

I have seen a lot of self-righteousness among men doing antisexist work, and I just personally find it very unattractive. I also think it's very counterproductive because we end up spending a lot of time talking to each other and feeling "more-feminist-than-thou" and there are bunches of everyday folk out there who aren't even listening to us! Seeing these kind of dynamics among men who say they are antisexist and who work with men who rape and batter women makes me wonder just what kind of change can one reasonably hope for in this situation. It's sobering to realize how much work we have to do on so many different levels. There are so many complexities associated with men trying to play an active role in antisexist, antiviolence work when one focuses on how to do that kind of work in ways that are truly accountable to women. It's disheartening to realize that some antisexist men arrogantly assume that they can help other men change when they themselves have not changed.

Only one man, Solomon, the anthropologist, included two separate contamination experiences in his life story. In the first episode, his father sexually abused him during childhood. Nothing positive came out of this humiliating experience. The second contamination experience was characterized by the disappointments he has experienced from rejection, in men's groups that discuss gender issues, by men born biologically male.

I tried to become a member of a Black men's group and was ostracized by the group. I was rejected as a member—particularly by a Black gay man who considers himself profeminist because I'm a transgendered man. The excuse given was that the men in the group were not yet ready to receive a transsexual man among them. How many times have White people asked Black people, "Can we go slow and wait until White people are ready for racial justice?" This rejection is what forces a lot of female-to-male transsexuals to pretend that they have never been in female bodies. When we tell the truth about our past trajectory into manhood and don't deny our genetic female history, people, especially biologically born men, typically reject us. When we deny our past, we deny a rich aspect of our growth into manhood that makes us who we are. Also, when we deny our past, we are forced to live a lie. I don't want to be rejected or have to lie about the experiences that have shaped my male identity. It's one of those "damned if you do, damned if you don't" situations. I currently belong to a men's group of female-to-male transsexuals like myself. . . . A transsexual man has to contend with what it means to be male in a female body, and we have to be very aware of how our female bodies have exposed us to female socialization, to the internalized sexism that females are prone to, and to the macho gender roles and attitudes that we often aspire to in our efforts to express our ideas of valid maleness. Instead of seeing the advantages of being transsexual men as meaning we have an opportunity to discuss difficult issues about what makes a man a "real man" in this sexist society, it has been a painful disappointment to see many transsexual men construct their male identities in ways that are harmful to women and to themselves. I believe that there are different ways in which we have to critique and construct ourselves as men outside of the larger male community, but this idea is largely rejected because of the profound need transsexual men have to fit in.

Although Solomon remains committed to feminist principles and action, his experiences with other men—even those who say they support feminism, if they shun him and exclude him from their all-male groups—have left him feeling wary. Like Chad, he doubts the degree to which feminist men demonstrate real change, particularly in the company of other men. However, that does not mean they can't change, don't change, and are totally hopeless about change. In fact, the disproportionately fewer contamination narratives in this study suggest that there is more reason for hope than for despair. Moreover, pain is not always necessary to bring about a revelation that leads some feminist Black men to change.

Peak experiences in narratives make clear that men understand positive life events in ways that produce other positive events in their lives, which further shape the development of their feminist outlook and practices. Peak experiences that became turning points for these men included participating in women's studies courses or conferences, meeting feminist women and men, and developing supportive and mutually respectful friendships across a variety of settings (see Table 4.1 for all examples).

Carlos, currently a graduate student in environmental studies, shares one of his peak experiences that included meeting a Black feminist woman; it led to another positive outcome when he took a women's studies course she recommended.

I dated a Black feminist woman for most of my undergraduate years at a predominantly Black men's college. She attended the Black women's college down the street. We had so many conversations and talked about everything! One day she kept talking about this Black male professor who was a feminist. So, I said, "Why is he a feminist?" She gave me her explanation, then I said, "Why can't I be a feminist, I can be that!" She replied, "Then be one." She recommended a feminist course at the Black women's college, and I took it. I ended up making so many friends with sisters who were on fire during that time period! They were mainly feminists and we were always debating different issues. I kept an open mind and started thinking about the sexist things that I did and I just loved that feminist class! A well-known Black feminist writer who was such a beautiful person taught it. We discussed the writings of Black feminist writers like bell hooks, Beverly Guy-Sheftall, and Audre Lorde. My feminist consciousness skyrocketed! Being in that class really positively affected me in so many ways.

Summary

Life in the raw is messy if not chaotic, comprehension is limited, and memory imperfect. People use themes that suggest redemption, contamination, and peak experiences for making sense of transitions in their lives. These themes and experiences contribute to the construction of identity in adulthood as people attempt to integrate disparate elements of their lives into life stories. "What actually happens" in a person's life matters, but it matters more, and in a complex way, how the person chooses to remember and understand it.

This study's emphasis is on how feminist Black men choose to remember their reality, yet each person's reality is different, in both subjective and objective senses. Personal selection and choice are significantly involved in the telling of any autobiographical story (e.g., what scene to describe, how to describe the scene, how to frame the circum-stances and the conclusion). The consequences may have actually occurred, but there are likely to have been other consequences as well, some of which the individual has chosen not to narrate. Therefore, it is likely that individual differences in the ways in which feminist Black men narrate life transitions reflect both differences in the objective past and differences in the styles and manners in which they choose or are able to make narrative sense of their lives. Individual narrative styles are also likely to be both the causes and the consequences of different levels of psychosocial adaptation, which psychologists—and the narrators—can interpret in different ways. Psychologists cannot rule out any of these interpretations, nor do we have to. All are valid assessments of how feminist Black men construct their realities and how those con-structions relate to their present and future behaviors and practices amid various institutional settings, social interactions, and individual feelings. The next chapter assesses how some Black men's feminist identities shape their romantic relationships with women, and how various institu-tions facilitate and constrain these interactions.

CHAPTER 5

Romantic Relationships with Feminist Women

Women who are self-identified feminists, or feminist-oriented in their thinking, are major influences in the lives of Black feminist men.[1] This is the most robust finding of the study. It is consistent with autobiographical writings of feminist men in general. Every feminist Black man's outlook was facilitated by interactions with a feminist woman at some point in his development. Sometimes the relationship was romantic and sexual. Other relationships were platonic—the woman was a college professor, supervisor, classmate, or friend. In all cases, their interactions with feminist women motivated the men, in some way, to confront their sexism and attempt to move beyond it. In addition, whether romantic or not, these relationships had an impact on and, in fact, *improved* their relationships with women in general and extended their feminist practices.

Directing attention to these practices, and the social interactions that make them possible, counters the popular tendency to view a person's gender identity as fixed or as developed primarily through childhood socialization.[2] Viewing gender identity as dynamic suggests that adults can and do change their gender identities, that is, how they understand themselves as men and women. Through feminist relationships—usually emotionally intense and unpredictable—and regardless of the outcome, the effects are perceived by the men as long-lasting.

This chapter presents examples of feminist Black men's social interactions with feminist women who were romantic partners. These involvements reinforced their intersectional understanding of feminist *practices* in relationship; their heightened understanding helped the men negotiate the other, competing factors that shape their identities (e.g., race, gender, class, and sexuality) and offset their patriarchal practices and traditional constructions of masculinity.

Heterosexual Relationships from Feminist Perspectives

Most popular literature on romantic relationship is aimed at women.[3] Magazine articles and books frequently encourage women to change—yet rarely does this advice encourage self-actualizing practices that challenge gender inequities at the personal and institutional level. Instead, women are encouraged to accentuate their physical appearance, "play hard to get," temper their independence and allow men to take control, focus on becoming engaged then married, and learn how to please men without "knowing too much" about anything. Women are supposed to accept that men cannot change because they are "born that way," "that's just how men are," and "biologically, they can't help it."[4] The stereotype is that women want a white wedding, while men get dragged into marriage.

However, empirical findings suggest that men typically benefit from marriage more than women—and often at their wives' expense. Most married women still "carry an inordinate share of the load at home...and men are likely to experience greater opportunities for leisure."[5] The female authors of a popular book entitled *The Rules,* which advises conventional behavior for women to avoid remaining single, claim to be feminists: "Antifeminist? No, as far as we are concerned there is no conflict between The Rules and feminism...we are feminists...all women have different definitions of feminism...Feminism is also about women believing in their own importance...but with all due respect, feminism has not changed men or the nature of romantic relationships. Like it or not, men are emotionally and romantically different from women. Men are biologically the aggressor."[6]

Feminist scholars, using an intersectional analysis, must address these popular, yet problematic, mixed messages because many women—even some feminists—turn to advice books when they are most vulnerable.[7] Advising a woman to "overlook" a man's faults and focus on "building up his ego" ignores the reality that these rules do not work for men any more than they work for women.[8] Worse, they ignore or deny women's entitlement to equitable treatment in relationships with men.

This study found that some men want to, can, and do change when they internalize and then act on feminist principles. Feminist Black men's narratives about their relationships with women challenge books like *The Rules* and spin-offs like *The Sistahs' Rules*.[9] They demonstrate that feminism can change them, through interactions with feminist women that help them in the process of seeing *why* they should change and understanding *what* they are changing into. Their narratives tell what they used to do in romantic relationship and how they changed. A Black feminist intersectional analysis of these narratives clarifies how individual acts, interactions with others, and progressive institutions mutually influence one another, despite the competing interests and constraints of mainstream institutions.

Partnered Status and the (Ir)relevance of Legal Classification

Feminist Black men's narratives offer multiple representations of heterosexually romantic feminist relationships, along with multiple meanings of marriage. Although most of the men in this study are married, limitations inherent in my selection procedures preclude knowing whether legally married partnerships are representative of feminist Black men's relationships in general. While I found diversity across marital and non-marital relationships in the narratives, the most obvious distinction among heterosexual couples was not whether the partnership was legally sanctioned but to what degree the relationship was based on a continuum of patriarchal and egalitarian principles.[10]

In describing the marital status of the men in this study, it is also important to mention their sexuality because that sexuality has shaped to what degree they can be considered legally married (for instance, Solomon, the transgendered man, identifies as heterosexual, but cannot legally marry a woman; some bisexual/queer men whose sexual orientation is fluid are involved in heterosexual, legal marriages).[11] Of the twenty men interviewed, thirteen described themselves as heterosexual. Ten were legally married, five were partnered and living in separate residences, three were currently not in a committed relationship, and two were partnered and cohabiting.

The narratives contradict simple equations, such as "marriage equals oppressive heterosexuality" and "cohabitation equals liberating heterosexuality," or "cohabitation signals a temporary relationship while marriage signifies a permanent one." I contend that heterosexual feminists have a variety of options for negotiating the significance of their romantic, intimate relationships with each other and that no particular practice or arrangement—marriage, cohabitation, monogamy, commuter-based—is intrinsically better than the others. I also agree with other feminists' observation that people don't avoid the legal power of marital contracts simply because they reject patriarchal, heterosexist politics. On the contrary, both married and unmarried heterosexual couples—and, increasingly, same-sex couples—must negotiate their relationships against a backdrop of cultural codes associated with social norms and titles, welfare policies, employment practices, expectations from one's family of origin, and other constraints on the partnership, given the interplay among various social institutions, cultural expectations, and practices.[12] Instead of separating romantic relationships into categories of married and not legally married, I try not to privilege marriage as a marker of truly committed feminist relationships. Also, my findings suggest similarities across feminist relationships, even if they are viewed differently—and thus affected differently—by society.

In some cases, whether the partnership was legally regulated (marriage contracts or civil unions) or resisted legal classification, the subjective experience of the partners and related pressures on them did indeed vary as a result of official status. Even though statistics suggest that marriage is in slow decline, since people are marrying later and divorce is more frequent than ever before, weddings still hold powerful sway over the popular imagination. Marriage remains the ideal standard of adult relationship achievement (hence couples are still "congratulated" for getting married).[13]

Ultimately, the underlying question, regardless of the relationship's legal classification, was: how are feminist principles and practices negotiated between the partners in contexts where power relations constantly shift within a couple? The following narrative excerpts provide an inside look at the concrete, lived experiences of feminist Black men and their partners and how these experiences shaped (and continue to shape) their feminist outlook.

Radical Intersectionality

Consistent with previous research on equity within romantic relationships among feminists, all the feminist Black men romantically involved with feminist women described their experiences of feminism as a part of a larger worldview that also includes social, political, and religious perspectives considered to be outside the mainstream, referred to here as "radical intersectionality."[14] Their exposure to open-minded and radical, social justice-oriented institutions (e.g., liberal universities, sociopolitical organizations, and politically progressive work environments) and their active participation in collective efforts to support racial and economic justice often provided the foundation for subsequent feminist views and practices. These progressive institutional settings, and their interactions with feminist women in such settings, gave them a framework for evaluating their interactions with women.

A civil rights organization exposed Jake, the human rights advocate, to feminist women.

I was active in the Student Nonviolent Coordinating Committee (SNCC)…. So, almost every woman I've had a relationship with was involved in the civil rights movement and was either an overt, self-proclaimed feminist or espoused feminism but didn't use the label. I met my first wife and the woman who later became my second wife in the civil rights movement.

For Carlos, the graduate student who cofounded a student profeminist organization for Black men, a predominantly Black university setting and its women's studies department led to interactions with feminists.

The woman who I dated for almost four years had the greatest impact on me and my efforts to unlearn sexism. She attended the Black women's college down the street from the Black men's college I attended. We met right after the Rodney King verdict and the uprisings in Atlanta in response to the verdict. We were on a chartered bus on our way to Washington, D.C. for a political rally. We eventually started dating. We would have ongoing discussions about a whole range of social justice issues in society and were both members of a Black empowerment student organization…. Shortly thereafter, I took a feminist course she recommended.

David, the English professor, reported diverse interactions as an undergraduate with women who were independent critical thinkers at a student-activist oriented, liberal arts college.

I've had a number of close friendships with women, but it wasn't until college that one of my friendships was with a woman and her friends who was very feminist in orientation.

For Edmund, the performance artist, leftist views regarding racial and economic equality were not the only prerequisites for feminist perspectives; they grabbed his attention when a feminist to whom he was also romantically attracted challenged him at a meeting sponsored by their socialist organization.

I had hooked up with the Young Workers Liberation League, which was a youth group of the Communist Party. We used to have "educationals" at every meeting where someone would present a topic to the group, then the group would have a discussion about it. At this particular educational session, the White woman I was dating presented on an international women's conference…. My buddies and I were talking and being

disrespectful—you know, acting childish and laughing during her presen-
tation. Afterwards, she said, "Edmund, you are weak on the woman
question." Instead of listening to what she was saying, her words became
a long-standing joke among my buddies and me. We would tease each
other saying, "Hey man, you are weak on the woman question!" She
couldn't get me to focus seriously on women's issues because I would
always deflect her arguments by emphasizing the superiority of my expe-
riences of racism. However, when I met my second wife, Ruby, who is
Black, emphasizing my experiences of racism to deflect from her argu-
ments about sexism didn't work because she had experienced both racism
and sexism.... I'm not saying a profeminist Black man needs a Black
feminist woman if he is to be challenged to grow. I'm saying that the
woman has to have his full respect and her arguments have to have merit
if they are to get through to him. I don't believe many men will put much
effort into correcting themselves if the person who is trying to correct
them is not someone who they are committed to and who is important to
them. If you meet a woman in a bar and she tells you that you're sexist,
you simply go to the next woman BECAUSE you're sexist! You're not
going to say, "Help me understand how I'm sexist." So, desire and my
commitment and attraction to [Ruby] also helped.

As Edmund's narrative reveals, a confluence of motivational, emotional, and cognitive factors, shaped by institutions and social interactions—including being physically and emotionally attracted to a
particular feminist—open a man to feminist perspectives and practices in
his romantic relationship. Also, two feminist Black men—unlike
Edmund—were able to sustain enduring romantic relationships with
White feminist women when they honestly acknowledged how systems
of oppression affect them in different and shifting ways. Thus, several
factors tend to operate within the progressive worldview that a feminist
Black man already holds regarding society, politics, and religion in his
romantic relationships with women. That orientation provides the foundation for practices of vigilance that helps maintain an egalitarian outlook in the romantic partnership. The following sections take a closer
look at the kinds of social interactions that shape feminist Black men's
practices in their romantic relationships with women.

Concrete Feminist Practices of Vigilance

Previous research suggests that feminist couples in egalitarian relationships practice a special kind of vigilance, defined as "an attending to and
a monitoring of equality, within and outside of their relationship."[15]

Most of the men in the study cited five processes of vigilance: (1) the critique of injustices from an intersectional perspective (ongoing conversations about incidents experienced in their daily lives); (2) public acts of equality (outward demonstration of the woman's equal status in the relationship, varying from the use of different last names to joint financial decisions); (3) support of the female partner's career or vocational activities (e.g., moving because of her new job); (4) reflective assessment (ongoing personal monitoring of one's contributions to the relationship); and (5) emotional involvement (communicating emotions verbally and otherwise, and not withdrawing from conflict). Reflective assessment and emotional involvement distinguished those couples who were also able to identify and correct inevitable relationship imbalances.[16]

"We Talk About the Scary Stuff"

Bruce, who used to beat women, currently works with male batterers. "Feminist-thinking-and-acting" women who dared to break *The Rules* challenged Bruce to be better, do better, and strive for a level of humanity based on mutual respect. His narrative provides rich examples of individual feminist practices. I quote him extensively to demonstrate how, despite childhood formation, adult men can be resocialized, changing their behavior by adopting feminist practices and beliefs.

The first "challenging" person I met during my dating life was a woman who was working on her master's degree in counseling....At first, we hit it off pretty well, but as time moved on I realized that I couldn't manipulate her like I had done so many other women....She would stand up to me and challenge me intellectually—so I thought—because she had more college degrees than me. I had dropped out of college temporarily in order to work. Even though I made more money than she, this status stuff was in the mix, and her educational experiences and sharp mind gave her a kind of confidence that pissed me off. I would try to be slick with her, using my sweet-talkin' bullshit, but she would stand her ground with me by refusing my demands for sex and my demands on her time. I'll never forget the first time she finally allowed me to have sex with her—I became impotent. It blew my mind! I wasn't accustomed to having sex with a woman who felt equal to me. I talked "women's equality" talk, but, I didn't "walk" what I "talked"—and she would question me about my assumptions and the advantages I felt entitled to simply because I was a man. I was making "long money" for a Black man back then, but that didn't impress her because she had goals for herself and wasn't dependent on me emotionally or economically.

Bruce's narrative demonstrates the degree to which he internalized patriarchal concepts of power before his exposure to feminism. In patriarchal systems, power is understood as *power over* something or someone and as a relation of domination.[17] As we saw in chapter 3, the "patriarchal dividend" ensures that even Black men will have power over the women in their same race and class subgroup. Bruce assumed he should have power over the African American woman he was dating because he was "making long money for a Black man back then"; he felt entitled to a certain amount of deference from her. Her perception of the two of them as equals (enhanced, no doubt, by her economic independence and higher level of education) left Bruce feeling "pissed off." The power she brought to their relationship, stemming from her own independence and human agency, did not enhance it; rather, Bruce interpreted her power as a threat.

Feminist perspectives on power do not necessarily assume that all forms of power are negative. In fact, feminist reconceptualizations of power include the capacity to produce a change that simultaneously enhances, rather than diminishes, anything from point A or state A to point B or state B;[18] the capacity to transform (empower) oneself and others, suggesting that one is transforming *power to* oneself and others or drawing on *power from within,* rather exercising a controlling *power over* others;[19] and energy and competence rather then dominance, such that one is acting in concert with others, *power with* in a collective sense.[20] Black feminist conceptions of power resemble the humanistic sharing of *power with* others in collectives and communities, expressed in, for example, the Afrocentric ethos "I am because we are" and the Black Women's Club Movement slogan "Lift (others) as we climb".[21]

Feminist standpoints on power suggest that when we define our power by whom we control or dominate, we ruin the opportunity to see how another person's power (and, thus, power sharing) can enhance our own growth as human beings. White patriarchal, market-driven, and heterosexist structural systems have taught Bruce and other African American men to define their masculinity as "power over" someone, offering as justification, "since the White man has power over me, I get to have to power over you—'cause after all, I'm a man, too." When gender (im)balance and other systems of power are understood as structures, however, their conceptions and practices can be seen in an historical light, varying over time and therefore susceptible to human agency. Thus, over time, as a result of Bruce's interactions with feminist women and staff at a feminist agency dealing with men who batter, his conception of masculinity did, indeed, change. Later in his interview he mentioned concrete examples of the alternative conception of masculinity that affected his practices. Moreover, feminist practices of vigilance increased the gender equity in his second marriage.

I've been in my current marriage for a little over ten years. My partner, Charlotte, is a woman who makes twice the money I make and don't take no junk off nobody! [chuckles]. She is brighter than I am intellectually, and my relationship with her has taught me more about myself than any other. Charlotte hyphenated her last name when we married, to let everybody know that she is still an individual person. She didn't marry in order to blend into me and lose herself. Our relationship has been good for me, because it is what I always needed but was too afraid to get.... It took me a long time to accept this about myself.

I can't dominate Charlotte, even though I have a history of abusing women both physically and emotionally that goes back to the time when I was about 12 years old.... Today, I feel disgusted about how I used to treat women.... Through couples counseling with Charlotte, I finally realized and accepted how I had been relating to women. I also learned that you could abuse a woman without even touching her—like verbally and emotionally. What's interesting is how after couples counseling and learning how to communicate better with each other honestly, our relationship improved without my manipulative games.... I started trying to learn more about women's reality—as opposed to emphasizing my reality and the reality of other men. So, when Charlotte had a chance to get national exposure in her field, we decided to live in different cities. Who am I to say, "Baby, I can't put up with that 'commuting crap' because I got to have someone I can lay up with every night in order to feel like a man." Women follow men all over the planet, especially when their husbands are in the military. Why is it that most people overreact to a scenario that involves a man following a woman and supporting her advance professionally?

The strength of the relationship is that we are really honest with each other. We talk about the scary stuff. I don't hesitate to say, "Hey, I'm scared, I'm jealous," and she feels comfortable telling me similar things. Honesty doesn't always feel good—but it gets us through the rough spots.

As Bruce's narrative suggests, a Black feminist intersectional analysis becomes a lens through which both partners critique each other's practices, on the basis of their experiences as African Americans. That analysis often moves them toward an arrangement they perceive as better than traditional marriage. In addition, couples in feminist relationships are willing to demonstrate publicly their equal status in the marriage. Public acts, symbolic or straightforward, announce that the marriage is not based on traditional assumptions of male preeminence.[22] For instance, Bruce supported his partner's decision to hyphenate her last name (a common practice in feminist marriages, along with wives keeping their original family name without using the husband's at all). Most obvious is Bruce's support for his partner's career. Marital studies indicate that when a woman's career organizes family life along with the man's, the chances of marital equity are significantly increased.[23] The middle-class status of most of the couples is an important contextual variable that assists in this process, and the men's partnerships with professional, college-educated women contribute to that status.

Bruce also practices "reflective assessment" by monitoring his contribution to his relationship with his partner and to their family life. When both partners reflect on what is fair and why certain choices are more equitable than others, imbalances that occur can be identified and corrected. In addition to this kind of "reflective vigilance," emotional involvement is critical. Without constant communication, equality cannot exist because equity within relationships is not static; it must constantly be negotiated and renegotiated through effective dialogue.[24] With the help of couples counseling, Bruce developed the interpersonal skills that facilitated emotional intimacy, which enabled him to address issues that commonly lead to resentment and frustration in partnerships. A marriage based on Black feminist principles requires the active participation of *both* partners, as well as a guiding ideology of equality in which race does not trump gender nor gender trump race during decision-making processes. Instead, race and gender are considered simultaneously.

"We Tapped into Fragile Places in Us That We Didn't Even Know Were There"

For Ralph, a 41-year-old social scientist who works for a federal agency, creating an egalitarian marriage with his African American feminist wife has not been automatic or simple. No single recipe exists for creating one, and a variety of social experiences have contributed to his willingness to practice feminist principles with her.

Even though I am a social scientist, it has not always been easy for me to communicate with women—but I have struggled hard to hear women and continue the struggle daily. There was one woman who, perhaps, found me the most lacking in my development with respect to understanding women. Our friendship evolved into something romantic, but she challenged me with such intensity—because she was going through her own turmoil and the realization of the pervasiveness of sexism—that our relationship became very tense and conflictual. There were also times when our ideas and practices converged quite passionately, but we eventually parted, even though we both grew.

I had another platonic friendship with a woman that led to marriage, and that woman is currently my wife. When we met, she was also going through this process of developing an understanding about what was happening with women, from readings and other sources that provided feminist perspectives.... We both have to deal with the fact that sometimes our actions are not consistent with our intellectual understanding of feminist ideas. We constantly grapple with how to find balance and, as a result, challenge each other to be better at this stuff than we are. The daily living and giving required in marriages based on feminist principles demands that you deal with feminism at a level that is more complex and goes beyond the theories presented in feminist literature. In marriage, feminism becomes more than an intellectual struggle to win a debate as if you are in a classroom arguing an intellectual point or idea; my lived experiences have become a struggle to reveal and allow my most intimate part of myself to live, in fact, coexist in a jointly created interdependent union of equals.

A feminist vision can guide couples through the murkiness of living in circumstances that are considered nontraditional. However, couples must "act" in feminist ways in order to realize their feminist vision. Ralph is used to using academic jargon to win an argument (he was a professor before he took his current job as a government researcher), but he no longer sees egalitarian marriage and other feminist perspectives as intellectual fodder solely for winning debates or earning "brownie points." Today his struggles and debates are grounded in his personal experiences and practices, not just "winning an argument" but winning back his right to experience the fullness of his humanity. Rather than simply celebrating—or, worse, pontificating about—how he is part of an egalitarian marriage, Ralph offers a complex analysis of marriage as an institution as well as a site for individual growth and holistic development. He continues:

When my wife and I lived together before marriage, I would say it was hard for both of us to remove our thinking and behaviors from those traditional ideas about male–female interactions. We tapped into fragile places in us that we didn't even know were there—which resulted in many conflicts. I won't dare suggest that we have it all together right now, but our faith in the process has continued. The process of her getting out of the relationship what she needs and my getting out of the relationship what I need is an ongoing one.

Since we've been married for thirteen years, I have a different sense of egalitarian marriage than I did when I was teaching about it.... I think marriages are both equitable and sharing to the extent that men and women really are involved in a process of self-understanding and

consciously choosing certain behaviors—even 'willing' them into exis-
tence—in an atmosphere of respect between the two partners. I think
that's a real hard thing to achieve, but to me, if I frame it that way, at
least I know what to work on. And that's where my wife and I are. We
realize that sometimes situations occur in a marriage that just ain't equal.
Sometimes we're at different places in our lives and in our feelings that
require us to behave justly and other times unjustly. So this thing about
equity, the way that we deal with it is we say that in the final analysis it
balances out. But, if you were to measure equity within a particular, dis-
crete point in time on a certain day at a certain hour, our marriage may
appear inequitable. Therefore, you have to observe our marriage over a
variety of situations and over time.

Ralph is exceptionally candid about the gap that often exists
between the ideology and practice of egalitarian relationships among
feminists. His narrative includes key points about how that gap can be
narrowed and possibly closed. He underscores the importance of communication and negotiation. Also, Ralph's narrative exposes an underlying vulnerability, along with resigned acceptance of the fact that
grappling with equity, justice, honesty, and one's partner's expectations
are not always warm and fuzzy experiences.

Like most couples who are relatively successful in feminist partnerships, Ralph and his wife are committed to egalitarian principles; even
when they fall short of them, they have an agreed-upon vision of the
philosophy and principles they are striving toward in the relationship.
Discussing actual practices of egalitarian marriages shows how change is
both resisted and accomplished over time when couples challenge the
institution of marriage as necessarily patriarchal.

Ralph's narrative exemplifies another aspect of feminist relationships that is a product of vigilant practices by both partners: the healing component. Enduring feminist relationships entail mutuality or
relative reciprocity, thereby allowing the emotional involvement and
openness characteristic of successful partnerships. In that climate, it is
possible to work through conflict and heal pain instead of denying or
avoiding. Humanistic psychologist Carl Rogers, elaborating on the
process of relationships characterized by mutuality or relative reciprocity and healing, noted that when healing is experienced, each individual is able to communicate both aspects of his or her divided self:
the façade and the deeper level of self-experience. Equality, per se, is
not what's fundamental; rather, two unique persons are in tune with
each other in an astonishing moment of growth and change.[25] This vulnerability, *in the context of acceptance*, is what is gratifying, healing,
and growth-promoting.

Thus, equality, equity, egalitarianism—regardless of the terms used—is a multidimensional phenomenon. Not acknowledging that these social interactions are a process, and that both equality and inequality are present in the process, is detrimental to ever discovering the richness of an evolving, dynamic feminist relationship.[26] Denying the inevitable ebb and flow is to engage in a pretense of egalitarianism that blocks its realization and the reality of being human, that is, being both fragile and strong simultaneously. Egalitarianism requires not perfection but *effort mixed with humility*. When human errors are made and inevitable contradictions surface, either party can admit being wrong and attempt honestly to do better by recommitting (in word and in deed) to a shared vision of justice. The couple's emotional involvement provides a foundation that can sustain them during difficult periods, hence its importance as a feminist practice in egalitarian relationships.

By admitting the difficulties and the ongoing, evolutionary process associated with egalitarian relationships, Ralph and other feminist Black men are able to experience genuine dialogue with their partners, instead of just paying lip service to feminism and making superficially equitable arrangements. Not all feminist marriages and partnerships will achieve this level of mutuality, but the chances are increased if the efforts are sincere and if appropriate amends for shortcomings are made and negotiated. Power relations, feminist awareness, and the willingness to shift in different ways on different levels depend on the emotional maturity of each partner.

Good intentions notwithstanding, one cannot assume that a marriage based on feminist principles automatically entails mutuality and will *not* end in divorce. I next discuss two separate marriages that helped a human rights activist gradually to develop his feminist outlook and practices.

"Every Relationship has Tensions, Even Relationships Based on Egalitarian Principles"

Jake's narrative illustrates two important points. First, if a feminist marriage ends in divorce, that does not necessarily mean one or both parties were not "truly feminists." Divorce might simply indicate the level of individual difference between feminist men and women that surfaces in their interactions. Second, irreconcilable differences between two feminists may or may not be related to feminist principles or ideology. A feminist who divorces another feminist may be doing so for various valid reasons, depending on the circumstances. Both possibilities can be seen in Jake's narrative.

My first marriage grew out of a relationship that I had with a Black woman in SNCC. After a couple of years of marriage, I wound up going to jail because of my refusal to be drafted. During the two and a half years that I was in jail for refusing to fight in the Vietnam War, my wife decided to become celibate in our marriage for spiritual reasons. So, when I got out of jail, I had to go outside of our marriage if I wanted sex.... I have certainly engaged in my share of blatant sexual opportunism in life, but today when I look back and analyze my serious relationships with women, one problem was that I considered anything that didn't have to do with politics as unimportant. Until my current marriage, I never put any real time and energy into my relationships with women. My attitude was, "We are about struggle, we are political comrades, and what do you mean bring you some damn flowers?" The things that I do today to make my relationship work—not only would I have not done them before, I would have considered them acts of heresy! But, over the last ten years, it just started to hit me how I had never really thought about building and enhancing my intimate relationships. I was so busy dealing with politics at the institutional and abstract level that I was denying the other person certain important things as well as myself at the personal level. So, there were times when I was involved in very emotionally, sexually, and other-wise unsatisfying relationships, but I would tell myself that those things weren't as important as our political ideology and community work.

My current relationship has forced me to really look at all of my con-tradictions. The first few years of our marriage were very stressful and intense because I had to face my shortcomings directly. Every relationship has its tensions, even relationships based on egalitarian principles. I tend to have egalitarian relationships but I know that they aren't perfect rela-tionships.... I wanted to be affirmed and respected in my past relation-ships with women, but I didn't know how to respect and affirm myself. I used to feel intellectually inferior to certain women, yet would come off as really macho when it came to who should protect the household—today, I can admit that I've been around women who could kick my ass and had to protect me! In the past, I used to think it unimportant as to whether I express my feelings to my partner. I'm sure that excuse was just a shield for me because of how difficult it was for me to do it. Today, it's not hard to do, but I had to learn how to do it, like any skill.

Jake's experiences with feminist women—in and out of marriage—are quite sobering. Feminist marriages are not perfect. All the married partici-pants readily admit this in their narratives, which provide concrete exam-ples of what relationships based on egalitarian principles look like and what practicing them entails. On the one hand, the men are trying to learn new interpersonal skills. On the other hand, they are simultaneously unlearning and discarding habits acquired by virtue of living in a sexist society. Neither these men nor their feminist partners have completed their evolutionary processes. Thus, in their daily social interactions, they bump heads, disappoint each other, and give up along the way, just like couples in nonfeminist partnerships. Most difficult and humbling, however, is the fact that even when both partners are feminists, there is no guarantee that the relationship will be successful. A commitment—even a firm one—to feminist ideology and process does not automatically erase individual incompatibilities or vestiges of sexist attitudes and practices.

On the contrary, feminist partnerships can be more challenging than traditional relationships based on rigid gender roles because no single blueprint exists for renegotiating roles and practices. Couples often find it easier to describe the kind of relationship they *don't* want than to realize the feminist vision of the one they *do* want. Most feminist men and women must acquire new skills without many role models. The experience can be overwhelming for both partners and almost always involves the shattering of illusions. In fact, feminist relationships may be experienced as especially painful because each partner's expectations regarding the other and the partnership may be higher—and the disappointments more devastating—than in traditional relationships that rigidly prescribe how a man and a woman ought to behave.

Victor, the former prosecutor and law professor, provided an example of some of the pressures feminist men experience in these partnerships.

My wife has come to expect a reciprocal relationship when it comes to nurturing. When she doesn't get it, she feels actually worse than when she didn't get it in her previous relationships because she didn't really expect it as much from those men. When I am not nurturing, it's really a problem because on top of whatever is actually bothering her, she's additionally hurt by the fact that someone who she believes has the capacity to be nurturing and believes that nurturance should be mutual is not demonstrating it.

Feminist practices of vigilance provide a process for resolving the complex issues that arise in relationships, as opposed to ready-made solutions—and processes must be practiced, not merely "preached" by both partners. The narratives suggest that partners often vary in their choice, experience, and understanding of feminist perspectives, and sometimes they find each other's maturity as feminists lacking. This uneven rate of feminist development within couples can result in conflicts that lead to the dissolution of their relationship. Therefore, engaging in self-analysis, also referred to in the marriage-and-family scholarly literature as the practice of reflective assessment, becomes crucial at all stages of the relationship.[27]

Reflective Assessment Before, During, and After Romantic Relationships

Chad, the 37-year-old youth outreach director, assessed his personal growth after several romantic relationships with feminist women, particularly White feminist women, realizing that conflicts and inconsistencies are uncomfortable aspects of change and touch on the social issues that result in redefining masculinity.

I attempt to have equitable relationships with women with the hope that at the end of the day, we both can honestly feel like we're sharing the burdens and sharing the joys.... All of my intimate relationships with women have taught me about ways that I need to grow, ways that I have grown, and ways that I haven't grown in terms of being able to match my behaviors to my principles, issues like the degree in which I intimidate women, sexually exploit women, play on their insecurities about their weight and other aspects of their physical appearance, and other stuff. So, I have been taught "this is not where I need to be" on this issue if I want to be congruent with my principles about what is right and wrong.... I've been able to witness and grow from interacting with "concrete-flesh-and-blood-feminist-women" who try to enact feminist practices in a world that pressures them to conform to the sexist status quo. I have pressured them to conform and they have pressured me to resist— sometimes successfully, other times unsuccessfully. I had to realize that some of the things I learned from my father about "what it means to be a man" regarding sex, not sharing my feelings, always trying to be in control, achieving a certain status to be successful have not been particularly healthy for me or my relationships with women. One good thing about dating feminist women is that they often have firm and high expectations of the world and how people should treat them. So, I have been with women who insisted that I change (like being more nurturing, attentive, expressive, considerate, and basically emotionally available) and, when I wouldn't, those feminists left the relationship. I've just gotten into a new relationship after not being in a serious relationship for a couple of years, and there are just certain mistakes that I'm not going to make again.

The personal growth that men like Chad experience in their romantic interactions with feminist women cannot be overstated because growth and change highlight how people create their social world, not only how they react to it.[28] Also, the reason change is often a slow, gradual process is that various institutions (such as church, family, and schools) establish expectations for individuals, order social processes, and influence our identities in ways that restrict our gender practices. Involvement with institutions and their standards creates and reinforces conditions that make gendered behavior patterns repetitive, predictable, and thus mainstream. However, while people are shaped by institutions, they also shape institutions themselves; thus, change is always possible, albeit difficult. What is learned can be unlearned through social interactions that counter previous socialization, as the narratives of Chad, Victor, Jake, Ralph, and Bruce show. A variety of social interactions, positive and negative, can influence growth and change.

Sometimes, the dissolution of a relationship creates significant growth in the man's life. Reflective assessment, so important *during* a relationship, can also offer hindsight *after* it has ended. Paul, the tax accountant (and, at age 58, the oldest man interviewed), affirmed that breaking up can bring about a new level of awareness that can be applied to the next relationship.

I was married many years ago at age 20 and was later divorced. Divorce happens, but one can also benefit from experiences that people say are negative. In the final analysis, we must live with the decisions we make as well as the decisions that we don't make. Although I am not currently involved in an intimate relationship, I'd rather be involved than not be involved in a relationship. Involvement, to me, means that there are things that... are conducive to creating the "two of us becoming one." When I am in a relationship, I ask myself, "Is my life more enhanced by being a part of this relationship?" "Is the other party's life more enhanced as a result of my part in the relationship?" These questions are not about economics, education level, or prestige. These questions pull from a deeper level where respect and trust form the foundation of the relationship. In many instances, women who I've been romantically involved with espoused views that not only paralleled my views but surpassed them. Over the last twenty years I have matured and evolved regarding my relationships with women and have learned from these experiences that patriarchy is not natural; it is a cultural choice and includes the assumption of male centrality. Women confronted me about my threatening tone of voice, my aggressive tendency to make all of the decisions and to assume my decisions were automatically the best. After years of growth, it actually feels good and even better to listen to somebody else, to allow decisions to be shared, to engage in a partnership, not a dictatorship.

Cabral added:

Traditional marriage, where roles are prescribed for men and women and a legal contract is used to define whether that relationship is legitimate, is akin to slavery and a convenience of government. I've come to understand that marriage, as we traditionally know it, is basically a government contract to sanctify and keep holy property rights. At the same time, it's important to personally commit to something larger than the self, whether it's the family, an organization, or whatever.... I don't think that marriage is the only way to demonstrate a commitment, but marriage can serve that purpose as well.

In the relationship I'm in now, we're not legally married. Zawadi just bought a house and we moved into it together. We may or may not become married. When I was staying in an apartment, Zawadi moved in with me. I'm not committed to "we must get married" or "we definitely must not get married." Instead of some abstract goal that we adhere to, my question is, "Zawadi, what do you really want?" What do I really want, let's figure that out and cocreate it.

Jake's, Paul's, and Cabral's narratives note that feminism is not a panacea for all relationship problems. Couples may need other social, political, psychological, even spiritual perspectives and interventions to understand how their past experiences affect the overall health of their current interpersonal relationships and cope with problems. Victor had to address the effect of a previous traumatic experience of childhood sexual abuse on his relationship with his feminist wife.

I haven't had many sexual relationships. My wife and I met through a mutual woman friend. I lived on the East Coast and she lived on the West Coast. We started our friendship by having real open conversations, minus the bullshit, because the childhood sexual abuse that I experienced kind of stopped or altered my sexual development. I wasn't interested in sex and saw it as this horrible thing that people do to others to hurt someone. So I developed a capacity to love and care for somebody based on things other than sex. Sex complicated things, so I had to resolve certain issues and my view of sex before I could engage in it. One good thing that came out of the traumatic experience was my ability to love a person deeply without sex. Once I resolved certain issues in therapy, I took sexual intimacy and made it a part of the love I already had for the person, as opposed to sex first, and then love.

Victor's narrative exemplifies the "healing agent" in some feminist relationships that allows people to become in tune with each other, on a level of self-actualization that one cannot develop on one's own. Clearly, Victor's past is related to how he actually practices a healthy relationship with his wife.

Past experiences also shape how and to what degree a man will periodically fall back on patriarchal assumptions that negatively affect his behavior. Feminist Black men's use of male dominant behaviors can be subtle, unconscious, and used as a coping device when they feel threatened. Hence, vigilant attention to feminist practice becomes especially important when these "growing pains" run their cycle. Alan, professor and minister, described how the old patriarchal self he is trying

to discard can compete with the new feminist self he is gradually growing into, in his interactions with women.

*Feminist men need to be around women who will put us in check
because we are constantly being seduced by the privilege of maleness.
My partner constantly puts me in check! Early in our relationship, I had
to deal with my attitude that suggested that she should be attentive to
me because "I'm the male person." Even in the bedroom, I initially
expressed the attitude that she should serve me sexually. She was like,
"What you want me to do gives me no pleasure and we will have none
of that until you start knowing that you have to serve me as well!" She
told me once, "I want you to really explore the kinds of experiences that
will make you grow because if you do not feel nurtured, spiritually
empowered, and satisfied in this relationship, you can't be a healthy
functioning partner for me."*

Alan's narrative reveals why vigilant practices are so important in
feminist relationships. Even though Alan teaches feminist courses and
radically identifies with the term "feminist," he admits how persistent
the slippage can be between his professed commitment and his actual
behavior. At some point, feminist men have to accept that feminism is
not an extracurricular activity to be practiced in their spare time. When a
man practices feminism only when it is convenient for him, his feminist
theory and rhetoric will not erase or compensate for his personal practices of dominance and shallow engagement in social change.[29]

Romantic relationships with feminist women often pressure these
men to live with integrity, which means the men are bound to learn
some troubling things about their own lives as well as society. These
relationships require men to reinterpret their lives in ways that are
uncomfortable, unflattering, and that demand action and personal transformation.[30] Alan continues his narrative describing a rough period after
the birth of their first child.

*My partner is also an actor, so she has to be away from the home
quite frequently.... I was working on a Ph.D. and she was working on a
master's degree in fine arts in acting when we had our first child. We
were both graduate students trying to finish our individual programs. It
was a difficult time. There was much negotiation and "nuts and bolts"
discussions about redefining what it meant for us to be in the relationship. She never negotiated from the standpoint of gender, she simply told
me once, "This is your child, too, and you have to do what's right for
your child."... I wanted to fall back on the excuse that she was the
"mother and was supposed to do these things."... When a man marries
an autonomous "feminist-thinking-and-acting" woman, he really needs
to know that things will not operate on his terms alone and that every-*

*thing will be negotiated. This defies the popular notion of the "tradi-
tional" marriage.*

The home is sometimes "the last feminist frontier" that men are
unwilling to explore or change in depth.[31] Like Alan, many feminist men
would rather attend a feminist rally, read a feminist book, or write a
feminist article than clean a toilet, do the laundry, change a diaper, and
bathe or feed an infant at night. Feminist women would rather do other
things, too, yet often end up performing most of the household chores
and childcare Many feminist women must constantly remind their feminist male partners to pull their weight in the home, not only in public,
activist-oriented forums. Too often, men—even feminist men—see
themselves as "helping" with the household chores and childcare
responsibilities rather than equally *sharing* in completing these tasks.[32]
These tasks require skills that can be learned easily; however, feminist
commitment requires changes in behavior, and setting up an egalitarian
household has challenged even the most committed feminist men. Alan
understands that the process is ongoing, based on repeated interactions
with a feminist woman who stands her ground.

An egalitarian marriage requires different politics. Alan explains
how the "politic of naming" is an important aspect of his marriage.

*My partner and I really work hard at maintaining our own identi-
ties, while simultaneously sharing ourselves with each other. In our marriage, my partner retained her last name, and I encouraged her to retain
it. We have two children and we hyphenated their last names to include
both of our last names. We want our children to know that the mother's
name should not seem subservient to the father's name. So, we began our
marriage with that kind of politic—the politic of naming.*

*I think it's also important to note that my partner does not use the
label feminist to describe herself. She's familiar with the literature,
but has a number of issues with White women and how they have
used the term. She feels that she is an autonomous being and doesn't
need the feminist label to express that autonomy. I have certainly
asked her to use the label since she represents feminism in practice, but
she replies, "I'm not going to serve your desire in that way. I am who
I am." I had to accept her decision even though I use the term feminist to describe myself.*

Alan's examples of the "politic of naming" show that there is no one
"right" Black feminist analysis. An intersectional analysis of the race,
gender, class, and sexuality issues in a relationship can lead two feminists
to two different conclusions on a particular issue. However, the process
of listening is more important than whether the couple comes to an
agreement about the "correct" answer on an issue.

Alan listens to his wife and how she chooses to define herself in nonfeminist terms; likewise, she listens to him and respects his choice to define himself in clearly feminist terms. Patriarchal masculinity, in contrast, teaches that men have the final word and authority on a topic, so listening to women becomes less important than listening to men, even when men and women may be saying the same thing. Hence, a common expression of male power is that men interrupt women more frequently than women interrupt men, take most of the speaking time in a conversation, and assume that what they have to say is somehow more important than what women have to say.

Abdul affirms how seriously the depth of male socialization goes; his everyday behaviors, desires, and beliefs are constructed and reinforced by patriarchy.[33] His previous practice of polygamy, coupled with his ingrained sense of male privilege, has presented major challenges in his current marriage.

I was never taught how to deal with the pain, confusion, frustration, and hard times in a relationship. When those difficult moments came up I fell back on that "male thing," you know, "my way or no way." I had to ask myself, how do I begin to work at my relationship differently? I'm more grounded in that "how" today than ever before in my life.... I really didn't connect with my own sexist influences and behavior until around seven years ago. I was only able to see my sexist stuff when my mind started to open up.... Equal partnerships are challenging because they require you to listen instead of simply calling all of the shots. They are worth the struggle because one of the things that I never want to do is crush someone's spirit.... If I'm making sure that I don't crush my partner's spirit, then I have to be figuring out how to make the relationship a safe place for both of us.

Abdul and his current partner attended couples counseling prior to their marriage and still go to counseling sessions when necessary. Interactions with his wife and a marriage counselor helped him develop some of the skills needed for an egalitarian, monogamous marriage. He had to admit that he did not have all of the answers and that he had to learn to listen actively in order to communicate better in his relationship. This required him to look inward.

I believe women have always said things to me about my behavior and their experiences with men, but because of my indoctrination and socialization, like most men, I just never really heard them! I've always been one of those men who had the answer before the woman even asked the question. I just figured I knew what she was thinking before she even opened her mouth. So, basically I was at a place where I didn't have an ear for whatever she had to say. My attitude was, "Hurry up and say it so

*we can move on, but don't linger on it because I'm gonna call you some-
thing you won't like if you say it too many times." To be honest, I didn't
really know how to listen to a woman. First, I had to learn how to listen.*

*Today, my strength in my current relationship and relationships with
other women is that I try to believe and listen to women's reality and
support their struggle for justice, freedom, safety, trust, and love. By
believing women's reality, I'm not saying that women are saints or
angels. I am accepting their reality without passing judgment! We as men
have to begin to think about what women say, respect what women say,
and even uplift what women say, in order to do the work that we need to
do in response to what they share with us. If I spend time trying to judge,
challenge, confront, and deny her reality—I'll never have to deal with
my role in her pain and anguish and how I have been socialized to ignore
her reality and overly promote mine.*

Feminist scholar David Kahane notes that understanding women's
realities and experiences results in a man's transformation regarding the
way "he experiences his own life, conceptualizes possibilities for personal and social change, and acts in the world."[34] Hence, feminist Black
men must constantly see their fate as linked to the fate of women and
other oppressed groups. Obviously, many feminist men will periodically
stray from their commitments and will have to be reeled in by their conscience if they expect to benefit from the rewards of feminist practice.

However, some men in this study, along with their feminist partners, are engaged in what can be considered radical practices, compared
to those of earlier heterosexual partnerships, and to these I now turn.

Institutionalized Heterosexuality, Coupledom, and Monogamy: Stretching the Boundaries

Some narratives, like Toussaint's and Solomon's, demonstrated diverse
approaches to relationships, despite similar visions of what is egalitarian.
Although most of the men emphasized the importance of monogamy,
Toussaint, the priest, did not.

*I have politically reinterpreted the label "queer" as a positive word
and describe myself as a "queer-identified bisexual man." I have been in
a long-term relationship with my woman partner who is a multiracial,
bisexual woman. After five years of marriage, we "came out" to each
other as bisexual. Over the years, living in close proximity with her and
participating in her research on the role of women in the early church,
sharing with her the struggle around raising consciousness about the
ordination of women, and working with her to challenge readings that
distort religious history have had a major impact on me. Living with and*

experiencing a sister who's very self-determining and who also provides a space for me to be a different kind of man is very gratifying. Our rela-tionship allows us to explore our gender expressions, and, together, we have created the kind of environment where we can actively work to dis-mantle gender oppression.

I have been in a polyamorous relationship for the last fifteen years or so. I don't call my relationships nonmonogamous because I have consis-tently had relationships with only two people at a time and all parties involved negotiate these conditions. In other words, I was not involved with anybody else outside of those two people. Therefore, if I am in a relationship with a woman and with a man, I am not dealing with any other woman or any other man. My boyfriend, who was a part of this three-way relationship, just left the relationship. Prior to the breakup, the three of us were living together. I know people who live in polyamorous relationships where both partners are involved with several people and for some people that seems to work. But it requires constant negotiation, openness, and honesty.

Toussaint challenges a variety of institutionalized assumptions about legally sanctioned partnerships, bisexuality, monogamy, and any "single-recipe ideas" about what constitutes an egalitarian partnership. For some people, openly discussed polyamorous relationships offer a greater chance of honesty with different partners.[35] Like Toussaint, some femi-nist women who support nonmonogamy argue that it is not a situation in which people simply do as they please, but one in which negotiations over ground rules and boundaries reach outcomes acceptable to all par-ties.[36] Rather than allowing their lives and the lives of others to be cir-cumscribed by negative emotions like jealousy, possessiveness, and insecurity, and viewing these emotions as "natural," feminist arguments for nonmonogamy suggest that these emotions are socially created and should be challenged.[37] They ask, "Why should sexual love be regarded as more exclusive than any other kind of love? No one suggests that a woman who has two children loves each of them less than a woman with only one, yet we assume that she cannot love two lovers. Why is having sex with someone other than a given partner equated with betrayal? Why do we call it infidelity? There are far worse forms of betrayal and faithlessness."[38] Feminist women who support these arguments say monogamy should be questioned because it suggests that a person cannot have more than one meaningful relationship.

As long as monogamy and the primacy of the couple are the norm, the privilege of heterosexuality is sustained. From a feminist perspective, the critique of monogamy remains important if we are to challenge insti-tutionalized heterosexuality.[39] The argument for nonmonogamous partnerships also suggests that if sexual relationships were de-prioritized as the basis for our most meaningful social ties, and if they were not exclusive, then who one related to sexually might come to be of less pervasive social significance. Heterosexuality would then lose its privileged, institutionalized status, and nonsexual friendships would no longer be regarded as intrinsically less significant than sexual ones.[40] The unarticulated assumption that nonmonogamy harms women ignores some of the damaging effects of monogamy, which pressures women to de-prioritize their friendships. Neglecting friends often results in putting all of their emotional investment into a single 'love' relationship that can impoverish their social lives.[41] Also, monogamy can limit how one socializes with friends, given that couples tend to socialize with other couples. The dominant notion of 'togetherness' leads to the assumption that friends should be friends of the couple, not of one or other of the partners.

Most critiques of nonmonogamy among African American scholars have not incorporated clear Black feminist perspectives and continue to favor Black men.[42] Monogamy has always been more binding on women than men. Moreover, some feminists believe that the privatized monogamous couple and nuclear family divert attention away from wider political issues and struggles that affect broader relationships. Hence, the critique of monogamy was never concerned solely with sexual exclusivity, but with the institutionalization of coupledom and the presumed "ownership" of another individual.[43] Jackson and Scott, two feminist women who support nonmonogamy, explain, "If we suspend the idea that sex is a special activity, defining a special relationship, we can see how ludicrous it is to assume that someone we have sex with is so different from friends we do other things with.... Yes of course sex is different—there are all sorts of emotions invested in sex—but we need to ask why and why they are so different from emotions invested in other relationships. It is worth reminding ourselves that this difference is not natural and should not simply be taken for granted.[44]

Although feminist women who support nonmonogamy are in the minority, they argue that it can be practiced in egalitarian ways and that the threat of loss, insecurity, and jealousy can be minimized or prevented by open, thoughtful discussion. They also challenge people in monogamous relationships to describe to what degree those emotions have been minimized or prevented in their relationships, noting that harmful, dishonest, and manipulative practices in a marriage may be the result of one party's refusal to commit to or act responsibly toward lovers.[45]

Solomon, the transgendered anthropologist, also challenges us to imagine other models of feminist, egalitarian relationships.

Most of the Black women I have dated have had feminist inclina-tions, even though most did not identify with the term. Most had feminist inclinations because they were willing to risk heterosexual privilege and being ostracized by people they loved. They were risking possibly never fitting into the Black community like they did before they met me. So, that's pretty feminist to me. They understood the risks, yet chose to be with me anyway. Transsexualism is relatively rare in comparison to homosexuality, so there's no script for it. Every relationship that I've been in has required me to clearly explain to my partners how I describe myself and what transsexualism means. I do this because my partner has to understand what it will mean for her to be in a relationship with me....

I became antisexist largely in response to the cry for help that I sensed in my female partners and my empathy for them. All of the women I have loved have served as profound motivation for me to develop an antisexist awareness. I never realized the extent to which I had grown up with sexist ideas about women and men. As a male-identi-fied person, I acquired many of the macho, sexist attitudes and behaviors that many men possess. During my early twenties, I used to hit women, and even beat one of my girlfriends. I have sexually forced myself on women. I have pinned women down on the floor against their will during a fit of personal rage. Feminist women helped me understand these acts as abusive, and my love for them helped me listen to them and their description of how my sexist ways caused them pain.... Eventually, I realized that if I wanted to have love in my life, I had to learn how to behave differently. So I became increasingly antisexist as a result of dating women who were becoming increasingly feminist in their con-sciousness. The more feminist the woman I was dating, the more she expected me to change my sexist ways. They helped me understand that a real man is a peaceful man and does not need to act macho in order to feel at home with himself.

Some female-to-male transsexuals like myself assume a dominant, macho male role in their relationships and attempt to be the head of the household in order to prove that they are real men. I acted like that in my youth, but not today. I want my wife to bring her whole self to the relationship and if I want her to do that, then I have to make room for her whole self. I also want to bring my whole self to the relationship. Khalil Gibran explains in one of his beautiful writings on marriage that couples "should be as two pillars, standing side by side." You can't be two pillars standing side by side if one is trying to tower over the other. I sin-cerely believe that the purpose of partners, of people coming together in a marriage, is to love each other, yes, and to enjoy each other, yes, but more important, to heal each other. My understanding of a relationship is that it's not just to have fun, sex, or share the bills with someone—it's about attempting to evolve spiritually with someone.

It is important to remember that, unlike genetic men, female-to-male transsexuals (FTMs) have lived parts of their lives as girls and as women; thus, many have experienced the oppressions to which girls and women are subjected.[46] In addition, some FTMs have long histories of participation *as women* in women's communities, in ways that men in general are not allowed to experience; some have spent years of living or "passing" as lesbians, heterosexual women, bisexual women, or all of these gendered positions, prior to medical or social transitions as transsexuals.[47] Thus, many have endured different kinds of oppression that other men and women generally do not experience, and a Black transgendered man like Solomon is positioned to offer a unique, intersectional analysis of the oppressions he has faced. While it is beyond the scope of this research to address the oppression of female-to-male transsexuals in U.S. society, the complex specificities of their manhood should be acknowledged.[48] Compared to men born biologically male, FTMs have advantages and disadvantages regarding feminist theory, politics, and practice. Solomon is clearly aware that his experiences as a transgendered man, different from those of genetic males, have contributed to his feminist outlook and development.

Solomon's creative reconstruction of manhood, like other feminist constructions of masculinity, challenges mainstream notions of a "real man" and a "real woman." Any man who identifies with feminism is still seen as outside the norm of manhood and manliness, according to everyday, popular, biological, cultural, and dominant concepts, but some feminist Black men experience this outsider status more than others because of their sexuality, physical appearance, mannerisms, marital status, age, socioeconomic class, and other socially constructed factors that convey privilege. Feminist men have to care more about moral and political values than they do about how people perceive their masculinity; FTMs may be in a better position than other, genetic men to engage in this task, owing to their unique experiences.[49]

The reconstruction of masculinity using feminist perspectives allows us to identify certain feminist values that amount to spiritual principles. Solomon identifies these as nonviolence, the absence of the need for dominance, and enlightenment. The narratives of Paul, Alan, and Toussaint also reinforce this point. However, those values do not evolve from gender construction alone. Feminist women and feminist politics also inform each man's spiritual perspective, and the vigilant practice of reflective assessment, as seen here, is consistent with egalitarian practices among feminist men in earlier research.[50]

Summary

Black feminist men's narratives of romantic relationship are snapshots of a particular time in their life history; they are therefore subject to change as their lives and stories about their lives evolve. Although not all the men were feminist at the beginning of their relationships, all currently offer a feminist outlook, making their personal lives political to the best of their ability and crediting feminist women with daring them to be fully human. Their narratives also confirm that while being a feminist does not magically inoculate men from patriarchal influences, such influences can be countered. Furthermore, although reflective assessment is critical, it is through both public and private acts that such contradictions must be negotiated.

These findings challenge popular books suggesting that women must be passive because men and women are *inherently* different. They also challenge some one-dimensional feminist notions about romantic relationships with men, exemplified by slogans like "[they] start with you [the woman] in his arms and end with your arms in his sink." Although it is a huge struggle to maintain egalitarianism in a romantic partnership, all the men in my study clearly state that they prefer this struggle to those of traditional relationships in which gender roles are rigidly prescribed. Feminist practices of vigilance found in previous studies on egalitarian man–woman relationships were also found among the heterosexual couples in my study: (a) critiquing daily forms of injustice from an intersectional analysis; (b) public acts of equality as a couple; (c) clear support of the female partner's career; (d) reflective assessment; and, (d) emotional involvement (communicating emotions verbally and otherwise, and not withdrawing from conflict).[51] Furthermore, feminism allows men to understand women's experiences, their partnerships, and *their own* individual experiences better. Such practices of feminist vigilance on the part of men, particularly Black men, allow them to become women's allies instead of competing with Black women over who is the most victimized by a White, male-dominated, and market-driven system.

CHAPTER 6

Platonic Friendships with
Feminist Women

Women friends who are feminists facilitate feminist Black men's outlook and practices as much as feminist romantic partners do. Here I focus on the importance, for the men in this study, of platonic interactions with feminist women: their college professors, supervisors, coworkers, classmates, or relatives. Feminist women writers—some of whom the men have actually met in person—have had a role in their development, too; their words have touched the men's lives and reinforced their understanding of various manifestations of sexism.

Earlier research on cross-sex adult friendships has shown that relationships between feminist Black men and feminist women have an ongoing effect on the men's self-perceptions and offer unique benefits that same-sex friendships do not. In particular, the unique components of social interactions such as platonic friendships with women have a noticeable impact on feminist Black men's evolving feminist identities and practices. Certain institutional factors and arrangements increase the chances that men will meet and have meaningful interactions with feminist women and their writings. University settings, in particular, as well as sociopolitical organizations and social–justice-oriented work environments, promote such friendships. We will see in this chapter how those contextual factors shaped the educational biases found in my study and in other studies of feminists in general.

Research on Adult Cross-Sex Friendships

Research on cross-sex friendships[1] is extremely helpful in distinguishing the generic benefits of friendship, cross-sex and same-sex, from the unique benefits of man–woman friendships during adulthood. The generic benefits reflect similarities between the two types of friendships, regardless of gender, whereas the unique benefits reflect their differences.

Both cross-sex and same-sex friendships offer comfort during difficult times, an outlet for the expression of fears, feelings, and fantasies; companionship, acceptance, and greater self-knowledge.[2] The unique, additional benefits of cross-sex adult friendships include (1) insider perspectives on "how members of the opposite sex think, feel, and behave"; (2) other-sex companionship without the pressures, demands, and expectations that normally accompany romantic relationships; and (3) information regarding some of the gender differences in communication that women and men experience.[3] These findings indicate that cross-sex friends can provide benefits not typically available in romantic relationships or same-sex friendships. However, not all cross-sex friendships are the same. Some friends choose to have sex with each other;[4] some actively avoid sexual contact;[5] some men and women receive more social support from their same-sex friends than from their cross-sex ones;[6] whereas others, often males, report receiving more support from their cross-sex friendships.[7] Some struggle frequently with issues of power and control, others do not;[8] some value insider perspectives provided by friends, and others do not.[9] Thus, it is important to recognize the variability within such friendships, as well as the trends they share.

Most important, studies unequivocally support the fact that men and women can be friends, despite various social and structural barriers that may get in the way.[10] Most of these friendships do not include a romantic or sexual component, and cross-sex friendships occur between heterosexuals as well as between pairs in which one friend is (or both are) gay or lesbian. This chapter focuses particularly on nonromantic friendships between feminist Black men and feminist women, mentioning, when relevant, the sexual identity of the people involved.

Heterosexual, bisexual, gay, and transgendered men's narratives frequently highlight the emotional intimacy at the core of their friendships with feminist women. The narrative excerpts quoted here show a range of experiences feminist men have had with feminist women that demonstrate the unique aspects of such friendships. Specifically, feminist friendships reinforce the social reconstruction of masculinity and the reinterpretation of gender relationships in each man's life. Consistencies across the narratives include each man's growing trust in women and women's stories about their lives, as well as a university setting being the place where most of these feminist friendships originated.

The Importance of Trust

Sometimes a man's prior close relationship with a feminist romantic partner helped open the door to other trusting, egalitarian friendships with women. Bruce shares the impact his feminist wife Charlotte had on his friendships with other women.

Charlotte was my buddy before we ever slept together. We used to hang out. She's probably the only good buddy I have. So, we are buddies and lovers—both aspects create a strong bond. Originally, I didn't trust women, so I really didn't experience platonic friendships with women until the last four or five years.

Bruce's loving and trusting interactions with his partner led him to being open to developing close, trusting friendships with other women. However, a feminist man must also trust that "he is still a man in his own eyes" when he is in a close friendship with a woman—especially a woman he finds attractive—that is *not* motivated primarily by his desire for sexual gratification. Research on cross-sex friendships suggests that the extent to which a person exhibits mainstream, traditional masculine or feminine personality traits influences subsequent success in cross-sex friendships.[11] Specifically, men who are less macho in their expressions of masculinity have significantly more cross-sex friendships than traditionally masculine men and traditionally feminine women. One explanation is that men who are less traditionally macho in their behavior may have better-developed interpersonal skills and be more flexible in their communication styles than traditionally masculine males.[12] Furthermore, traditional men may be more inclined to see women as (prospective) dating or sexual partners and less inclined to view them as platonic friends. Some friendship studies suggest that openness to cross-sex friendships allows both men and women to develop a broader range of communication styles than do same-sex friendships.[13]

Insights as to how sexist thinking and behavior work against friendship with women can also be learned from public figures. Hearing certain Black feminist writers like Toni Cade Bambara, Angela Davis, and Pearl Cleage speak—as well as reading their books—also helped Bruce understand women's experiences better. He states,

Black feminist writings and speakers helped me see why my mother, sister, and other women experienced and interpreted their lives in ways that represented their reality in sexist contexts. In the process, I learned to

*recognize the various layers of oppression and developed empathy for
people who experience oppression in ways that I do not.*

Although Edmund, the performance artist, was a prolific reader
before meeting his feminist wife, he admits that he "didn't trust or pay
attention to the writings of women." Ruby, his wife, an African American
writer and performance artist, opened his eyes to women's experience.

*I was exposed to feminist writing through Ruby's poems, essays,
plays, and her performances. Once Ruby made it clear how sexist I was, I
started reading books by feminists that she suggested, like Marion
Zimmer Bradley. Ruby suggested that I read "The Shattered Chain" and
I was surprised to find out that almost every sexist thing the guy in the
story did was what I had done previously. Reading feminist literature put
out by the National Organization for Women (NOW) and magazines
like* Ms. *and* Essence *have been invaluable when it comes to helping me
understand women's perspectives and relating to them better. Also, feminist literature has helped me understand—and finally believe—that men
do so many things casually that women find completely offensive.... So I
had to willfully deal with this belligerent ignorance and set an example
for other men... but the process is like being a recovering drug addict
providing drug rehabilitation counseling for other addicts.*

Eddie, 36, an urban planner, also said his feminist wife exposed him
to her friends (who later became his friends). Their real-life stories, along
with nonfictional feminist work by revolutionary writers like Assata
Shakur,[14] helped him trust women's reality.

*Probably my contact with progressive women has been even more of
an influence in my antisexist outlook than any readings and my political
study in my organization. I've been influenced so much by my relationship with my wife. However, my wife also exposed me to women who are
my close friends now, due to the friendships that she developed with some
of them through her work. As a social worker she works with lots of
women who were in abusive situations.... I've had enough exposure that
would make it very difficult for me not to feel that I should do something
differently as a person, as a man....*

*So it's the reality of a sister telling me the story of her life that has
affected me. Women's real-life stories are much easier for me to understand and are [more] difficult to refute or challenge than some of the fic-
tional feminist literature. These are platonic friendships with women who
I consider good friends. They have shared their serious struggles in relationships involving abuse and all kinds of horrible things that have
stayed in my mind. Their experiences mold me and are, hopefully, changing me in positive ways.*

Bruce's, Edmund's, and Eddie's experiences are representative. The feminist Black men in my study had to develop trust in their friendships with women before the women could have any impact on their beliefs and behavior. This individual factor was further influenced by the women's expectations during these interactions and by institutional arrangements that made the friendships possible.

For the majority of the Black men in this study, their nonromantic friendships with feminist women offered benefits identifiable by four interrelated themes in the narratives: (1) a practicing ground for evolving alternative masculinities, (2) a safe space and place to be vulnerable and human, (3) a site for constructive criticism from allies who are both personally and politically invested in the men's well-being, and (4) mentoring. Examples of the four themes are given throughout the rest of the chapter.

Feminist Cross-Sex Friendships in University Settings

Previous studies indicate that universities provide a rich opportunity for initiation and maintenance of cross-sex friendships, offering facilitating conditions such as proximity; nominal equality in status; a supportive, open-minded, and often liberal environment; and time for interacting.[15] As in earlier studies, the majority of the men in this one developed platonic friendships with feminist women in university settings.

For Cudjoe, a 29-year-old Black (Seminole) Native American born in Oklahoma, the university provided an extremely rich environment for cross-sex friendships, as well as other important feminist connections during his time as an undergraduate and graduate student. All four themes appear in his narrative evoking the unique benefits of man–woman feminist friendships.

When I was in college in the early 1990s, I was walking with two really good friends of mine—two White women who were feminists— and they were talking about how they were taking a women's studies class; and the first thing I thought was, how stupid! Why would anyone ever take that kind of course? They responded by saying how important it was and how they should be able to study themselves as part of the curriculum. They also said that I should take the class. At first I was really resistant because I was thinking that if I took the class, someone was going to think that I was gay, weird, or something negative. In my early high school years, a lot of people always teased me about and questioned my sexuality because I had really good friendships with women.

Cudjoe's narrative shows how much gender, as structure, affects our individual, interactional, and institutional experiences.[16] The expectations that Black men face each day (e.g., "men act in ways that are the opposite of women," "men can have some women friends but not too many women friends unless they are gay," and "only White women and some White men take women's studies courses") play a huge part in the development of their individual identities, the people they choose as friends, and the degree to which they feel welcomed in certain institutional settings. Thus, when they do not follow the racialized, patriarchal heterosexist, and class-based rules and behaviors expected of them, they are judged gay, too White, or too soft. A subgroup of men in the study, seven in all, were bullied and taunted as being sissies or gay on a regular basis during adolescence, despite their heterosexual identification.[17] Thus, men's choices about how they practice masculinity are made within social constraints, and nonconformity often involves major personal sacrifices. Interestingly enough, these same men in the study often had the greatest and most rewarding number of friendships with feminist women. As Cudjoe's narrative continues, I indicate the themes he touches on, in parentheses:

I continued having many friendships with women in college, and my best friend, who was Palestinian and Salvadoran, would actually tell me things like, "You really shouldn't say the word pussy in the company of women." (constructive criticism) *I'd be like, really? She would tell me what women liked and didn't like about men.* (practicing ground) *Another feminist friend would engage in intense conversations with me about gender and question my views by finding fault in my argument in ways that didn't say, "Not only are you fundamentally wrong, but you are also stupid for thinking like that."* (constructive criticism) *Her kindness helped me see that I was wrong, but not in ways that suggested she was always right.* (safe space) *She wanted me to think about what I was saying, and was definitely a feminist.*

During that same period of time I was also learning that men could be feminists and that the feminist movement is not closed to men. So I ended up taking Intro to Women's Studies with my best friend who was a feminist woman! There were probably eighty people in the class, and about five guys. I found the subject matter interesting. I guess I felt like I had a stake in addressing gender issues, especially because I also have a lot of women friends. The professor became my mentor and was really encouraging and helpful. (mentoring)

Cudjoe's narrative and the ones that follow most commonly described the pleasures and deep camaraderie of these friendships. They also show how feminist Black men learn to perceive their fate as men as truly linked to that of women. Although difficult and uncomfortable interactions occur, especially when a feminist friend is voicing her concerns or displeasure regarding sexist behavior on the man's part, most of the men in the study who had feminist friends talked about how they delighted in and treasured these friendships—in fact, more so than their friendships with men. Why this tends to be the case will be discussed in the next chapter, on participants' friendships with men.

Taking women's studies courses at the university exposed Cudjoe to a variety of feminist friendships.

In graduate school, I also took a lot of women's studies classes and befriended a lot of the women in those classes.... Between undergraduate and graduate school, I heard Naomi Wolf speak while she was on the college lecture circuit promoting her ideas and book about "The Beauty Myth."... Today, I also love to read Black feminist Patricia Williams's column in The Nation *because I just find her so funny and athletic with words. Her delivery is brilliant and many of her articles are about gender from the eyes of a Black feminist trained lawyer—but I still love Naomi Wolf!*

I also worked for a Black feminist psychology professor in graduate school. She was so kind to me and was the book review editor for a feminist journal. We worked in a women's research center that was this hyperfeminist environment with posters on the wall like Rosie the Riveter and contemporary feminist art everywhere. I spent most of my time there, whether I was working or not! Another amazing feminist psychologist at the center was also unusually supportive of me. She would assure me that what I was doing was fantastic and made me feel like I was doing the greatest thing and that there was nothing wrong with me or any man who was interested in how women view and contribute to the world.

Finally, I became the house sitter for two elderly Jewish lesbians who were so much fun. I took their classes and had a lot of fun with them and would house sit during the summers when they would go away.

Thus, the university setting provided Cudjoe with feminist friends who were peers, feminist professors who became mentors, and older feminists who became like family to him. All four themes appear in his descriptions of these relationships, consistent with other research in this area. Specifically, previous research on cross-sex friendships suggests that, compared to university students, individuals who do not go to college seem to be at a structural disadvantage for developing cross-sex friendships in general, and with feminists in particular.[18] Some researchers speculate that college-educated individuals tend to marry late, and usually have cross-sex friendships by the time they marry;

while working-class people tend to marry soon after high school and do not get the chance to cultivate many cross-sex friendships before marriage.[19] Studies also suggest that married couples tend to have fewer cross-sex friendships than single individuals because spouses spend most of their free time together rather than separately, couples are less dependent on friends for meeting their social needs and tend to become more dependent on their spouses, and spouses are often jealous of their partner's cross-sex friends.[20] The partner may end such a friendship because of the stress it places on the marriage. Finally, young adults appear to have more cross-sex friendships than most other individuals, and Cudjoe is representative of this group. However, even most of the older men in the study who had many feminist women friends met them as young adults or while studying at a university.

Feminist Women as Peers

Carlos, currently a graduate student, says his feminist outlook grew as a result of platonic friendships with Black women during his years as an undergraduate at a Black men's college. These friendships helped him reconceptualize what it meant to be a man. In the excerpt that follows, Carlos touches on at least three of the themes characterizing the unique benefits of cross-sex feminist friendships.

One summer a platonic friend of mine and I were volunteering for a conference sponsored by the National Black Women's Health Project at the women's college down the street from the men's college I attended. We met at the conference and afterward we got together and talked about feminism, women's health, men's health, sexism, and the different ways that men and women perceive things. She thought I might be interested in meeting people who do reevaluation counseling, to explore my emotional health as a man and as an activist. Reevaluation counseling is a process [in which] people learn to free themselves from the effects of past painful experiences. The process teaches you how to emotionally express your pain and then move beyond it. By learning to express yourself emotionally, you become more effective in looking out for your interests and the interests of others. Plus, you learn to act more successfully against injustices because you are not emotionally blocked. I participated in men's groups where they would ask you "What do you like about being a man?" "What don't you like about being a man?" I took some of the material discussed in reevaluation counseling and used it in the discussions of the Black men's antisexist group I had cofounded on campus. I really grew that summer. The feminist woman I was dating was away for the summer, so the woman that I met at the conference and I just hung out all summer, going to different activities with people who were doing reevaluation counseling.

I used to just think of social justice issues as being only political and as something that was outside of my personal life. I didn't question how I felt inside about such issues. Reevaluation counseling sessions helped me see how political issues had affected me emotionally. As a result, I developed an interest in changing how I felt as well as changing the external political conditions. I also came to realize that there were things that I did to other people that perpetuated the system I was organizing against! So I started to make these connections that summer, thanks to my friendship with this woman.

By exposing him to reevaluation counseling, Carlos's Black feminist woman friend enabled the creation of a practicing ground, safe space, and site for constructive criticism in the context of their friendship. One might even say she mentored him that summer. The institutional factors that shaped his interactions with his friend must also be noted. Carlos's predominantly Black men's college was just down the street from the predominantly Black women's college his friend attended. The close proximity of the schools encouraged cross-sex friendships, platonic and otherwise. Through his feminist woman friend Carlos developed a network of men who questioned traditional notions about masculinity, which they felt hurt men and impaired their ability to do activist work in social movements. As Carlos began to redefine manhood, he took what he had learned from the reevaluation counseling group back to the feminist Black men's student group he cofounded, encouraged by his Black feminist woman friend (see chapter 8 for details about the student group).

Toussaint's narrative turns on a historic moment: when a women's institution goes coed, men are exposed to feminist cross-sex friendships and can begin to reshape their perceptions and practices of manhood.

I went to two different universities for my bachelor's degree. I went to an all-male college in Massachusetts during my first year. Big mistake! It was an East Coast old boy's club. After my first year, I left and was admitted to a women's college. I think that was the first year the women's college started accepting men... transferring from the men's college to a women's college was one of the turning points in my life. Being at an historically women's institution, seeing women in positions of power, being in classes where I was the minority because I was a man, and being around sisters who were on the cutting edge of feminism and sexuality issues contributed to a rich intellectual environment that I had not experienced at the men's college... the sisters were fierce and helped me rethink so many issues.... I was very, very happy there.

Sometimes my college friends would make little remarks that trans-formed my level of awareness. For example, when I was in the bathroom in a coed dorm, I was in one stall and there was this sister in another stall. All of a sudden she said, "I can't stand men who will not put the toilet seat down!" That was an epiphany in my life. I have never left the toilet seat up since! It takes simple acts of solidarity to acknowledge that not everybody in the world pees standing up.

Later when I lived alone, I kept sanitary napkins in my bathroom for women. Guys would come over and see the sanitary napkins in the bathroom and say, "Oh, you are really going too far with this antisexist manhood stuff, you are tripping." But the sisters would say, "I'm so glad you had these sanitary napkins in your bathroom because I needed them tonight." I take antisexism seriously at all levels.

Narrow, binary ways of looking at gender (male/female, mascu-line/feminine, heterosexual/ homosexual) limit our ability to be fully human and whole. Cross-sex friendships with feminists have allowed these men to reconceive what it means to be a man, and to develop new interpersonal skills and creative practices that enable them to discover a previously denied aspect of their humanity. It is human, not simply "feminine," to be thoughtful and considerate, to empathize, to base friendships on equity, and to care for and nurture another. When one is pressured to view one's humanity in terms of " being a man" or " being a woman," what it means to be human is lost, truncated, stereotyped, and taken less seriously.

Getting in touch with one's full humanity is not merely a "touchy-feely" New Age experiment. It is the serious task of striving to become as good a person as possible, using feminist perspectives as a guide. Moreover, cross-sex feminist friendships provide feminist Black men with an interactional context for practicing masculinity differently. The more feminist friendships one has, the more contexts there are in which to practice. As a result, feminist masculinity becomes the new norm as, over time, the men themselves internalize the new expectations of their feminist friends.

Alan knows his platonic friendships with feminist women in gradu-ate school gave him a safe space to be vulnerable and permission to become more fully human.

During graduate school, I was the only male student activist in a group of White women Ph.D. students called the Feminist Forum. My closest friendships have been with women who are feminists. These pla-tonic relationships contain a real sense of honor and respect, whether that feminist is of color or not. When women who are feminist see me as a potential ally, a friendship usually emerges. These friendships have been life-affirming for me. They influence me in ways that relationships with men have not.

Ralph's narrative dovetails with Alan's.

Most of the women to whom I've been closest since graduate school have been feminist women. I genuinely desire being around women who have an understanding of themselves as women constrained by patriarchy who also challenge traditional notions, categories, and boundaries that constrain men. They also free me from harmful, debilitating popular notions of "what it means to be a man" in sexist settings and additionally recognize, are open to, and fully appreciate my attempt to practice alternative conceptions of manhood.

These interactional experiences in adulthood may be better predictors of a man's ability to embrace feminism than his childhood gender socialization as male. Cross-sex feminist friendships have a way of putting these men at ease. Such interactions also challenge feminist Black men to deepen their feminist outlooks in ways that create discomfort, doubt, anxiety, and sometimes grief. Within their feminist friendships, constructive criticism from political allies becomes possible.

Soyinka describes the mix of feelings and experiences that ultimately create what some researchers call a "mutually understood and shared relational reality that affirms another's identity."[21] The affirmation of identity as "a member of the group" is what comforts feminist men during both pleasant and unpleasant experiences that occur in the context of these cross-sex feminist friendships. Soyinka's narrative portrays how the uneasy feelings—arising from the contradiction between what he believes and how he behaves—motivate him to do better and strengthen the bonds of the friendship.

During my graduate school years, I met many women who willingly dragged me along—kicking and screaming—on the path to my true self. It was during this time that I was shot by my (former) wife and was exposed to Black womanists and feminists. My friendships with women—platonic and nonplatonic—have had a profound impact on me. Today, most of my close women friends are womanists and feminists. We have formed an informal community that allows men the rare opportunity to sit in "women's space" with our mouths shut, listening to what women think, feel, and say about their experiences. Over the years, these sisters encouraged me to participate in discussions with them. It's a different kind of hearing and a different kind of learning from what many men are used to experiencing. If something comes out of my mouth that is sexist or wrong, these sisters are on it! Even though I am constantly being challenged, I am blessed because these friendships constitute one of the richest areas of my life. I'm still struggling, but I have a deep sense of peace about it. These friendships are very fortifying. They serve as a compass, guiding me where I need to go. Like a rudder, they keep me moving in the right direction.

Soyinka's descriptions of these friendships as being like "a compass" and "a rudder" are reminders that feminist Black men are, indeed, swimming against the current. Feminist Black men are resisting tremendous pressures associated with patriarchal, heterosexist, institutional rules, Black cultural norms, and everyday practices, which suggest that listening to a feminist woman's—or any woman's—views about "how to be a man" is necessarily destructive to a man's masculinity. Yet the reality, as described by the men themselves, is that the process is instructive, often constructive, and affirming. In the next passage, Soyinka exhibits a level of honesty and humility characteristic of most men in the study.

I still have weaknesses that I really need to work on. Basically, they include struggling with my own sexism and challenging other males to do the same. It's easy to fall into a "good-guy" mode, where I feel like I've already arrived since I'm less sexist than most men. Well, as soon as I get smug and overconfident, more sexist skeletons fall out of my closet! Sometimes, I also have to struggle with how reluctant I am to hear sisters raise criticisms about my behavior—especially when I think I already have a particular problem licked. As long as we are men and live in a system that makes the male experience the norm, it's going to be hard to hear what women have to say. So the struggle will continue, no matter how much progress I think I'm making personally, because until the institutions have changed, not much has changed. Changes must occur at both the personal and the institutional level.

To Soyinka's credit, he has made the connection among his individual problems, popular notions of masculinity, and the institutionalized structures that reinforce his problems. I discuss the importance of collective activities in chapter 9. Here I deliberately focus on individual social interactions, in order to convey the practical and emotional aspects of feminist friendships in men's lives. These social networks tend to fuel the men's motivation to engage in collective action supporting feminism and to join formal feminist movement organizations.[22]

Youth director Chad's narrative also mentions the ebb and flow of friendships, which have challenged him to grow and develop feminist sensibilities.

In graduate school, I gradually began to feel relaxed around women and developed close friendships with them that became sites for further gender-related explorations. Witnessing their experiences helped me to become invested, in a very direct kind of way, with grappling with gender issues at all levels. I have feminist friends who have made clear to men that they have high expectations and that those men can try to meet those expectations or they can hit the door. These women have taught me that feminism can exact a price from feminist women that has profes- sional and personal implications, but the price of colluding with patriar- chal injustices is higher. Today, [the price of] colluding with patriarchal injustices is also higher for me than trying to engage in equitable practices with women.

David, who teaches literature, reported diverse interactions with women who were independent critical thinkers at his student–activist- oriented liberal arts college. Later, in the context of graduate school, he discovered similarities across various forms of oppression and the importance of coalitions through his friendships with feminist women. His narrative exemplifies how in addition to abstract theoretical writings about intersectional politics, men in my study who interacted with Black feminist women, in particular, were exposed to the concrete reality of their friends' lives. Different interactions provide different kinds of fem- inist exposure, and an earlier interaction may reinforce a subsequent one.

By the time I had graduated, worked full-time, and gone back to graduate school, my feminist friends had increased. They were mainly White feminists in graduate school, and we had in common our disruptive politics. Although my emphasis was more on race, we were able to discuss our similar reactions to a history of exclusion and persecution, and together challenge the ideas of institutions that reinforced our exclusion.

I was also encouraged to read feminist literature during college. Works by Black feminists such as Audre Lorde, Barbara Smith, and Alice Walker stand out in my memory. I was first exposed to the works of Black feminists in African American literature classes. Then, I started reading feminist works on my own. I was really challenged by the read- ings, given the rather narrow Black nationalist politics I was pursuing. Once I got to graduate school, I had to read feminist literary criticism by both White and Black feminists. I was also exposed to socialist and other leftist political literature.... Barbara Ehrenreich influenced me because she is a White feminist Marxist, and, of course, reading and meeting bell hooks made a very big difference in my thinking....

I've had a number of close friendships with women, but it wasn't until college that one of my friendships was with a woman who was very feminist in orientation. Although she later became my wife, it was a very challenging friendship because I was trying to pursue a narrow kind of Black nationalist agenda at that time. I remember asking her and a couple of other women who I was close to, "What's more important to you, being Black or being a woman?" I dared to suggest that those two aspects could be separated. They responded with some really complicated

answers and showed me how unfair the question was. Furthermore, they
pointed out how my asking the question was another way of exercising
my male privilege. The question allowed me to indirectly reinforce sexism
by minimizing its impact in their lives and assuming that it had to be less
important than racism.

David's narrative indicates that feminist literature enhances a man's
understanding of the various ways that feminism can be useful to him.
However, developing feminist practices requires a supportive network
of feminist women who will recognize when he is off course and
demand that he live it, not just read it or speak it. David's social interactions with living, breathing feminist women helped him move from a
fairly rigid strain of Black nationalist thought and activism to a broader
understanding and practice of coalition politics.[23]

Feminist Professors: Authority Figures, Coworkers, and Colleagues

Feminist professors teach and mentor many Black college men, another
reason why university settings provide a ripe environment for exposure
to and friendship with feminists. Rex, a social worker, narrates his graduate school experiences with feminist mentors.

A supervisor I had in graduate school was very much a feminist, and
listening to her and reading stuff that she would suggest that I read
helped develop my consciousness. She exposed me to so many interesting
feminist writers. I especially love listening to and reading bell hooks and
Kimberle Crenshaw. In fact, most of the feminist writings I've been
exposed to were by Black women. That really has been important because
I know that I made conscious choices to look for any presentation of fem-
inist issues that had race, sexual orientation, and class issues as part of the
discourse, like Audre Lorde's writings. That was really important to me
as a Black gay man.

Rex mentions later in the interview that reading "out" Black lesbian
feminist writers strengthened his understanding of Black feminist analysis; he learned the importance of an intersectional analysis that did not
exclude sexuality. He quoted Black lesbian writer Cheryl Clarke, who
wrote in 1983, "Homophobia divides black people as allies, it cuts off
political growth, stifles revolution, and perpetuates patriarchal domination."[24] Most important, these writers supplied theoretical perspectives
that he has been able to apply to his professional life as a social worker
who works with men who batter women.

A mélange of feminist-inspired intellectual, emotional, and spiritual
experiences during graduate school changed Alan's life and professional

direction. His exposure to a feminist professor led him to write a dissertation that reflected his reconstruction of masculinity, mentored by another leading feminist in his field.

In 1985, I took a graduate course in feminist literary criticism taught by a White feminist woman. The course exposed me to African American feminist bell hooks and her book Feminist Theory, From Margin to Center. . . . *bell hooks's words spoke to me as a Black man. It was at that point that I embraced feminist ideology because it was presented from a Black woman's point of view and it spoke to men's role in the struggle to end sexist oppression. The chapter on men as comrades affected me so profoundly that I changed my dissertation project to a topic that allowed me to learn about other men who shared a consciousness of feminism. I made a decision that my scholarly work from that point on would be pronouncedly feminist.*

Writing the dissertation on Black feminist forefathers and ultimately, having bell hooks direct it, empowered me as a Black feminist man. After the dissertation, I started to use a Black feminist standpoint in my writing and my teaching. . . . The acceptance of Black men as feminists—and, thus, the humanistic enterprise of Black feminism—radiates so deeply within me. . . . Black feminists have historically emphasized the activism of Black male feminists and what feminists should be doing to eradicate various forms of oppression. This activist orientation helped me to see that if I was going to speak to Black men about embracing a feminist sensibility, I would have to go beyond writing and articulating the message—I would have to act. I would have to live it.

As Alan's words suggest, feminist professors, supervisors, and mentors validate each man's evolving view of himself and increase his confidence as he seeks interactions with other feminist women. Alliances with those women may result in subsequent romances, platonic friendships, and work relationships. Alan's experience with a Black feminist lesbian colleague is a typical example of feminist cross-sex friendship between university coworkers who are professional equals.

My relationship with a Black lesbian feminist woman who worked at the university with me was one of the most holistic and gratifying friendships I ever had. In addition to teaching me about feminism, she taught me about the importance of collegiality, the importance of a liberating pedagogy, the significance of scholaractivism, and what it really means to be a human being. She impressed upon me the importance of self-analyses and helped me understand how men really don't listen to women. Even the men who purport to be feminist, profeminist or antisexist don't always listen to women. When my feminist friend pointed out to me how I didn't listen to women, it was a critical moment in our friendship. I now realize that when men truly learn to listen to the voices of women, we will go beyond being simply "politically correct" to being human. For instance, I have to work hard in my efforts to not interrupt women. I talk right over men too, but the effects are different because women are listened to less than men in general. So talking right over men and interrupting them doesn't have the same political ramifications, though I shouldn't talk over anyone.

Alan's narrative exemplifies, in yet another context, how friendships with feminist women allow—indeed, require—feminist men to develop new skills. Although institutions organize our lives in ways that support the status quo, cross-sex feminist friendships allow a space for men to shape new responses in their gender relations.

The narratives also call attention to how important it is for feminist men not to make excessive demands on their feminist women friends. Renate Klein notes that when budding feminist men use these friendships solely to seek absolution for their "worst sins and excesses in oppressing women" the interactions can become tedious for the feminist woman friend.[25] Thus, a balancing act becomes necessary in these friendships to prevent the woman from feeling drained by her enthusiastic male friends, the kind of exploitive interaction between women and men that feminism challenges. The following excerpt from Victor's narrative suggests the kind of healthy balance that feminist men and feminist women can cocreate.

I stopped practicing law and became a law professor. My male colleagues were so busy competing with each other that they could not imagine working together to help each other publish articles. I would even ask Black male colleagues to look at my articles, and they would always manage to say no. I was becoming extremely frustrated trying to get my articles published in academic law journals. One day, I ran into one of my former law school professors and told her how much trouble I was having. I hadn't seen her in a while, so I was surprised when she said, "Give me your article." She talked to the members of her writers group and they invited me to one of their meetings. This was a really sophisticated and productive group. Each meeting always included the discussion of two papers. Every participant brought food for the potluck dinner. We would discuss the first paper, and then eat. When we ate, we would talk about our personal lives. Then, we would spend the second half of the meeting discussing the second paper. . . . It was a Black woman's group; so the plan was not for me to join the group on a regular basis. Their understanding was, "The brother's in trouble, let's help him out because nobody else is helping him." I was so thankful for their feedback. Later, I got a letter in the mail and it read, "Dear Sisters and Victor" and announced the next meeting date. My former professor called and said,

"We decided to invite you to the group because everybody's really comfortable with you." After the third or fourth meeting, the conversations during dinner became even more personal. I learned things about women that made me a better person. Their concerns became my concerns.

When Black men demonstrate their awareness that the playing fields are not yet equal for Black men or Black women as well as respect Black women's time, space, and initiative, in general, a feminist friendship becomes possible and even pleasurable for both parties. Moreover, a Black feminist intersectional analysis can be transformed into concrete practices in the context of these friendships. Victor was aware that men are socialized to expect a variety of services from women—even when these women are their professional equals or superiors in a work setting. For example, Victor learned to wait for his former professor to volunteer to read his paper, rather than expecting this service from her as if he were entitled to it. It would have been insensitive of Victor to burden her unduly just because the men couldn't get their act together. He also waited to be invited to the group, instead of assuming that he *should* be invited because he was also a Black professor of law. He made an effort to fit in, as opposed to standing out, and brought his covered dish for dinner like the others—not simply expecting to be served. He did not try to change the subject, demonstrate his knowledge of feminism, or flex any other "intellectual muscles" during dinner, the time set aside for discussing personal life matters. At the end of the event, he did not try to push the women's guilt-buttons or charge them with "reverse sexism" or any other such nonsense. He was welcomed because, as the letter stated, "everybody's really comfortable with you."

Victor's interactions with Black feminist women have heightened his awareness *and* his discomfort with some of the privileges he experiences as a middle-class, married African American man trained as a lawyer.

My close women friends are feminists and have influenced me tremendously. These friendships have certainly heightened my awareness regarding women's experience of sexism, but they have also kept me honest. There are times when I want to deny my own privilege as a Black man because it makes me uncomfortable to admit privilege. For example, in the writer's group, it was easier for me to get published as a Black man than it was for the Black women in the group.... Law journals would look at my stuff more because there was a thrust to publish the works of Black men. These same journals didn't publish a lot of articles by women anyway. In the writer's group, the fact that it was easier for guys to get published than women came up during a discussion, and I didn't want to be viewed as someone with privilege. But there are places where I do have privilege and it's an uncomfortable place for me. My feminist friends and my wife have helped keep me honest because that privileged place can also be a place where I am insensitive to the concerns of women—even when I don't mean to be insensitive. I'd rather feel sorry for myself or only focus on the circumstances where I have been mistreated and marginalized than openly admit the places where I have privilege. By not acknowledging that I have certain privileges in this society—even as a Black man—I am less understanding and less aware of particular issues. So I'm kept honest by these friendships.

Victor's experience of honest communication echoes Johnetta Cole and Beverly Guy-Sheftall's call for "gender talk" among African Americans: "Individual change begins with greater awareness, which can be painful. Sometimes it hurts to open our eyes and face reality about ourselves, our homes, and our communities. But we must look unflinchingly at what ails us."[26]

Feminist Coworkers and Colleagues in Other Settings

Although most men met feminist women at a university, some met feminist women in other settings, such as community cooperatives and sociopolitical organizations, and one during his military service. Like any friendships that develop in the workplace, men's friendships with feminist women must take into account: (1) differences in power, requiring additional caution to avoid coercion and intimidation; (2) the blending of work and personal relationship, requiring awareness of appropriate boundaries; (3) potential career implications, positive or negative; and (4) third-party perceptions, among other factors.[27] While these issues are beyond the scope of this study, I have to assume that the relationships discussed here included those dynamics and were dealt with in ways that contributed to the positive effects that the men reported.

Donny describes working relationships and friendships with feminist women in which mutual respect and reciprocity were critical for establishing trust and duration. Although these friendships are a part of his work environment, he met most of the women when he was a student.

I am co-owner of a restaurant with a White woman. The restaurant was opened in the 1970s and initially was run by a collective of sixteen people. There were thirteen women—the majority were lesbian feminists—and three men. I was one of the men. We tried to establish a business that embodied "cooperative economics." So I had a cadre of feminist coworkers who checked me on my sexism daily. They kept a check on me because they cared about me and because we had this agreement to build the business in ways that demonstrated our concern for each other and other people. Being co-owner of the restaurant also helped me become attached to and support many local women's organizations. When the restaurant is closed, we allow community groups to use the space as a center for their meetings, parties, fund-raisers, poetry readings, and so forth. Many women's organizations use our restaurant space for these purposes....

I've also learned so much just listening to the music of Sweet Honey in the Rock or from Linda Tillery of the Cultural Heritage Singers, about the lives and struggles of Black women. I've also studied the writings of a number of feminists like Audre Lorde—who I think is one of the smartest, coolest folks who ever picked up a pen—bell hooks, Angela Davis, Sister Lute, Pearl Cleage, and lots of women writers whose perspectives I take seriously....I also have women friends from childhood to the present who consider me their best male friend. They trust me and count on me....I get a little choked up when I talk about these friends because they care about me and I care so much about them.

Donny's experience shows how friendships between feminist men and feminist women can help each person develop creative, sensitive practices, as well as new expressions to convey the profound intimacy that characterizes these unions. He used the word "femtor" later in the interview to describe one of his Black feminist mentors, and the word "sistren" referring to his network of women friends. These cross-sex feminist friendships can be transformative because of the knowledge, compassion, and emotion they generate.

Donny was not the only participant who became "choked up" when talking about his feminist women friends; Paul asked the interviewer to stop recording as he described how his participation in civic organizations with feminist women affected him. It helped him forge platonic friendships and hands-on experiences that were professionally transformative and personally self-actualizing. Feminist friendships in these settings expanded his understanding of leadership and had a tremendous impact on him as a political organizer and entrepreneur.

I'm a member of the League of Women Voters and my involvement with women in this organization and the labor movement exposed me to feminist thinking....I'm also interested in writings by Black feminists such as science fiction writer Octavia Butler, Angela Davis, and the woman who spells her name in small letters—bell hooks. Their writings have been very influential regarding the beliefs that I subscribe to today and have shaped the models that I use in my politics, business, and personal life. Black feminists have certainly taught me that there are issues that must be articulated by women. The people who are most affected by certain issues not only deserve—but have an inherent right—to be at the table during the decision-making process. I do not differentiate too greatly between the problems of sexism, racism, homophobia, or economic exploitation. At one level it's essentially the same—you are denying an individual the opportunity to self-actualize.

Similarly, Jake's friendships with coworkers and with women in civil rights organizations challenge him, as a human rights advocate, to respect their leadership and practice masculinity in feminist ways.

I work in a politically progressive human rights organization where a number of White feminists work and challenge me on issues of sexism in the organization—despite their racism. So my consciousness is mainly a function of peer pressure from women in social movement organizations and interactions with women in my personal relationships [who were] either overt, self-proclaimed feminists or espoused feminism but didn't use the label.

Some feminist men strive harder to maintain these friendships than others; the depth of their commitment to feminism may correspond with their efforts to sustain such friendships. Sometimes the friendship came first and influenced a person's initial commitment in important ways. Solomon's exposure to feminist women and feminist literature began when he lived and worked at a feminist bookstore.

When a woman who I loved and cohabited with died, her family told me to get out of the house that we had shared together because it was in my lover's name. So I was homeless. Some White feminists allowed me to sleep on the couch in a feminist bookstore. That's how I got introduced to feminism. There was a food co-op next door to the feminist bookstore. I started working in the food co-op and the bookstore. I was able to feed myself and finish my dissertation during that time period. I don't think I would have finished my dissertation if they hadn't given me that space.... While working in the bookstore, I started reading a lot of feminist literature and found words to describe a lot of the experiences that I had undergone as a man in a female body.... That experience allowed me to associate myself with anthropology and women's studies programs when I became a college professor.

Living there also had its difficult moments. Many [women] feel betrayed and threatened by me because I'm too "male-identified" and too "masculine." They want me to identify as female and think I'm just confused. I'm "wrongly identified," in their view, so they experience a loss. However, my biological sister who I am closest to is a lesbian and a feminist. Other feminists who are close to me tend to be lesbians. I have two sets of close friends who are lesbian couples and play a very strong role in my life. They are the only lesbians I know who accept me as a transsexual. All of them are practicing saying "he" when referring to me. I also have many friendships with women who are heterosexual and have feminist orientations. I have a very close and important friendship with a Black heterosexual feminist. Our friendship has always been platonic. She accepts me as a transsexual man and we are both professional colleagues and confidants.

Published autobiographical essays by female to male transsexuals (FTMs) suggest that when enduring cross-gender friendships develop, they can have a profound impact on the continued commitment of these men to feminist expressions of gender.[28] Some feminist women continue to judge FTMs as women passing as men in order to obtain the privileges that men have, as people who get to enjoy the best of both worlds, as gender traitors, or as "spies" who were really men in women's space before their transition.[29] Others, like me, welcome FTMs as credible political comrades who are developing alternative masculinities that individually and institutionally challenge all gender hierarchies.

Finally, a friendship between a man and a sex worker reveals the truly transformative power of feminist knowledge when transmitted from one heart to another, regardless of the context. Cabral was exposed to global feminist perspectives and their relationship to international economics during his service in the armed forces.

Throughout my life there have been strong women caring for me and teaching me. Every step of the way they supported me—even when they didn't necessarily agree with me. They not only created a major part of me, they also created the emotional space for me to be myself. This is why women often speak in my poems.

I joined the armed services and was stationed in Korea. I became friends with Em who was in her early thirties and a prostitute. She was one of the most intelligent women I had ever run across. She spoke Korean, Japanese, Chinese, and English.... She was the sole support for her family and sent money home for the education of her younger brothers and sisters. Like so many other Korean women, Em had made a conscious decision to sacrifice herself so that her brothers and sisters could make it in life. She helped me understand gender politics more quickly and more directly than any understanding I could have gotten by just reading. There is not enough discussion of prostitution as a form of imperialism or as the international exploitation of women. After my discussions with her, I began to realize the extent to which the U.S. armed services and the government in general are responsible for the development of prostitution. A country like Thailand has been turned into a brothel as a result of the Vietnam War.... The majority of Americans have no idea of what the American government has done to other countries around the world....Em opened my eyes to some of these injustices.

When I was in the army, I had sex with prostitutes many times in Korea, and I don't think those women wanted to be intimate with me. Most people would think sex with a prostitute is a consensual thing, they paid their money and that's it. But, for me, it goes back to the question of whether people really want to do something versus whether people are simply submitting to the material conditions before them. Just because you "choose" to do something, doesn't mean you "want" to do something. Once I returned to the United States, I vowed that I would never, ever engage in sexual relations with a woman based on money or based on me being a superior force, after those experiences in Korea.

The influence of feminist women and feminist organizations on me has been more intellectual and ideological than anything because I read a lot. I was an early supporter of Black women writers like Alice Walker and Ntozake Shange. Also, because I've been a publisher, I published a lot of stuff on and about women.

However, my most significant experiences with women tend to be like the relationship I had with Em, rather than the "romantic" variety. You can only learn so much from romance. We tend to look at personal relationships only in terms of individual relationships and depersonalize all other relationships as a way of distancing ourselves from our responsibilities to others. Once we understand that every relationship is a personal relationship, we begin to see our responsibility in all human relationships.

Cross-sex friendship research confirms what these feminist Black men's narratives claim: that men and women friends can care deeply for one another and in many instances "love" one another.[30] This love is not synonymous with romance. Rather, it is a love rooted in mutual respect and egalitarianism. In platonic friendships between feminist men and women, intimacy has less to do with sex and more with shared emotional involvement and openness. It allows each person to experience the other and him or herself at a deeper level that promotes interpersonal growth and self-actualization. My observations were consistent with previous research, which suggests that feminist friends negotiate how their relationship is to be defined and what role romance and sexuality will have within that definition. As they create that definition, they consider the circumstances of their lives, their commitment to others, the incompatible parts of their personalities, and their life goals, as well as their sexual preferences.[31] While some cross-sex friendships do become romantic relationships—and some romantic feminist relationships end up as platonic—close, affectionate ties between women and men need *not* necessarily involve sexual or romantic relationship. Many friendships, particularly Cabral's, challenge prevailing assumptions about what man–woman relationships ought to be like.

Summary

In the process of overcoming sexist behavior, Black men are able to forge friendships with feminist women and reconstruct masculinity in private and public situations that deepen their feminist commitment and practices. As feminist writer David Kahane explains: "'getting it' means no longer being able to see or live your life in the same manner. It is to reinterpret your history and your identity in ways that can be profoundly uncomfortable and also to reinterpret your place in the world in ways that permit and demand new forms of action."[32] These friendships require trust and serve as practicing grounds for emerging feminist masculinities. Feminist friendship gives the men a safe place to be human (and thus vulnerable), constructive criticism from political allies who have an interest in their development, and opportunities for informal and formal mentoring.

The narratives indicate that most of these friendships were formed in university settings, consistent with the findings of cross-sex friendship studies. However, some developed in social–justice–oriented organizations, work settings, or community cooperatives. The next chapter discusses the role of friendships with other men in feminist Black men's rejection of patriarchal expectations and habits.

CHAPTER 7

Men as Friends, Brothers,
and Lovers

Once a man begins to apply feminist principles to his everyday practices, his relationships with other men are also affected. With few
exceptions, the Black men in my study, particularly the heterosexual
men, experienced noticeably more difficulty in establishing close friendships with men than they did with women. Indeed, the majority of the
participants had closer friendships with women. However, gay and
bisexual study participants were more likely than others to have as many
close friendships with men as they did with women, or more. I also
found that each man had to grapple with a broad range of heterosexist
assumptions and practices, including sexuality issues, before he was consistently comfortable having healthy, loving friendships with men—platonic or romantic.

Given these complexities, the participants' interactions with other
men shaped the creation of entirely new thoughts, reinterpretations of
old thoughts, and different, less homophobic and heterosexist practices.
For the most part, change in everyday practices was a slow, contradictory, and uneven process.

Homophobia in African American communities is reflective of the
broader homophobic culture in which we live and is not unique to
African Americans or any specific racial-ethnic group in the United
States. However, Black feminist lesbian and gay scholars researching

134

African American communities have paid particular attention to the fact that heterosexism—the notion that sexual involvement with opposite-sex partners is natural, right, and superior—continues to inform what is considered a healthy Black identity, particularly a healthy Black masculinity.[1] The degree to which individual Black men believe that healthy Black masculinity is heterosexual affects their relationships with other men and feminist Black men are no exception.[2] If, as recent research suggests, being a Black woman, having feminist attitudes, not being heterosexual, and not attending church regularly are all associated with empathy for the plight of gay men among African Americans,[3] straight Black men, including churchgoers, need to work on their attitudes toward their gay brothers. There is an extremely close link among patriarchy, homophobia, and heterosexism; to be feminists, Black men must evolve to the point where they understand that connection.[4] Before Black men's relationships can benefit positively from their adoption of a feminist outlook, their patriarchal, homophobic, and heterosexist attitudes and practices must undergo radical transformation.

Patriarchy, Homophobia, and Heterosexism: Institutionalized Links

Homophobia is an irrational fear or prejudice based on beliefs that sexually diverse people (homosexuals, bisexuals, etc.) are sinful, immoral, sick, or inferior to heterosexuals; heterosexism refers to institutionalized, unjust practices exercised by those in power against sexually diverse groups.[5] Homophobia and heterosexism reinforce rigid notions about what is "manly" or "womanly" and, thereby, patriarchal beliefs about gender. As a result, both homophobia and heterosexism force the repression of anything that seems "feminine" in men and regulate the entire spectrum of what are deemed "appropriate" gender relations.[6] Since male domination is not simply a system of men's power over women but also hierarchies of power among different groups of men, sexualities that diverge from the dominant, heterosexual male norm are also discriminated against.[7] Thus, a key component of maintaining gender inequality and heterosexual privilege is upholding and highlighting differences in appearance and action between men and women and subsequently internalizing those differences within our gender identities.

As we saw in chapter 4, a common pattern in men's stories about how their self-definition of masculinity changed is the occurrence of one or more key events that trigger their attempt to change. These events lead men to reevaluate whether their sexist attitudes and behaviors are congruent with their perceptions of themselves as feminists. A similar process occurs with homophobic and heterosexist attitudes and behaviors: these discriminatory stances become incongruent with how feminist Black men view themselves and how they would like others to view them. When that happens, the old ideas and practices create an uneasiness (or dissonance) and motivate them to change in order to alleviate the discomfort created by the contradiction. Such was the case with Soyinka, when he came face-to-face with his heterosexist assumptions at a public lecture.

I think that meeting African American feminist bell hooks in person was a notable experience for me because it was certainly an unpleasant one. I remember her coming to our campus, and a sister who I was dating at the time asked me if I wanted to go see bell hooks. I didn't know bell hooks from "Adam's house cat." I considered myself a political activist and had a desire to be on the right side of what I understood to be "the woman question." So, I attended the lecture. Well, meeting bell hooks really challenged me. She challenged me publicly. After her public lecture I asked her, "How can we avoid being homophobic yet encourage young Black children not to become homosexual?" She looked at me and said, "I think the first thing that we need to do is make sure we are not in the business of trying to regulate people's sexuality." There was complete silence in the audience.

For a couple of weeks after that I was struggling, really "chaffing" because I was mad at her because of the way she answered my question. I tried to get one of my best friends, who was also struggling with some of these issues, to agree with me. I went to him—as men very often do—looking for some support against this woman's response. Well, he didn't give me any…he looked at me and said, "Maybe she thought you were homophobic." I replied that I wasn't homophobic! Then he said, "Are you sure?" Then I was mad at him for a couple of weeks. Finally, I had to be honest with myself and acknowledge that both of them had really pushed me to grow. Ultimately, it was one of the best experiences in my life.…I saw bell hooks again and talked with her about it and thanked her. She replied, "I respect you for coming back and telling me."

Soyinka's emotional ups and downs on these issues are not unusual. Institutionalized heterosexuality means that our cultural expectations teach us to take for granted that a person's spouse or significant other must be of the opposite sex, and that one spouse should be *the husband* and the other must be *the wife*. We also expect, as Soyinka's question to bell hooks indicated, that young people should not only *be* heterosexual but *they should want to be* heterosexual and *we should want them to be* heterosexual. These routinely unquestioned assumptions, expectations, and practices are what institutionalize heterosexuality and its operation in our daily lives.

The narratives of the men in the study expose institutionalized expectations regarding gender and sexuality that affect individual experiences and practices, particularly with other men. These attitudes and practices are supported—directly and indirectly—by the church and by law, particularly when it comes to defining a legal, and thus recognizing a legitimate, marriage. Each man in the study had to unlearn patriarchal and heterosexist assumptions, and each continues to unlearn them.

Like Soyinka, Edmund had an embarrassing and confrontational experience with one of his college instructors.

I had a teacher in college who helped me understand my homophobia. She taught first-year English in college and asked me what was my major. I told her that it was Mass Media,[and] that I had originally majored in English and drama but there were too many faggots in those areas. She replied, "Oh, so you think you have punk appeal?" I was crushed. She said, "This is college, don't you think homosexual men have a right to go to college just like you do?" I still couldn't believe we were having this conversation, but I nodded yes. She continued and said, "Do you think that these men are going to overpower you and rape you? I want to know exactly what you are afraid of because I think I can help you." I told her that I wasn't afraid of anything. In reality, I was trying to bring the conversation to an end. She said, "Don't bullshit me! If you aren't afraid of anything, then why did you change your major?" She helped me to understand how irrational homophobia was. I didn't fully understand how irrational and misdirected my fears were at the time, but over the years I finally understood how completely incorrect I was.

As Edmund's narrative suggests, achieving long-term, sustained changes in attitudes and behaviors often requires repeated efforts and extended periods of time, even for a single behavior.[8] People who experience identity changes in adulthood report considerable degrees of negative emotion, including irritation, hassles, frustrations, feelings of hopelessness, and even anger before and during the change process; the narratives quoted here are consistent with those findings.[9] In the following sections, feminist Black men describe some of the emotions that accompanied their experiences of change. These experiences affected their attitudes and beliefs about gay men, which affected their interactions with men in general. Their narratives reflect how patriarchy hurts not only men's relationships with women but also men's relationships with other men.

The Power of Institutionalized Attitudes and Practices

Opponents of feminism have historically questioned the "gender credentials" (manhood and womanhood) of feminist supporters. The day after Frederick Douglass gave his passionate speech about women's rights at the Women's Rights Convention in 1848, he was vilified in Syracuse newspapers as an "Aunt Nancy Man," an antebellum term for a "wimp."[10] Today, many people assume that a feminist man is automatically gay and a feminist woman automatically lesbian.[11] In fact, homophobia is a major deterrent for many men, straight and gay, who want to claim feminism publicly, just as it is for closeted gay men.

Therefore, feminist supporters must come to grips with their homophobia—as well as the homophobia of others—if they hope to sustain their feminist commitment and challenge homophobia and heterosexism systemically. Some feminist Black men have grappled with such issues more successfully than others. Soyinka painfully recalled the following experience:

During college I became friends with a brother who I really cared a lot about. I think I loved the brother because I never had a brother and when I got to know him and saw the kind of person he was, I really grew to care about him. After knowing him a couple of years, I said to him one day, "You know, I really love you, man." Unfortunately, he couldn't handle it. He told people on campus that I must be gay. That was a real source of pain for me, and anger, much anger. We never had the opportunity to talk about it, but it was a real learning experience for me. It was unfortunate that he felt the need to respond to my honesty that way. Ultimately, after some time, I came out of it feeling that I was okay and that nothing was wrong with me for being honest and expressing my feeling for him that way.

It is critically important to acknowledge that men are fully capable of experiencing nonsexual intimacy with other men. Friendships between men can include the self-disclosure and vulnerability that characterize the man–woman platonic relationships described in the previous chapter. Some feminist Black men have experienced this level of intimacy with men, or yearn for more male friendships along these lines. However, most of the men admitted how much easier it is to establish emotional intimacy with their women friends in order to avoid homophobic judgments by their male peers.

Other men's homophobic perceptions of him helped Victor understand that different systems of oppression reinforce each other, years before he was exposed to Black feminist viewpoints.

I have experienced heterosexism and homophobia from people who perceived that my sexual orientation was not heterosexual.... Race, class, gender, and sexuality injustices interact in such a way that one has to look at how they work together to exclude various people. I think people who are oppressed by these various systems are looking at different parts of the same elephant. Ultimately, we have to get across the point that your oppression, whatever it may be, is intimately connected to my oppression. So we have nothing to lose—in fact, more to gain—when we fight for social justice on many levels.

"Out" Black lesbian feminists Barbara Smith, Audre Lorde, Cheryl Clarke, and Pat Parker have written some of the most incisive essays, poems, and manifestos about the necessity of understanding the connections among different oppressions; their lived experiences guided their intersectional approaches to injustice.[12] Barbara Smith, a founder of the Combahee River Collective, writes, "I have little difficulty seeing how the systems of oppression interconnect, if for no other reason than that their existence so frequently affects my life."[13] Similarly, Ralph's experiences of racism and heterosexism helped him see the interconnecting factors in the domination of some humans by others and the importance of feminism to men and their struggles for social justice, even though he is heterosexual.

I have experienced two forms of inequality and discrimination that help me empathize with women's oppression. The first one being the obvious, being Black, and realizing that no matter what I do, I'll never be seen as good enough and somebody's always trying to define who I am and where I can go and what I can do.... The second area is in being what I consider a different kind of man. I remember times when I was a boy—as well as times since I've become a man—when people have evaluated me as "less than a man" because I don't do what other men do in terms of various macho behaviors. I don't want to act that way, and I don't feel that I have to act that way. I also speak in tones and inflect my voice in ways that other people characterize in ways suggesting that I'm not as masculine as other men or "masculine enough" and that hurts at times. These unfair characterizations of my manner of being a man have helped me understand how sexism and heterosexism affect women and men. These experiences led me to conduct research on how these interconnected systems also hurt men.

Regardless of whether one identifies as gay, other people's homophobia can oppress a man if he is *perceived* as gay. Alan explains how other men perpetrate harmful heterosexist behavior.

Heterosexism has brought a lot of pain in my life. I still have a lot of issues around my father because he was the classic representation of brutal masculinity that "othered" and denigrated me. His comments about what real men do versus what I did as a boy and my chosen profession as a man contributed to my feelings of inadequacy as a man. This "othered" status (for example, his accusations that I was something "other than a man") has been a source of deep pain for me. During childhood, I was always the one who was picked on and hurt by somebody because of his or her perceptions of me as gay. I was called a punk and other similar terms. Although I view gender as fluid, in my case the person with whom I am partnered is female, so I have been afforded privileges associated with heterosexuality. However, I think sexuality is about a fluidity of movement along a sexual continuum and that belief most aptly describes my sexuality and my current politics.

Homophobic and heterosexist practices rank who is a "legitimate" or "real" man or woman, in order to keep people in their place in oppressive hierarchies. Unquestionably, being a feminist man requires taking a stand that challenges such practices. As each man's definition of masculinity changed from popular notions to radically feminist ones, his friendships with women *and* men changed. Toussaint recalled:

Growing up, I think I ended up with all of these friends who were girls and women because I was a safe boy. I wasn't the kind of boy who was trying to jump in their drawers and everything. So, I became their confidant. We engaged in conversations that had a broad range of content. We could discuss ideas, act silly together, and do a whole range of things together. The scope with my male friends was much more limited, the exception being those men friends who were really close during my boarding school years and current close male friendships that are mainly with gay and bisexual men. My best friendships are ones that have a sense of intimacy and a feeling of safeness—friendships where you can wonder out loud and still feel like your friends are providing a safe space for you to be yourself. I have always felt safer in a context where I could be myself.

Donny, who agrees with Toussaint, also points out that gay men have internalized some of the dominant and destructive notions about masculinity and thus experience difficulty in their attempts to establish meaningful, intimate friendships.

I hunger for more close friendships with men. It's been easier to have close friendships with women. . . . Of course, I value my friendships with women and they are very important to me. However, I've had to work harder for relationships with men. My friendships with men can cross the border into intimacy—and even as a gay man, it's always easier to find a man to have sex with than to find another gay man to think with, be close to and to talk to about the gritty, intimate details of our lives. This form of intimacy has nothing to do with sex, so, whether it's another gay man or a heterosexual male friend, it's taken a lot of work to push past the male conditioning to find closeness. However, when I find it and when we achieve levels of it, it's exciting!

These comments on the transformative power of male friendships emphasize the importance of intimacy and emotional support among men. The men in my study frequently remarked that the different communication styles men and women have learned are a barrier to emotionally supportive friendships with men. Cudjoe describes his experience of this difference.

I like the way that women talk to each other. It's definitely different from the way men, on the average, talk. Women cross lines in their friendships that men don't cross as frequently. The guys that I know rarely have a lot of close male friends like the women who I know—or if they do, they're work buddies as opposed to friends they call and talk about their relationships with, like many of my women friends do.... I appreciate the ways that women talk to each other about how they're feeling. A lot of times when I want to talk about an emotional issue I talk about it with my women friends instead of my men friends—especially if it's over the phone cause if I'm talking to guys over the phone I've only got between three to seven minutes to talk! Our conversation is usually about when we are going to meet, when are they coming to town or what time are we meeting! It's more like the phone is for planning, not sharing feelings. However, there is hope, because I recently had a really good conversation with a male friend. I think he sensed that we were talking in ways that people associate with women, because we were talking about our romantic relationships with the women in our lives, our hopes and dreams about them and it was so different and so nice! I think I know how to talk like this with men because I learned how to talk like this from my women friends.

Victor also provides a telling example.

My conversations with my close men friends are often different in style from my conversations with my women friends. Not everything is a problem to be solved; sometimes, I just want to vent. It's easier to vent with my women friends than with my men friends. For example, I was having financial problems and I was talking to this one male friend about it and a few days later I received a check from him in the mail. It was a lot of money with a note that read, "Don't worry about paying me back, I know you will when you can." The check solved a lot of immediate problems, but that wasn't the problem I was discussing in our conversation! I always knew that I could ask him for the money and I didn't think I was going to lose my house or anything. I was trying to share with him the fear that I was experiencing that my business would fail. At the time, things weren't going well. My expectations were unrealistic and I was panicking and trying to vent with him. He just sent me a check. I appreciated the check, but what I really needed was to vent and hear somebody say that my fears were unfounded and that I needed to give the business time to grow. I didn't need him to fix the problem. I just wanted to talk to him about it.

David compares the depth and quality of his conversations with male and female friends.

My closest male friend and I do not have similar values and similar ideologies with respect to women. I think that a lot of it is because he's not been challenged in the way that I have. I occasionally share intimate details about my relationship with him as well as gender issues in general. I have to work harder in my friendship with him to get what I need than in my friendships with women. It's certainly harder for me to get my male friends to express themselves in terms of their feelings, although I've had some successes because we work hard at it. Many men feel we have to really know the other man pretty well and that the other man wants to do it too and is willing to work at expressing himself that way. It's hard to get past all the other macho stuff and fear to get to that point, but it's possible, and I try hard to do it with my male friends. However, from junior high until I got married, I have always had at least one close female friend. These friendships provided a level of honesty and intimacy that I don't find easily in most of my friendships with men. My closest male friend and I have discussed this, and he describes our friendships with women as ones that don't require a narrow sense of masculinity, as most of our friendships with men do. I tend to explore different dimensions of my personality with female friends that I can't explore when I'm just hanging out with my basketball buddies or my football buddies. The conversation range is pretty narrow with most of my male friends.

Underlying these various fears, heterosexist beliefs, and homophobic practices are issues of trust. To open up emotionally to a man or a woman requires trust. Bruce, Alan, and Victor say their lack of trust in other men affects their ability to form close relationships with them. Bruce honestly admits:

I don't have any close male friends, even though I still live in the city where I grew up. I fear men like an alcoholic would fear a bunch of drinking men. I love a good argument and I can argue my positions very well, but it's difficult to bond with most men because so many of them are where I was twenty years ago—and that is very painful to see. We men have the ability to revert to earlier sexist ways so quickly that being around men who haven't come to grips with their sexist monsters is hard for me. Hell, his monster might jump up and try to get me! I already got to fight my own monster. I don't know if I can beat two of them—his and mine. One monster is enough. So my closest friends are females. Originally, I didn't trust women, so, I really didn't experience platonic friendships with women until the last four or five years. Now, I trust women considerably more and men considerably less.

Alan describes the debilitating effects of distrusting other men.

Men are so self-conscious, and our homophobic, macho belief systems often prevent us from going beyond the small talk and superficial topics. It's difficult to be vulnerable with another man because I often have to worry about whether he will still think of me as a man after I expose myself. I have so many issues about having friendships with Black men such that I come to the relationship with a lot of baggage and with a lot of fear. I'm afraid that I will be hurt, so, rather than be hurt, I remain disconnected and uninvolved. The closest Black male friend I have is always telling my partner, "I don't understand why Alan doesn't call me, I'm always calling him, what's up with him?" My partner just says, "That's between you and Alan." This fear of being hurt is so debilitating. I have some potentially good Black male friendships that I just don't pursue. I don't know how to negotiate these friendships. I can envision the kind of friendship that I would like to have, but it's hard to know where and how to start. My closest Black male friend lives in another city and is our daughter's godfather. He's just the most wonderful, gentle Black man I've ever met, but I always have this sense that he doesn't really care that much about me. Sometimes I feel like he's just calling me to talk to my partner because they are also really close. There's just this persistent feeling that there's something in me that is not worthy to be loved by another Black man. As a result, I undermine my friendships with Black men. I think most of these feelings of inadequacy go back to the early relationship between my father and me—that early absence of love and care. My male friends tell me that they care about me, but I tell them that I don't think they do. So a lot of them say, "Alan, we can't win with you."

Victor describes his ongoing battle to reestablish trust in men after being sexually abused by a man. His narrative suggests that if a man knows another man fairly well and believes that they both want to work at expressing themselves emotionally, one can help the other by taking the initiative.

I still have issues of trust with men. I have two close male friends, but I'm more apt to talk about certain things with women friends, than with male friends. I might not tell my male friends something until I've already worked it out, whereas I talk to my women friends while I'm working it out. Most recently, I've been doing that less and can confide in my close men friends when I'm in the process of working some issue out. One of my close men friends confronted me at one point and said, "What makes you think you're better than I am—I tell you everything that's important to me, but you don't tell me at all what's important to you!" He was actually offended and it was amazing. So, the two of us are actually beginning to transcend my usual limited level of trust with men.

Victor's narrative shows that men are capable of developing emotional intimacy in their friendships and that such interpersonal skills can be learned. Although patriarchy influences various social interactions between men and women and among different groups of men, negative influences can be resisted, and feminist men's friendships with other men can achieve an emotional intimacy akin to that in their friendships with women. As Abdul put it,

Some of my closest male friends are engaged in the struggle for justice, equality, and safety for women in this world. However, I have other men friends who are not yet on the same page. I appreciate these men because we need to struggle with these issues together.... They help me and I help them.... I'm working a lot more on male friendships than I ever have. I mean, until recently, I never had male friends, I mean serious friendships. What I realize is that if I want to have true male relationships in this world, then it's my responsibility to make that happen.

The next group of narratives specifically document how Black men exercise agency in interpersonal relationships with men as they redefine expressions of masculinity along feminist lines.

Creative Agency Despite Institutional Constraints

Ralph, the social scientist, was one of the few heterosexually identified participants who had experienced close friendships with men from various backgrounds and walks of life. Those friendships, particularly with gay and bisexual men, further transformed his view of himself and other men in positive ways. Unlike Toussaint's disappointing experiences at a predominantly White men's college, Ralph flourished at a predominantly Black men's college; there he met Black men who expressed masculinity in diverse, less popular ways. Some were gay, others were not. He credits the openness of some of the Black gay men with helping him feel comfortable with his nontraditional tastes.

I attended an all-male, predominantly Black institution during my undergraduate years and that period of my life was the first time that I began to develop male friendships because I had never been around a

whole lot of Black males. My pre-college schools were predominantly White and there weren't many Blacks and there were always more females than males. Also, because I was much more academically oriented than athletically oriented, that narrowed the numbers of Black males that I came into contact [with] as well. But during college, I was exposed to a large number of Black males who I had something in common with that didn't have to include sports. I think that environment freed me then to initiate relationships that I had not previously been able to initiate. There were a number of men I became really close to and am still close to and what I've subsequently come to understand is that we were all looking for each other. We all felt odd or different in one way or another and we all felt our values really required that we have honest relationships with people.

Ralph's experiences exemplify the homophobia that in African American communities "continues to create real barriers to the prospect of Black men comforting each other."[14] Ralph continues:

There was another male professor in graduate school, my advisor, whom I love. I mean, he is just a real special man, and he's White! He is truly committed to social justice and he believes in leveling the playing fields, transforming the way we approach traditional social sciences, and has challenged himself to learn and to grow from his students... he has always made me feel as though we weren't competing and that whatever I said and whatever I did, did not detract from his sense of his own importance and value as a human being or mine. He was also a man who was struggling with his own sexism, so he was a model to me as I began that process of struggling with my own. And it was really during that time that I began to read the feminist literature and to engage in friendships with feminist women.

Donny, who is gay-identified, also expresses the importance of a range of friendships with men, particularly ones that cross boundaries of race and sexuality.

I gather men together from time to time to have support groups to talk about their lives and what it means to be a man in this society. Most of the groups are with Black men, so we also talk about racism and sexism and the various ways we've been set up by these systems. When I can, I attend and present at workshops at conferences sponsored by anti-sexist men's groups such as Black Men for the Eradication of Sexism in Atlanta and the National Organization of Men Against Sexism.

I have many male friendships. My best friend and I support each other to read and to discuss certain issues. For instance, I remember sitting at his house because his wife had him read Deals with the Devil and Other Reasons to Riot *by Black feminist writer Pearl Cleage. I was reading it and we both found it really harsh writing. I like Pearl Cleage, but something about that book just got to me. So, we decided to drive to the lake and hang out for the weekend in order to talk about all of the shit that came up for us after reading the book.*

From Donny's and Ralph's narratives it is clear that feminist Black men friends can create a support system as they deepen their commitment to feminism. Also, as in friendships with feminist women, these connections between men provide a safe space for practicing alternative expressions of masculinity. In fact, even men not committed to feminism can teach important lessons, depending on the circumstances. They may express values and model behavior that a feminist man needs to learn. For instance, a feminist man may work on his behavior with women and incorrectly believe that feminism has nothing to do with how he treats men. Victor's story illustrates how his feminist vision had to broaden and be applied also to interactions with men.

During college, I still had a lot of pent-up anger about the child abuse and how other boys and men considered me an oddball for so many years. Prior to college, my view of Black men outside of my family was very narrow. I always expected to be attacked emotionally by men. After developing close friendships and a sense of family with brothers in the dormitory, my friends helped me to see that I wasn't handling my anger well in certain situations. For instance, I played sports in college and had a fight when I was playing in a football game. I had trained in the martial arts, so the fight was brutal and wasn't your typical football fight. I kicked the guy's legs out from under him and did things that he didn't expect. Then, I had him in a chokehold in such a way that no one could get me off of him. I just kind of snapped. So the brothers who were my friends sat me down and said, "Yo, man, that wasn't cool, you could have killed that guy—even though the people in the stands were cheering and everything—that wasn't cool." There was talk of disciplinary action. One of my closest male friends was the head of the student disciplinary committee. He basically told me that there would be a decision of no liability, but he also told me that he didn't think that what I did was cool. So the brothers publicly supported me, but they told me in private that it wasn't cool and that I needed to deal with things differently. I had never had that kind of experience with brothers my age. Usually, the people who watched out for me were older or were family. It had a profound effect on me. They actually cared about me.

Victor's experience demonstrates that when men are teachable, and thus open to being different kinds of men, a variety of other men can point them in that direction. However, I found that the gay, bisexual, and transgendered men in my study seemed more adept at transforming their friendships with men than the straight men, regardless of the sexuality of their male friends. Malcolm, who is gay-identified, describes his close friendships, most of which are with heterosexual men.

I haven't had any significant gay romantic relationships, so, in one sense, my sexuality is not necessarily a major part of who I am. However, if people ask me if I'm gay, I tell them that I am. In my friendships with men, I insist on exercising my ability to communicate without stereotypical masculine barriers. My male friends call me to talk about things they don't feel they can talk about to anyone else. Most of my male friends are heterosexual. I encourage them to think and talk about stuff they haven't thought about before and talk openly with them about my various issues.... Despite my openness, I'm probably more reserved with my heterosexual male friends than my gay male friends because of the homophobic myth that "if you are gay, you are attracted to ANY man." So, I'm probably overly cautious in my attempt not to give that impression. Although I have more women than men friends, there's not much of a difference between my friendships with women and my friendships with men.

Even the straight men in the study, like Ralph, admitted that they learned to develop their own emotional expressiveness and grow accustomed to nonsexual intimacy through their friendships with gay men. Alan also specifically recalled:

Gay and lesbian people have had an extraordinary influence in my life. They helped me understand the totality of the human experience. During college, I got to know some really good Black men who were gay. They were my closest friends. It was the first time in my life that I had any Black male friends. They represented a different kind of manhood that was not brutal, macho, or threatening to women. I could identify with this gentle kind of manhood. When I was being ostracized by men who felt that my expressions of masculinity were too feminine, too gentle, too soft, Black gay men befriended me and gave me the courage to live and the space to be myself. I agree with feminists who believe that feminism should be antisexist as well as antiracist and antihomophobic. I don't know where those men are today—I had four very close Black gay friends during college—but I honor them wherever they are.

Some gender scholars who specialize in men's friendships have found that gay men "do friendships differently" than do most straight men; they tend to be more expressive of their emotions, more willing to be vulnerable and protective of each other, and communicate personal and emotional intimacy, including love and trust as well as anger and hurt.[15] They also engage in behaviors similar to those in heterosexual men's friendships, including watching and talking about sports, going to bars, pursuing hobbies and leisure activities, and competing intellectually and sexually.[16] Gay men's friendships with each other and heterosexual men may even reproduce dominant notions of patriarchal masculinity; researchers have noted how these friendships uphold mainstream notions of gender, sexuality, and power, given certain stereotypes of women, specific types of gay men, and gender roles in which some gay men continue to believe.[17] However, various types of men—heterosexual feminist Black men, heterosexual men who don't identify as feminist but are also not extremely masculine or macho by mainstream standards, and men who have questions about their sexual identity—report feeling comfortable in what scholars refer to as cross-orientation friendships. Heterosexual men who have developed deep friendships with gay men often say they learn a lot about themselves in these friendships, particularly how to be "straight but not narrow." That is another way of saying they do not worry if people perceive them as gay (the "guilty by association" homophobic judgments of others). They also learn not to be ashamed of being heterosexual when women confide in them (as if they weren't "real men") about "what bastards men are."[18]

Solomon, who has worked at his friendships with men of various backgrounds, admits he has had some successes and some setbacks as a heterosexual transgendered man, depending on the degree to which the other man is open to a deeper level of relating.

My closest male friend is a Black man who's heterosexual, who I also don't see that often. However, he is someone from my hometown who I've developed a close friendship with for over three decades. When you develop a relationship with somebody over decades, you sometimes take different paths. We both are involved in antiracist struggles; however, we differ in the sense that he hasn't read the feminist literature or thought deeply about feminist issues. He probably doesn't understand the extent to which feminism poses no threat to Black community development. However, he knows and accepts that I'm transsexual and feminist. In fact, when I told him about my transsexualism, he gave me a book about this White male transsexual who was active in the civil rights movement. He told me that I wasn't the first transsexual to be active in the liberation struggle. His positive response to my telling him that I am transsexual is why I love him and am still friends with him. I don't know any other Black man from my hometown who would have responded that way.

Although most of my female friendships are with Black women, most of my male friendships are with White men. This is largely because many Black men don't want to be friends with a transsexual. They don't wish to understand transsexualism, and it probably threatens their sense of themselves as men to be close to me.... So it's a big pain in my life. My male friends also work on their sexism, whether they claim feminism or not, because I'm not going to grow if I'm hanging out with men who are sexist.

Solomon's narrative reminds us that people who write off Black transgendered men as "not really men" are unwilling to expand their definitions of gender and sexuality, even when reevaluating those definitions would serve the interest of social justice; such are the effects of institutionalized heterosexuality. Gender scholars are beginning to question common beliefs about transgendered people; calling them "mistakes of nature" reveals more about the "mistakes of society" in not being open to different variations and expressions of gender and sexuality. Thus, just as homophobia (as opposed to homosexuality) is currently being researched as problematic, "transphobia" (as opposed to transsexuality or gender variance) is currently being researched as problematic.[19] Solomon's friendships with other men, particularly Black men, will improve to the extent that those men redefine masculinity, emphasize compassion and empathy in their relationships with each other, and work to dismantle institutionalized patriarchal and heterosexist values and practices.

Rex, the only feminist man in the study who had very few friendships with women but many with men, summarizes the attitudes and beliefs that lie at the heart of men's emotional distance from each other.

My closest male friend holds most of the views that I have, not all. First thing, he agrees with the fact that we are in a male-dominated society and that women aren't looked at as being on par with men. He's also able to do some retrospective work regarding how most Caribbean men treated women negatively when we were growing up. He's been my best friend since I was 14 and is still my best friend today. He is heterosexual and married. We have discussed the period of his life when he was abusive to women, and I have challenged him on that issue. He knows that I am gay, and I share intimate details with him about my intimate relationships. He still lives in the Caribbean, and I'm here in the United States. When we talk on the phone our conversations are mainly about the intimate details of each other's lives.

I don't have as many female friendships and that's one of the interesting ironies given the influence of women in my life and my chosen profession as a social worker. My family of choice is mainly Black gay men and is tied to a need to affirm myself as a Black gay man.... One of the messages that men get growing up is that the worst thing in the world is to be gay.... You're called a "fag" or a "sissy"—it's a way of putting down women and other men who remind men of women. So, to come to grips with being gay means one also comes to grips with one's attitudes toward women, at least that is what happened in my case. And, you know, what's so awful about being like a woman—what's so awful about that anyway?

Empathy, Not Apathy

Although social scientists are still in the early stages of understanding, empirically, what constitutes healthy attitudes among African Americans toward people claiming variations of gender and sexuality, I have found that empathy is a major component. Let us recall that empathy can be defined as "putting yourself in the place of others, orienting to objects in their world as they would, not only as you would." As the African proverb puts it, "I am because we are"—our fate is linked regardless of race, gender, sexuality, and class.

In addition to the students at his historically Black men's college, Ralph met supportive African American male faculty members who modeled diverse expressions of masculinity. He empathized with them and they with him.

There were also several faculty who had a profound impact on me personally and academically. Some professors were nontraditional because people at the college knew that their sexualities were not necessarily heterosexual—even though some of them were married. I'm a little hesitant to discuss this topic because I truly would not want to besmirch any of their reputations or images, but some of them were attracted to men and others were attracted to men and women.... One professor specialized in religion, so that had a positive impact on me because it was another incongruity when compared to what I had been taught. He as well as other professors exemplified different ways of being a Black man and how diverse Black men could be.

Ralph calls "incongruous" the behavior of those the Centers for Disease Control and the National Institutes of Health have euphemistically termed "men who have sex with men"; the more popular term—for Black men who engage in same-sex practices but do not claim a gay identity—is "being on the down low" or "D.L."[20] This new, stigmatized identity draws particular attention to the "risky" sexual behaviors in which these men participate, rather than to the culturally sanctioned homophobia that keeps gay identity "down low." That focus precludes the affirmation of any nonheterosexual identity and variation of sexual expression in African American communities.[21] Because they often promote homophobia and heterosexism, various Black religious institutions also reinforce the link between patriarchal structures and homophobia, implicitly fostering so-called down-low practices. Black Christian churches, along with the Nation of Islam, and other Black nationalist politicoreligious sects (e.g., the Black Hebrew Israelites and the former Universal Negro Improvement Association) have historically institutionalized homophobia within Black communities.[22]

Alan speaks as a Black feminist, a minister within the Church of God in Christ, and as partner in a committed, monogamous marriage, even though he perceives his sexual identity as fluid/bisexual.

I sit opposed to the view of the Church of God in Christ that gays and lesbians are unholy. At the center of my view of human liberation is a spirituality that stresses inclusiveness. The level of ignorance about the politics of sexuality is so entrenched to such a degree that I think the homophobia in the Church of God in Christ exists so deeply because there are so many gay men in the church! People frequently make comments like, "Look, the choir is full of gay men, the organist, the pianist, and some of the ministers are gay, Lord, what's the world coming to?" The notion of gay men in the church is very much like in the military—if you don't tell anybody, then there's no problem, just keep it to yourself. I know so many people who are in the closet, and that closeted existence leads them to engage in some really self-destructive behavior… because the person is literally living in the dark.

Alan understands it is "the closet" that is problematic, rather than the sexuality itself. Black feminist lesbian and gay scholars have found that culturally sanctioned homophobia, not same-sex sexuality per se, puts Black gay, lesbian, and transgendered people at risk for substance abuse, suicide, and other health-related problems.[23] However, even the "closet" can serve as a protective shield and offer opportunities for creative agency to Black lesbians, gays, and transgendered individuals. They can take advantage of its privacy to form networks and coalitions of like-minded people while keeping individual discrimination at bay and carving out autonomous spaces for themselves that are inclusive.[24] This phenomenon is not new. Histories and memoirs by lesbians and gay men recall how earlier generations created supportive community "in the life."[25]

In contrast, Abdul, a heterosexual-identified man, has never been pressured to remain closeted about his sexual identity. Like the other feminist Black men in the study, he calls for acceptance, beyond mere tolerance, of alternative sexual identities.

I feel that gays, lesbians, and bisexuals should not have to be in the closet. But I also know that it needs to be safe for them to come out. I can't speak for them and the experiences that they have. So, I understand

*that when and where they choose to come out is their choice. My role is to
respect that choice when and wherever they decide to exercise it.*

In particular, the Black feminist gay, bisexual, and transgendered
men in my study demonstrated a political sense of agency often ignored
by scholars, insofar as they were able to strategically "come out" in
varying degrees and remain closeted in certain contexts, according to
what was safe and/or advantageous at a given time. Their creative sense
of agency demonstrates, again, how institutional constraints (homophobia, racism) that oppress African Americans may concurrently create
opportunities for new social interactions and the development of alternative social institutions (e.g., the National Black Lesbian and Gay
Leadership Forum and the Unity Fellowship Church).[26]

Bruce's humanistic vision reflects a broad definition of social justice
characteristic of Black feminist thought as he challenges other heterosexual men to justify their lifestyle and sexual practices.

*A gay man is another human being who has his preferences, just like
I have my preferences. Who really has the right to say that what I like to
do in the bedroom has some sort of lofty moral advantage over what he
likes to do? Who am I to say that my life as a heterosexual man is inherently better than his life as a gay man? Every time I learn to get past my
bigotries and prejudices I make another step toward someone else's
humanity—and my humanity as well. Growth and political awareness
keep me going in life. I can look back and say, "Yeah, I used to have the
most stupid ideas about people, but I have grown and have prevented
transferring such ridiculous ideas to my children."*

Victor (the married lawyer turned entrepreneur who perceives his
sexuality as fluid) applied his Black feminist perspective to law courses
that grappled with race and gender (a field currently referred to as
Critical Race and Gender Studies).

*I think we need to develop a politic of Blackness that says anything
that interferes with the collective happiness and love across the diversity
of Black people has got to go. Therefore, heterosexism has got to go,
woman-hating has got to go, and a whole bunch of prejudices have got to
go. Race, class, and gender injustices connect in such a way that you have
to look at how they work together to exclude various people.*

The "politic of Blackness" to which Victor refers is at the heart of
the most vitriolic expressions of homophobia among certain Black
nationalist intellectuals and self-proclaimed "revolutionaries," who associate "gayness" with "Whiteness" and a less authentic Black identity.[27]
Furthermore, the level of homophobia among extreme Black national-
ists, and African Americans in general, is predictably higher among
Black men than among Black women, regardless of class.[28] These find-

ings support the complaint of Black lesbian feminist activist Cheryl Clarke, who observed more than a quarter-century ago that certain middle-class Black nationalist intellectuals played a key role in institutionalizing homophobia within Black *political* communities:

> It is these black macho intellectuals and politicos, these heirs of Malcolm X, who have never expanded Malcolm's revolutionary ideals beyond the day of his death, who consciously or unwittingly have absorbed the homophobia of their patriarchal slavemasters...rest assured, we can find his homophobic counterpart in black women, who are, for the most part, afraid of risking the displeasure of their homophobic brothers were they to address, seriously, and in a principled way, homosexuality. Black bourgeois female intellectuals practice homophobia by omission more often than rabid homophobia.[29] Feminist lesbians in the Combahee River Collective, represented one of the first Black organizations to place a defense of same-sex sexuality explicitly on its political agenda; they boldly issued a challenge in 1974 to White mainstream feminism, Black Nationalism, and the predominantly White gay liberation movement.[30]

On the personal level, most of the men in my study currently respond to issues involving other men and sexuality in new ways based on reinterpretations of their previous homophobic behavior. The insights they express are often the result of interactions with political allies of all sexual orientations who confronted them about their heterosexism. Many men in the study expressed righteous indignation regarding the assumptions heterosexual men make. Alan's narrative sums it up:

I think we need to understand that Black liberation, like any true form of liberation, cannot be piecemeal. We can't take any high moral ground by saying, "I first must be liberated as a Black man, then I'll bring you Black women along, then you children, then, maybe the gay and lesbian people." Also, the "don't ask, don't tell policy" is very prevalent outside of the military. This policy and the attitude associated with it remind me of comments that heterosexuals frequently make such as, "I'm fine with gay folk as long as they don't try to come after me." Now the heterosexual male who is usually saying this is usually unattractive as hell, has nothing to offer anybody, but assumes that every gay male would be chasing after him. I'm like, what dog would want to come after you? Please! Heterosexuals assume that gay and lesbian people are ready to sleep with anybody who is willing. Ha! I don't think so.

When a straight man is comfortable with his own sexuality and desires to do no harm, dealing with propositions from gay men is no longer a big deal. Soyinka, for example, has developed a peaceful, accepting perspective.

If a gay man finds me attractive and wants to be with me but doesn't know that I'm heterosexual and that I don't want to be with him, I should respond just like I would if I were responding to a sister. I should say, "You got good taste but I don't want to go there with you." It's really the same kind of thing. There's nothing vile or unnatural or particularly creepy about this man wanting to have a very deeply personal, intimate sexual relationship with me. If I don't want to do that, I simply say no. I didn't understand that during an obviously unenlightened period of my life. I know that I'm not completely homophobic-free. But I understand enough to know that we have to go beyond mere tolerance. It's no longer just a question of saying, "as long as gay people don't put it in my face, what they do is their thang and I'll do my thang." I have a number of gay and lesbian friends who are very graciously helping me to grow out of my homophobia. I'm reaching for that point in my life where I will, without reservation, be able to say that we need all of us on this planet to be just the way we are in terms of our sexuality.

The importance of that feminist attitude must not be underestimated. Solomon adds:

If I'm trying to liberate myself only on the basis of my experience, what's that liberation going to look like? My liberation might end up being your bondage.

Summary

Sexism, homophobia, and heterosexism are linked, and feminist Black men must evolve to the point where they understand how they connect. The homophobic and heterosexist beliefs that most men learn during socialization lead them to deny the real importance of their friendships with men and to shun open expression of tender emotions and affection among one another. To be masculine in today's U.S. culture requires distancing oneself from any behavior that may indicate homosexuality, including emotionally close friendships with other men.

Emotionally intimate friendships among men raise questions about the power structures that maintain patriarchal, racial, and gender hierarchies. Some feminist Black men have experienced this level of intimacy with men; most still yearn for more male friendships along these lines, but find them difficult to establish. However, just as many women offer feminist male friends a safe place to be vulnerable and to practice alternative masculinities, some gay, bisexual, and transgendered men (most readily encountered in academic environments) offer feminist men that space. My interpretation of their narratives is that the more comfortable a man is with his own sexuality and with the diverse sexualities of others, the more his life includes close friendships with other men. Next, I explore how the black feminist men in my study attempt to transform parenting and inter- pretations of a healthy family.

CHAPTER 8

Sweet Daddy

Nurturing Interactions with Children

Traditional models of fatherhood reinforce patriarchal definitions of masculinity: they focus on sociobiology and rigidly defined gender roles, marriage as the ideal union between a man and a woman, and men's economic responsibility for children.[1] Feminist parenting models challenge the belief that men and women must adhere to distinct gender roles: they show that a wide variety of family configurations can support positive outcomes for children, and that fathers' involvement fosters child development as well as promotes gender equity.[2] Feminist fathering allows men to recast masculinity in flexible ways, thus strengthening their ability to nurture their children *without* reasserting male authority.

Although no single way of being a father will work for all men, African American men have come to represent the most negative ones.[3] Historical, economic, and sociocultural factors complicate the efforts of African American fathers who are trying to engage actively and responsibly in their children's lives.[4] However, those who defy the odds are largely missing from contemporary discourse and literature on fatherhood. Scant information is available on responsible African American fathers who radically redefine fatherhood without adopting patriarchal models of the family.

This chapter critiques patriarchal assumptions and practices within U.S. society that shape men's definitions of fatherhood and masculinity, and highlights their implications for African American fathers. Five interrelated themes emerged from the Black feminist men's narratives in my study: (1) nurturance and emotional intimacy with children; (2) politically conscious parenting; (3) nonviolent discipline; (4) supportive social arrangements; and (5) open attitudes about who can raise a child. Each man's commitment to feminist principles implied that his parenting practices went beyond wanting the best for his child—they included, as well, what was good for women and for African American communities, broad societal change, and the psychosocial development of African American men. My findings, based on the personal experiences of Black feminist fathers who connect with their children despite societal barriers, offer practical insights and recommendations for best practices that any man can use.

Patriarchy's Impact on Masculinity and Fathering

A patriarchal society is organized in ways that emphasize the supremacy and power of fathers.[5] Within such societies, concepts of masculinity and femininity—what it means to be a man and a father, a woman and a mother—are inextricably intertwined, rigidly defined, and considered biologically determined and "natural." Any redefinition of fatherhood automatically redefines notions of masculinity and related gender ideologies. Also, because of the varying ways the intersectional "matrix of domination" affects individuals, fatherhood has different implications for different groups of men as well as different groups of women.

Polarized ideas about gender and roles often limit men and the range of fathering behaviors available to them by constraining the development of emotional and other psychological skills strongly connected to the ability to nurture a child.[6] Traditional, patriarchal fathering models view nurturing children as feminine behavior that mothers do best; fathers are expected to help mothers with nurturing occasionally, but they are not judged incompetent as long as they earn a good living.[7] However, studies on single fathers (particularly men whose wives died or deserted the family) suggest that fathers who cannot depend on wives for childcare can and do develop parenting behaviors, particularly nurturing skills, similar to those of women.[8] Thus, any redefinition of fatherhood also reshapes what can be considered appropriate expressions of "manly" behavior and either accepts or challenges the heterosexist notions that underlie current definitions.

Finally, acceptance of violence as a means of dominating others is reinforced in patriarchal societies by symbols of manliness, ranging from the brave soldier in combat to the staunch disciplinarian. Worse, "manliness" (particularly being a husband or father) is associated with dominance over women and children. Men's use of violence against women and children, including at home, is a common way of exerting male authority. However, a father's abuse of his intimate partner negatively affects the father–child relationship and the child's development.[9] Also, violent discipline of children (e.g., spanking, slapping, and hitting) contributes to physical aggressiveness and other antisocial behaviors among children.[10] Yet corporal punishment is viewed by many parents as consistent with, and even necessary to, fathering within U.S. society.[11] For those reasons, any redefinition of fatherhood must address the degree to which "manliness" and violence are intertwined, and either justified or shunned in the domestic context.

Patriarchy and African American Fathers

Today in U.S. society, one of the most critical ways of proving one's masculinity (and also one's heterosexuality) is by being a father, and a good father is first and foremost an economic provider for his family.[12] Yet, in every decade since slavery, African American men have experienced higher rates of unemployment, lower wages, and lower levels of education than have their White counterparts.[13] The most consistent finding of research on African American fathers is their struggle or inability to fulfill the economic provider role.[14] Underlying these findings is the complex reality that patriarchy within the United States operates in the midst of racism and socioeconomic class disparities.[15] Redefinitions of responsible African American fatherhood must consider individual factors (e.g., gender attitudes and parenting practices) as well as institutional or structural factors (e.g., employment and educational opportunities) that shape the sociocultural context.[16]

Scholars frequently attribute African American fathers' current unemployment rates and related statistics to structural changes in capitalism and to persistent racism.[17] However, they routinely ignore how sexism and global patriarchy stigmatize Black fathers and negatively affect African American families. Patriarchy deeply affects the degree to which African American men's fathering behaviors are validated; it limits what is considered "appropriate" and valued parenting for African American men, within various social institutions such as the judicial system,[18] the academy,[19] the church,[20] and the welfare system.[21] As a result, Black fathers are often described by policy makers and popular media according to what they lack, rather than what they possess.

Black feminist legal scholar Dorothy Roberts notes that while critics of "the absent Black father" focus on marriage statistics, "little attention is paid to the actual involvement of Black fathers in the lives of their children, male mentoring by grandfathers, uncles, church elders, women who share mothering responsibilities, and other distinct styles" of Black parenting.[22] I agree with Roberts's observation that we cannot "judge Black fathers until we address the institutional forces that keep marriage a patriarchal system, devalue the work of child rearing, and deprive families of the social resources necessary to raise healthy children."[23]

Uncritical acceptance of patriarchal, heterosexist, and economically driven fathering models fosters a lack of appreciation for the "best practices" of African American fathering and suppresses motivation to explore healthy, radical alternatives.[24] Nancy Dowd, one of the few White feminist scholars who acknowledges what African American fathers can teach U.S. society in general, stresses the importance of extended family for positive childrearing outcomes and the social, nurturing aspects of fatherhood: "patriarchal ideology and politics ignore or judge as 'second-rate' Black fathers' flexibility regarding family roles, commitment to multi-generational kinship bonds for support, and use of other cultural resources such as racial consciousness and spiritual beliefs in fathering."[25] Emerging studies on families who adopt feminist parenting models challenge preconceived notions about fatherhood and masculinity and suggest new ways of fathering that benefit children, parents, and society at large. All point to the need to address race and gender inequities that affect father involvement in childrearing, redefine masculinity and fatherhood, and implement changes in the workplace that value and support both mothers and fathers.

Feminist Models of Fatherhood and Father Involvement

A combination of individual and institutional factors help men reconstruct fatherhood in ways that counter patriarchal beliefs and practices. Correlational studies using self-report measures indicate that androgynous gender-role orientation and profeminist attitudes among men are positively related to father involvement, particularly a father's ability to nurture his children emotionally;[26] however, findings in this area have been inconsistent.[27] Remarkably consistent are studies based on in-depth interviews with families characterized as "fair," "feminist," "postgender," or "egalitarian"; that research reports a positive association between men's egalitarian attitudes and their involvement with their children.[28] Such studies confirm that father involvement can include nurturing, and that certain feminist attitudes are related to men's nurturing behaviors. Feminist concepts of fatherhood remove the stigma of calling men "too soft," "feminine," and "henpecked" when they care for the physical, emotional, intellectual, and spiritual development of a child.

In addition, narrative studies on feminist families suggest that father involvement is related to partnerships with women who bring similar or stronger egalitarian attitudes to the marriage, as well as higher education, income, and status.[29] Specifically, men who engaged in feminist fathering (defined as equal parenting partnerships with their spouses) had at least one of the following facilitating social arrangements: (a) the mother had equal or better opportunities for work success compared to the father, thereby providing economic support; (b) the mother emotionally supported and actively encouraged the father to become equally involved, rather than allowing him to rely on her as the primary caretaker; and (c) the father's job allowed sufficient flexibility and autonomy to allow time and space for equal parenting.[30] Thus, a mix of individual and institutional factors—higher education of both partners and an ability to earn a good living—facilitate father involvement and contribute to personal growth (e.g., emotional development) for the men and gender equity for the women. Some studies based on interviews with children reared in feminist households suggest that they tend to adopt the egalitarian views of their parents.[31]

Violence has not been explicitly investigated in research on feminist-oriented families, perhaps because feminist egalitarian philosophies are antithetical to the ideas of violence and dominance. However, parents who espouse egalitarian values seem to use corporal punishment less than parents who adhere to "traditional" values; egalitarian parents are more likely to engage in lengthy, nonthreatening discussions that promote common understandings and autonomy in their children's development.[32] In my research I specifically inquired about the use of corporal punishment among Black feminist fathers, given its high prevalence among Americans generally and African Americans disproportionately.[33]

In a review of the literature, one of the few studies including both dual- and single-parent feminist families characterized contemporary feminist parenting styles as (a) challenging the notion of hierarchy itself, particularly male privilege, racism, heterosexism, unnecessary adult authority, and the heterosexual, two-parent family as the ideal family; (b) emphasizing mutual respect through "inclusive," "democratic," parent–child communication; (c) stressing the sharing of household responsibilities in ways that foster empowerment of all family members; and (d) viewing nurturing of children as the responsibility of caregivers regardless of sex.[34]

A man was considered a father in my study if he referred to himself as a "father," "parent," or "primary caretaker" in his relationship to a child or children, regardless of the biological relationship. Of the four-teen who were fathers, nine were married (two were no longer living with their adult children); two were in committed partnerships but not living with the mother, their current partner, or their children; one was in a committed relationship and living with a romantic partner who was not the mother of any of his children; and two were single parents living periodically with their children. Nine were heterosexual, two gay, and three described their sexuality as fluid or bisexual. Most partici-pants had one child, although the average man had two and one man had ten.

Nurturing Emotional Intimacy with Children

All participants were gainfully employed and financially supported their children. Whatever their responses regarding the value and necessity of their economic support, their narratives overwhelming emphasized fathering as a personal and relational experience. Specifically, the narra-tives confirmed that when nurture is placed at the center of fatherhood, multiple levels of care—physical, emotional, intellectual, spiritual—are emphasized, rather than a father's biological or economic status.[35] Victor, the former law professor and entrepreneur, provides examples.

My wife, Violet, and I have a two-year old.... I do potty training, I change diapers, I cook, I take her to school, I read books to her, I hug her when she falls down, I put Band-Aids on her, I help her learn her alpha-bets.... I comfort her when she's crying, take her temperature, and make sure she has her medicine.

The feminist fathers' narratives counter the myth that only women can be nurturers. The depth of their feminist commitment can be mea-sured by their efforts to engage in nurturing acts as *routine* childcare, not just "helping out." Participants consistently said they reflect seriously on their parenting. Eddie, the 36-year-old urban planner, shares:

Both of my children are adopted.... I spend a lot of time, energy, sweat, and tears thinking about how I can be a good parent...[and] about the influence I am having on my son and daughter about what a man is like. I want to expose them to revolutionary and equitable models of relating to others. I remember having a long discussion with my wife about whether I should let our children see me cry, and if I did, how to explain to them, without frightening them—that men get upset and that's healthy and doesn't mean that they are not strong.

Nurturing fathers like Eddie are challenging heterosexist definitions of masculinity by expanding "what it means to be a man" to include for-merly "woman-identified" traits and behaviors (e.g., crying, comforting children, and admitting vulnerability). In addition, Black feminist fathers challenge the idea that fathering has to be different, separate and unique from mothering, thus resisting the hegemonic tendency to define manhood in opposition to womanhood and homosexuality. The feminist vision of "degendered parenthood" and increasing empirical evidence suggest that men and women are equally capable of performing and sharing most childcare activities.[36]

Sometimes a divorce or separation of partners facilitates new awareness among men of their nurturing capabilities. Earlier studies have noted that men learned to nurture their children quickly and competently when they were forced to raise them alone.[37] Thus, even a man who does not live with his children full-time can be an actively engaged, nurturing father. Paul, the tax accountant, describes the dedication of some divorced feminist fathers.

When my [now-adult] son was a child, I changed his diapers, prepared formulas for him, and did whatever was necessary. I was with my son when he first used the bottle. He was initially breastfed. His mother and I had prepared for this event, but she was at the beauty salon when he woke up. He was hungry, so I gave him his first bottle. His mother and I shared childcare responsibilities as well as household responsibilities. It was years before most people who were close to me were aware that his mother and I were divorced because I bought a house across the street so that I could carry out my responsibilities to the fullest.

Jake, the human rights program director, describes how he remained emotionally involved with his children after a divorce.

To me, taking care of my kids when they were younger meant more than sending a check and visiting on weekends. I cooked for them and went to their schools. Even when I was in a new relationship with a woman, I never thought, "Now, that I got me a woman, the mother can take care of them and I'll skip my weekend."

Paul and Jake, like many feminist men and women, recognized that economic support is critically important to children and is owed to them, whether the support is private or public; however, nurturing support is a relationship that cannot be bought. Sometimes even complex parenting situations can be resolved when a man accepts his role as nurturer, not simply as financial provider. Abdul, the 50-year-old counselor, describes his family ties after his failed experiment with polygamy during the 1960s.

I am responsible for ten children financially and have been actively involved in their lives. I basically have two sets of children: one set outside of Georgia and the other set here with me in Georgia. I have the children in Georgia every other weekend and on Thursdays. Thursday is my day with the children from pick-up to drop-off that evening. But every day I see them because I usually pick them up from school. I'm involved with their extracurricular activities by going to performances and taking them to practices. Interestingly enough, I do more of that now than when I was in the home with them. I just need to say that because I'm sure something shifted in me that brought that about.

Indeed, some divorced feminist fathers are able to work with the mothers of their children and to parent in ways that are emotionally involved.

In general, these Black feminist fathers' engagement in nurturing aspects of parenting challenged heterosexist notions of "manliness" and the narrowly defined "economic provider role," promoted gender equity, and questioned or limited the use of corporal punishment. Their childrearing practices are related to their broad, radical ideological beliefs and efforts to parent in politically conscious ways.

Politically Conscious Parenting

Although much has been written about the politically conscious ways in which African Americans try to counter the effects of racism on their children,[38] very little is known about how they attempt to counter the effects of sexism and heterosexism on their children. Black feminist fathers' narratives provide sorely needed insights. All participants in the present study actively raised their kids to oppose racist, sexist, and heterosexist beliefs and practices.

In particular, and consistent with research on the childrearing styles of egalitarian parents,[39] the parenting styles of Black feminist fathers were characterized by ongoing discussions as opposed to threatening lectures; they required their children to be accountable to others by understanding the consequences of their attitudes and actions on others. Rather than yelling at their children, resorting to hostility, or putting them down for expressing attitudes that counter feminist values, these fathers are likely to engage in dialogues that affirm and foster their children's ability to develop critical thinking skills and self-discipline. The high-quality nurturing relationships these fathers have already established with their children create a supportive context for "teachable" moments. As their children mature, Black feminist fathers demonstrate respect for kids' honest questions and refrain from using their parental authority to coerce or shame them into "politically correct" compliance.

For example, participants frequently commented about the need to challenge their sons regarding homophobic and heterosexist attitudes. Abdul, the father of ten, recalls:

I talked to one of my sons recently about his teacher, who he believes to be gay. My son said, "He's a gay teacher, Dad," like by definition that was a problem. . . . I asked, "What does that mean to you, how is that affecting you, how is the teaching and what you're learning in that class different?" I worked hard to get him to appreciate his teacher as a person, regardless of his sexuality.

Alan, the 44-year-old Pentecostal minister and college professor, described with some anguish the early signs of homophobic, rigid beliefs about "manliness" that he noticed in his 12-year-old son.

My partner and I have people of various sexualities in our home. So our son has been exposed to its fluidity. . . . When he was 10 years old, he had some male friends over and I called him from another room saying, "Sweetheart, come here, I need you to do something." He yelled, "Dad, who are you talking to like that, stop acting like a woman!" I was shocked, but could tell that he felt like I had embarrassed him. As opposed to internalizing the variety of ways that a man can express himself, I could see how he was being influenced by the rigid concepts of masculinity that I have always rejected. When his friends are around, I try to watch what I say and to remember that he's going through preteen stuff.

Alan and his wife also had to negotiate who would engage in sports with their son as they struggled with the notion, still widespread, that fathers have to be athletic with boys.

I never gained high self-esteem about my physical self, so I never really played sports. My partner is very physical. She was a swimmer, played basketball, and really got into sports throughout high school. She is the one who shows our son how to dribble the basketball and excel in sports. I take my son to games, but sometimes it can be embarrassing when there are father–son games. My son was enrolled in a basketball camp that wanted the fathers to play against the sons. I told my son that I would support him by going, but that I wouldn't play. He now realizes that his father is a sideline person and his mother is the athlete.

Alan's examples demonstrate how a key component in maintaining patriarchy and heterosexism is upholding and highlighting differences in behavior between men and women; it is primarily when men do "female" things (e.g., using certain terms of endearment, like " sweetheart") or when they don't do things considered "male" (e.g., playing and enjoying sports) that questions about their sexuality come into play.[40] Heterosexuality, along with rigid gender role norms, gets enforced through stigmatizing any alternatives to it; a man who crosses those boundaries is threatened with the loss of masculine, heterosexual privilege and is "homosexualized."[41] It becomes apparent that patriarchal norms rest on the everyday conflation of gender and sexuality, the connections between heterosexual masculinity and homophobia, and "heterogender" dynamics, rather than gender dynamics alone.

As African American feminist men challenge society's expectations about their parenting roles and practices, they specifically have to confront the powerful effect on their children of patriarchal beliefs and assumptions outside the home. Many feminist parents watch with grief as their children's friends, teachers, relatives, and the media pressure them to act in accordance with conventional gender beliefs. Feminist parents cannot completely cloister their children, and parental influence is only one of many sources of gender socialization. Bruce, a 47-year-old father of six who counsels abusive men, says:

When I hear my children use gender-specific derogatory terms or see my daughters taking gender inferior stances when it comes to their male friends, I correct them. I can remember when a woman who I was involved with would constantly ask me, "Do I look okay" or "Does this dress look good?" Well, who the hell am I to say if it looks good? I ain't wearing it! I don't want my daughters to grow up seeking the constant approval of men on every little issue and thing.

Yet Bruce's daughters, like children in general, are influenced by what others think; they experience conflicting social pressures as they both act and react to the gendering process, within and outside their parents' home. Another way to interpret some of the inconsistencies between how these children are raised and how they sometimes behave is to see the children as seeking a balance between their parents' egalitarian views and society's patriarchal ones.[42]

In their efforts to envision a radically different society not necessarily dependent on gender, some participants explored gender-neutral ways of raising children in an egalitarian home. Toussaint, the bisexual priest and professor married to a bisexual feminist theologian, defies convention in an attempt to dismantle "heterogender" dynamics:

My partner and I gave our child a gender-neutral name and decided to parent in ways that would allow our child to express its gender as it chooses or doesn't choose. However, what has been so amazing to me is the way people demonstrate their need to put a gender category on this infant, and the different things they will say once they have made certain assumptions about our child's gender. For example, if the baby is eating a lot and they assume he is a boy, they will say, "I can tell that's going to be a nice strong brother!" If they see the baby smile and think it is a girl, they will say, "You're going to have to watch out or she's going to cause you some problems later!" Rigid ideas about gender would click in.

Despite the range of practices feminist men implement to instill their political beliefs in their children, Black feminist fathers, like all parents, have to shed their illusions about the degree of control they have over their attitudes, given other influences in the kids' lives.

In addition, these fathers have to deal with how their views may differ from those of their partners, who may favor different feminist schools of thought and ways of applying them. Ralph, the social scientist married to a feminist university professor, gives an example of difference in their parenting styles.

What we try to do…is teach that boys are not better than girls. Regardless of sex, whatever one wants to do, one should be allowed to do that. However, my wife and I still wrestle with how do we prepare our children to be well rounded? I have a son and a daughter and make distinctions in parenting them because…my children's personalities also affect how I teach them and treat them. My wife says she doesn't like the fact that I'm always telling our daughter how pretty she is and calling her "Princess." I tell my wife "I also tell her how smart she is and that she can be anything she wants to be." I tell my son how good looking he is and how he can be anything he wants to be. But my wife thinks that I will instill a "Princess" complex in our daughter and doesn't want a daughter who is prissy. But our daughter is prissy, because that's her personality.

As Ralph points out, personality differences exist between parents, and how they respond to their children's personalities may differ too, regardless of feminist ideology. Thus, the men's parenting, even when politically conscious, is also affected by their own temperaments and personal preferences.

Challenging Violent Discipline

The use of corporal punishment (e.g., spanking, slapping, hitting) in American homes is not unusual. Straus and Stewart[43] found that 67% of American parents still use corporal punishment on children, and those numbers are reportedly higher for African Americans.[44] Yet all of the Black feminist men in this study shun its use and unequivocally believe in a violence-free home. The American Academy of Pediatrics, the American Psychological Association, and the American Medical Association oppose the use of corporal punishment as a disciplinary strategy because empirical findings associate its use with negative outcomes: violence permits and encourages behaviors inconsistent with nurturance.

Abdul explains a comprehensive concept of childrearing that includes directly nurturing his children, allowing them to see him and his wife nurture each other, and learning creative, nonviolent parental practices.

Children can learn how to nurture from their parents by seeing their parents nurture and respect each other…and men can be nurturers and disciplinarians. However, I believe discipline should take nonviolent forms. Taking away privileges, using "time-outs," curtailing activities, and setting up systems so there's no physical abuse are nurturing, yet effective disciplinary acts. To me, violence starts in the home at that moment when I decide to hit a child. For instance, when that child goes to the plant and starts pulling out all the dirt and throwing it all over the house and making a mess of things—how much trouble does it take to put newspaper on the floor, sit down on the floor with your child, and say, "Let's take this plant apart!" How do we cultivate that creativity? We have to learn innovative nurturing ways to be there in the room emotionally and physically with our children, as opposed to thinking, "Damn, the football game is on right now, why the hell are you messing with that plant?" Turn the TV off and think, this is my future—not some football game—so I must nurture and develop my future.

Bruce's comments dovetail with Abdul's.

A man must learn to be physically and emotionally available to his children and his mate, and they should not be afraid to tell him when he's wrong. My children have permission to "call me on my stuff" and, believe me, they do. I've learned a great deal from them and how to hear their honest criticism of me instead of adopting an overly authoritarian parental attitude. When I talk parental bullshit, they don't say it's parental bullshit, but they'll ask me a question that will help me see when I have fallen short. They have powerful truths to offer, even at their tender ages. I'm trying to be antisexist, nonviolent, and noncontrolling as a father. It's tough, because I had a lot of practice being the exact opposite.

Inclusive, democratic communication, which is characteristic of feminist households, is facilitated by environments in which the threat of violence (verbal or physical) for handling disagreements or conflicts does not exist.[45] The fathers in this study were neither authoritarian (marked by harsh punishment, excessive levels of parental control, and frequent resort to physical discipline and yelling) nor overly permissive (marked by high levels of parental support with low levels of parental control). These fathers appear to be comfortable with the gradual dismantling of adult privilege that occurs as their children mature and become increasingly autonomous, responsible, and socially equal persons. They appear to relate to their children in ways that positively affect their children's development, and their children's development, in turn, affects their own development, as Bruce's narrative demonstrates. Feminist parenting appears to change men in ways that require greater accountability and self-monitoring regarding their behavior, particularly their practices of nonviolence. Children in feminist families also grow to challenge gender hierarchies and practices beyond their parents' own understanding and feminist visions, such that the parents often find themselves learning from their children.[46]

Supportive Social Arrangements

Participants said often how grateful they are for supportive people in their lives. A network of social supports assisted these men in being responsible parents. As earlier research also found,[47] men with working partners, flexible jobs, and people willing to help them raise their children (e.g., grandparents, friends, and other relatives) had major advantages.

In this study, as in previous ones, all of the men who were able to care for their children full-time for certain periods were married to partners who had equal or higher education, income, or professional status.[48] Careful planning was critical. Victor explains:

My wife and I were both working in our professions when one of us had to take a backseat, given the birth of our daughter. There was no assumption on either of our parts as to who had to take the backseat. At that point in my career, I was really disenchanted with teaching law. She loved her job, so, during one period I was home with our child and my wife was working outside the home, then my wife was home with our child and I was working outside the home.

Toussaint, like Victor, took time off to care for his child.

I was home with our child the entire first year and a half of its life, on academic leave. My partner and I planned it. I think a lot of brothers—probably because our fathers were in the streets—don't even consider taking time off to be with their child. It's rare that I hear brothers say, "I'm going to take the year off from whatever I'm doing because we're having a baby and I want to really be there."

Sometimes other creative arrangements are negotiated. Edmund, formerly a public health specialist who is now a writer and director of a theater guild, describes how he and his wife handled it.

When my son was born, I took a night job at a hospital in order to take care of him during the day. My wife taught school during the day, so she took care of him during the night. When my daughter was born, my wife and I maintained the same schedule... until our daughter was seven.

These fathers demonstrate most clearly how institutional factors shape individual choices. The men's educational levels and the working status of their partners allowed them to choose professional work that was flexible enough to allow them additional time for childcare. Only a small, elite group of African American fathers has the opportunity for such choices. Alan provides another example of the complexities that led to the social arrangement he and his partner negotiated, and how they changed over time.

My partner and I have a son who is 12 and a daughter who is 4 years old. In addition to her acting career, my partner has an academic job that requires that she be away in Florida every fall semester. The boy stays with me and the girl goes with her. This year, because my mother now lives with us and helps with childcare, both children stayed with me. Our careers and our children are both significant parts of our happiness. We negotiate who can stay at home and who can be away. Childcare and household responsibilities flow from one person to the other on a continuum because we are both away for certain periods.

With some embarrassment, Alan recalls an earlier period when he and his wife experienced difficulties negotiating childcare arrangements.

I had a lot of head-trips around the birth of my first child. It was like I was saying, "I produced a male child, I'm a man, now!" I used to call him "The Prince."... My fractured self felt vindicated because friends and relatives used to wonder about my sexuality and whether I was a "real" man. I felt like I showed them. I begged my partner to have our baby even though she told me that she didn't want a child at the time; I told her I would help out one hundred percent.... After all of that begging, pleading, and showing off, when it came to the day-to-day responsibilities of caring and raising our son, we were having a very difficult time. We were both exhausted and ended up taking our four-month-old to my parents in Arkansas until we could deal with the additional pressures of being parents in graduate school. I kept telling my partner how I felt that it just wasn't right. Then she told me, "This is the last year of my master's program and I need to finish; you're starting on your dissertation and have classes during the day and evenings. So, whether you feel it's right or not, I'm not dropping out of school, and unless you plan to drop out, we need your parents' help." So we bundled up our infant, got on a plane, and left him with my parents for six months.

Alan's narrative shows that when fathering is tied to a traditional definition of manliness, such that the mere ability to produce a child demonstrates one's virility, caretaking and nurturing are deemed irrelevant. Feminist men must unlearn the "sense of entitlement" characteristic of most men in patriarchal cultures. Black feminist men's fathering is facilitated by living with women who reject notions of themselves as childbearers, mothers, and wives always willing to make sacrifices for the family. These men often have to admit under pressure how patriarchal notions allow them to shirk responsibility.

When men become actively involved in providing for their children beyond their own self-interest and egos, their motives can become feminist.

At that point, they begin to negotiate parenting responsibilities without falling back on traditional gender roles; and, in an impasse, they may have to make special arrangements.

Cabral and his former wife also negotiated a creative, nontraditional household with several support mechanisms in place. They were building on some counterculture history: during the early 1970s they were founding members of an activist-oriented collective that ran an alternative school (preschool through third grade) and a food co-op for fresh fruit and vegetables. They also operated a bookstore and a press.

I was married for sixteen years. Safia, my former wife, and I have five kids. Our collective had a school, so, we educated our own kids through the third grade. . . . I drove the bus for our school and they would be on the bus with me. When they started going to public school, I also took them to school. Safia taught at the school. . . . We had a totally nontraditional household. The previous owners of the house had converted the garage into a one-bedroom efficiency apartment. Safia and I stayed in the garage, the kids stayed in the house. Everybody had certain responsibilities—washing, cleaning, and preparing food. On certain days it was your turn to prepare food; if you didn't cook, you didn't eat. So the kids learned to cook and wash their own clothes. Other kids who were part of our collective had clothes here and our kids had clothes in their friends' places. It was a communal society. Our kids had a real sense of freedom to do whatever they wanted to do and live how they wanted to live, relatively early on.

One way feminist fathers can escape some of the limitations imposed in the workplace is by strategically creating their own work environments to facilitate close contact with their children. Although Cabral's case—like the elite group of professional fathers who were able to take time off to spend with their children—is exceptional, he demonstrates "the value-driven creativity"[49] needed to reject patriarchy.

Challenging Conventions About Who Can Raise Children

Value-driven creativity can also be seen in the men's radical responses regarding who can parent a child and what constitutes a family. Feminist African American fathers are well aware of the backlash against feminism and gay rights. At the heart of their narratives is the call to expand the idea of what constitutes a "legitimate" family and to dissociate responsibility for childcare from both gender and heterosexuality, in radical ways. Without exception, all believed that a gay or bisexual man could be an effective father. Toussaint most eloquently exemplified this point.

As a bisexual parent, I have one biological child who is 2 years old and an adopted son who is 21. I adopted the 21 year old in 1991 when he was a teenager. I didn't go through an agency but through traditional Black-style adoption, meaning I raised him for a Black woman friend who needed some help. I drove him to school, went to see his teachers, and had to drive him frequently to doctors' appointments because he is HIV-positive.

Malcolm, a gay college student and community youth organizer, adds:

When my sister died, my grandmother and I ended up taking on the childcare responsibilities for my sister's son and daughter. I attend college full-time; however, I also work full-time. I am one of the most financially stable persons in my immediate family. Children need to be taken care of, so, if it falls on you, you should seek a system of support from whoever is in your immediate circle.... My niece and nephew live with me in Georgia during the summers and during their school vacations, and they live with my grandmother in Alabama during the school term. I'm strict, but my ideas of discipline are by no means physical. Also, in my parenting, I want my niece and nephew to know me as a person, not just as their provider. I also believe you should give children emotional support so they know that they have your attention and time. I try to spend an entire day per week with my niece and nephew to show them my concern for them. That's their day, and they can talk about and do whatever they want us to do together.

Malcolm's financial stability, emotional maturity, and feminist belief that men can learn to nurture children—as well as his openness to an extended family caregiving network—contributes more to his ability to provide adequate childcare than do his biological sex, sexual orientation, marital status, or biological relationship to the children. Donny, too, emphasizes the need for people to expand their concept of who can "parent" a child. Although he currently identifies as gay, he recalls one heterosexual relationship he had years earlier.

Being gay does not preclude me from being a thoughtful parent. A woman whom I had a two-year relationship with a decade ago has three children. During the time that we were romantically involved, I got attached to her children and they got attached to me.... Two children were near adulthood when I came into their mother's life, but there was one who was quite young, who still thinks of me as her father, and I still think of her as my child. I did everything from changing diapers, cooking, being involved in their school lives, to disciplining and instructing them.... If men could get the support that they needed to parent full-time, that would be great.... I would have wanted to parent full-time.

Responsible, involved gay and bisexual Black fathers like Toussaint, Malcolm, and Donny challenge deeply held, popular patriarchal beliefs that good fathering can occur only in the context of heterosexual marriage.

One man, Soyinka, the instructor specializing in Black women's labor movements (and whose first wife shot him in self-defense), honestly acknowledges that his acceptance of gays, bisexuals, and lesbians as parents is an ongoing process. He was the caretaker of two stepsons in that same marriage.

Intellectually speaking, I think that gays and lesbians should have the same rights to adopt children as heterosexuals. I say intellectually because I'm being honest about the fact that I still struggle with the idea in some ways. But when I read how Audre Lorde, as a Black lesbian, struggled to raise her son so he wouldn't be a sexist male, I was literally in tears because of the integrity that she brought to her parenting. There are a lot of bad heterosexual parents. A person's sexual orientation doesn't make that person a good or a bad parent. We all—lesbian and gay couples as well as heterosexual couples—have a lot to learn about parenting.

Despite his ambivalence, Soyinka, like the other participants, accepts the legitimacy of diverse families. Their views are summarized by Bruce:

Gay and lesbian relationships should have the same legal rights as heterosexuals...and should also be allowed to adopt children. They can't do any worse of a job parenting than heterosexual parents. Parenting is not about sexuality. It's about patience, love, being there for your children, and being a damn good driver!

Summary

African American feminist fathers seek radical solutions to fatherhood issues without excusing themselves from financial responsibility for their children or reinforcing any patriarchal, heterosexist, or economic principles that feed the system. They emphasize important aspects of fathering often ignored by researchers, policy makers, and the media, such as practicing nurture as everyday acts rather than as unique, episodic behavior. Their efforts to raise children in ways that radically challenge conventional attitudes and practices—even in the face of multiple, strong, opposing influences in and outside the home—demonstrate their deep commitment to politically conscious parenting and broad social justice.

In addition to individual feminist attitudes and beliefs and internalized commitment to egalitarian principles, external factors are associated with these men's involved fathering experiences. All have a support network that involves the cooperation of partners, extended family members, and sometimes work colleagues. They frequently mentioned how their partners expected them to discuss, negotiate, and plan strategies regarding visitation, parental leave, and work-related commitments. Also, the married men's educational and financial resources, coupled with the feminist commitment, education level, income, and work status of their spouses, facilitated their high level of parental involvement.

Men who took care of their children full time at some point in their lives were able to choose jobs that allowed flexibility. Poor, working-class, and even most middle-class families do not have the choices available to some privileged professionals. Here we see the consequences of individual and institutional factors that interact to facilitate or retard both social change and individual choices. Social policies that encourage flexible workplaces free of penalties for involved parents (regardless of gender or race) and promote equal economic opportunities for women and equal parenting opportunities for men are essential to feminist practice in fathering, not only for Black men but for all men. Companies must be pressured to institute family-friendly work policies—otherwise, the level of nurturing associated with feminist fathering will remain a limited option chosen only by a small group of socioeconomically privileged men.[50]

Openness regarding *how* to parent extends to ideas about *who* can parent. By challenging the patriarchal notion that two heterosexual parents married to each other are necessary to raise well-adjusted children, the men in this study, gay and straight, are redefining fatherhood. The narratives of the gay and bisexual Black feminist fathers and the nurturing experiences of all the fathers add to a growing body of empirical evidence supporting gender-neutral parenting. Neither fathers nor mothers per se are essential to positive childrearing outcomes; rather, having *any* consistent, loving caregiver, regardless of biological sex and sexual preference or orientation, is what matters.[51] Finally, Black feminist men understand that redefining fatherhood must rest on the premise of a violence-free home; they shun the use of corporal punishment as a disciplinary practice. African American professional organizations would be well advised to take a strong stand on this issue, as well as educating African Americans about other, nonviolent disciplinary strategies in childrearing.

The Black feminist fathers in this study have taken the lead in applying radical, alternative childrearing practices that other fathers may want to consider. Although the men I interviewed are atypical, the issues they face are not. Their narratives reveal a desire to pass on a positive legacy resulting from parenting that cannot be separated from other political and ethical commitments. Those commitments involve a feminist vision of what is best for children, women, community, society, and their own psychosocial development. Next, I explore how the black feminist men in my study attempt to transform institutions, as well as their individual lives, through social and political activism.

CHAPTER 9

Private Commitments,
Public Actions

Feminist men who are truly committed to social change understand that challenging institutionalized forms of oppression is a necessary outgrowth of reclaiming their right to be fully human at the personal level.[1] Even though the present reality in the United States seems far from the just society they envision, they also understand that history consists of imagining the remotely possible and then struggling to achieve it. All the men in my study, to varying degrees, were aware that multilayered power imbalances—which Black feminist scholar Patricia Hill Collins calls "the matrix of domination"[2]—make it necessary for men to act both privately and publicly to resist sexism and other forms of oppression. Public acts of resistance challenge an unwritten commandment of systemic injustice, "Thou shalt conform and not confront."[3] However, there are no hard rules or written guidelines that teach Black men how to counter social domination. Often, they find themselves fumbling through the dark, and these twists and turns are reflected in their narratives.

Here I focus on the wide range of feminist Black men's participation in organized collective action. In this chapter we will see to what degree their private and public lives become indistinguishable, and how they recover from, and sometimes even avoid, certain pitfalls in their public political practices. The men's activism is characterized by at least three

175

major themes: (a) violence prevention, and holding men accountable for stopping it; (b) involvement in multiple issues and coalition politics; and (c) an ongoing concern with shifting power dynamics between themselves and women in diverse public settings. Although some of the men in my study have been active in predominantly White men's profeminist organizations, most of them, like many Black feminist women, are active in separate, parallel campaigns around violence prevention in African American communities and predominantly Black organizations.

Most interesting, their activism demonstrates that so-called identity politics can be focused on multiple issues and driven by coalition work when a broad ideology encompassing race, gender, class, and sexuality (such as Black feminism) is linked to other social movements.[4] Black feminist men's collective actions speak to specific manifestations of the intersecting nature of power, and, like all Black feminist political practices, their aim is to challenge unjust power relations. The next section presents an overview of the profeminist men's movement, African American men's participation in it, and separate profeminist activism within African American communities.

The Profeminist Men's Movement and African American Men

The profeminist men's movement in the United States has operated mainly through local communities in decentralized ways.[5] Many profeminist men's collectives advocate for the prevention of violence against women through community education via training workshops, men's support groups, protest rallies, antiviolence parades, mass media campaigns, and fundraising programs for women's shelters (e.g., Men Stopping Violence in Atlanta, Georgia; Men Stopping Rape in Madison, Wisconsin; and Men Emerge in Cambridge, Massachusetts).[6]

In addition to various local networks, the profeminist men's movement in the United States is associated with a nationally recognized organization, the National Organization for Men Against Sexism (NOMAS). Founded in the early 1980s, NOMAS is the oldest and most politically progressive profeminist, gay-affirmative, and antiracist men's social movement organization in the United States. Unfortunately, aside from organizing an annual conference, its meager resources hamper its ability to establish political priorities in alliance with the broader feminist movement and to mobilize local, grassroots chapters.[7] Thus, NOMAS remains a predominantly White, middle-class social change organization.

Some men in my study—notably Abdul, Bruce, Chad, Donny, Rex, and Soyinka—are active (or have been active) in NOMAS and local profeminist organizations loosely affiliated with it. However, most African American feminist men (and profeminist men in general) do not belong to any profeminist men's organization. Black men may be particularly reluctant to join NOMAS because of their unwillingness to submit to what they may perceive as "White male authority" on matters regarding their manhood—even though joining or forming coalitions with organizations like NOMAS might be congruent with their social justice interests.

Recently, however, an indeterminate number of profeminist Black men have begun to participate in a network of left-leaning, predominantly African American social-movement groups loosely affiliated with an umbrella organization called the Black Radical Congress and its Black Feminist Caucus.[8] Organizational autonomy allows Black men the ability to challenge predominantly White political and economic leadership arrangements that heretofore have required their deferential compliance. Furthermore, this autonomy has led some profeminist African American men to become organizers and participants in feminist collective action. Some have founded organizations, whose objectives converge with those of the predominantly White profeminist men's movement, as well as with radical feminist strains of the Black Nationalist Movement (e.g., Atlanta Committee for Black Liberation; Black Men for the Eradication of Sexism; and Brothers Absolutely Against Sexual Assault and Domestic Violence).[9] Feminist masculinities scholars are beginning to document the growing influence of the profeminist men's movement on its members, gender politics, and society at large.[10] This chapter emphasizes what feminist Black men, specifically, have contributed to that movement.

Public Activism as Accountability

Focus on Violence Prevention

Consistent with the profeminist men's movement as a whole, feminist Black men's activism tends to focus on preventing violence against women and stopping violence in general, particularly in African American communities. Violence is understood to include verbal and emotional as well as physical assault.

Carlos, the graduate student in environmental studies, became a founder of a Black profeminist men's student organization as a result of personal experiences that eventually moved him to act publicly in ways he had never imagined. His relationship with a feminist woman forced him to develop consistency between his private and public life.

My partner accused me of being antisexist around her privately, but "trying to look cool around other guys" instead of checking them on their sexism when I was in public. She asked me, "How are you going to confront the sexism of other guys in addition to being antisexist around me?" She suggested that a Black men's group against sexism would be a good idea and that I should organize it. At first I was like, "Say what?!" It took a while for the idea to take root, but it eventually did, and I coorganized a group at a Black men's college.... Although we both graduated and went our separate ways, given our different career interests and plans, she brought me the farthest on the road to feminism.

Carlos's feminist partner challenged him to oppose sexist beliefs at all levels of relationship. Once he realized he should not limit his commitment to personal issues at the expense of political mobilization, he contributed to real social change by organizing men on historically Black college campuses in Atlanta. His narrative includes specific examples of what can be accomplished.

I took a feminist class at the Black women's college that my girlfriend recommended.... The Black feminist professor whose class I was taking always had her students organize some feminist activity at the end of the course. My class decided to organize a speak-out on Freaknic, the Black college spring break weekend where nudity and the lewdest, "freakiest" behaviors [are] encouraged. It is also a weekend where many women are raped, sexually harassed, and generally disrespected by the male participants. I decided to announce the starting of an antisexist men's group at the speak-out.

Carlos's positive interactions with the instructor and other women in the course heightened his consciousness and thoughts about Black feminist issues. Both his girlfriend and the professor had affirmed that Black men could be feminists, and his classmates reinforced the idea that he was, indeed, becoming one. At this point, Carlos's narrative reflects the confidence he gained as a result of these positive experiences:

I waited until the end of the speak-out, got up, said some things about Freaknic, then told the brothers present that we need to organize a group that would help us correct our sexist behavior and put in check the sexist behavior of others.... We sat in a circle and planned our first meeting. That was how our Black men's antisexist group got started.... The next year our group held a protest march during Freaknic, sponsored informal discussion groups on gender issues—coed and single-sex dialogues, presented panel discussions, conducted antisexist workshops, and held a conference entitled "To Be Black Male, and Feminist/Womanist."

Carlos's next example makes an important point: One can never know what is possible until one acts publicly on behalf of women by challenging men.

During my first year of college, a group of sisters from the Black women's college down the street came to my dormitory room to hang out with me, but I wasn't there. A guy in the dormitory started harassing one of the women. She wanted him to leave her alone, but the guy wouldn't stop. None of the other guys on the floor did anything or said anything to help her. She was really afraid that he was going to hurt her because he had pushed her up against the wall, and the dude was big! Some of the other women helped her get away from the guy. They told me about it the next day. So, I wrote a note and posted it on the dormitory floor. I don't remember exactly what it said, but it was something like "ALL OF YOU SHOULD KNOW BETTER AND SHOULDN'T BE DISRE-SPECTING A SISTER. IF YOU HAVE A PROBLEM, MY NAME IS CARLOS AND I LIVE ON THE SECOND FLOOR IN ROOM 224." That night about five brothers came to my room and said, "Do you know who wrote this note?" and I said, "Yeah, I did." They confronted me for about 10 minutes. I think I did most of the talking, even though I was nervous and didn't know whether they came to talk or fight. They tried to play down the seriousness of what they did, eventually left, and denied any wrongdoing, but guilt was written all over their faces.

Carlos's actions make clear that in order to truly humanize society, men must take risks. To their credit, other participants in my study also mentioned, in their narratives, the importance of challenging other men to be publicly accountable for their behavior. In a separate study I conducted on Carlos and another African American male founder of a pro-feminist men's student group, Albert Bryant describes how he prevented an intoxicated female friend from being gang raped at a party, then later cofounded an organization to prevent sexual assault. When Albert "saw what the other men were up to, he grabbed her by the arm, and walked her home."[11] When men stand up for women against other sexist men, they stand up for themselves and, in my opinion, for all of humanity.

Some researchers believe that exposure to community violence, which can spill over into intimate relationships, may partially account for disproportionately high rates of intimate violence among African American high school and college students.[12] The men in my study who were involved in antiviolence feminist activism noted that the works of Black feminist scholars such as Beth Richie, Carolyn West, and Evelyn White had introduced them to a contextualized analysis of gender violence, rooted in a broad understanding of how social dominance operates; their own radical critiques of violence in general had been

strengthened by their reading.[13] Yet reading is never enough. Alan publicly calls on male students in his classes and colleagues in his field to
move beyond ideas into action:

*Profeminist Black men cannot simply think that because they are
writing from feminist perspectives they are advancing the agenda of
Black feminism in significant ways. Black feminism has to go beyond the
intellectual, creative writing level to where a Black man says to another
Black man, "I'm not down with your sexist behavior." Black male feminism isn't just about writing, it's about speaking out, it's about living the
life, and it's about Black male activism. As Black men who embrace feminism, we can't hide behind the text. I write about Black women's novels
from a feminist standpoint, and it's in vogue right now, but I also speak
out and place myself in the often uncomfortable position of calling brothers on their sexist crap. Brothers need to write about sexism, but we also
need to talk about it, then do something about it, particularly regarding
the rape and domestic violence in our communities.*

Toussaint agrees and adds:

*I remember seeing a brother getting loud with and raising his hand
to a sister in public. I asked her if she needed anything. I didn't jump up
and beat his ass or what-have-you. It's hard to teach a brother that there
are other ways to resolve this thing when you're beating his ass and physically over powering him. To tell him that he shouldn't be jumping on her
while you're physically beating him down makes it difficult to really
teach a person about alternatives to violence. There are other nonviolent
ways to intervene....*

*A lot of times people just get caught up in what's proper etiquette
regarding sexist language and what-have-you. A man may think, "I'm a
nice man, I'm not sexist, I don't abuse women." That same man rarely
looks at sexism as intricately linked to the sociopolitical economic system
that also promotes racism in very complex ways.... I can't stress enough
the importance of men who claim to be progressive, to take very seriously
women's issues and not just in lip service.*

Edmund weighs in with a similar experience in his efforts to get men
to engage in workable, concrete solutions to violence against women in
African American communities.

*My wife, Ruby, her daughter, and I were going to the movies one
day and I was driving. I was getting off of the freeway when I saw a
crowd. A woman was running and saying, "He's got a gun and he's going
to shoot me!" A man was running right behind her. He caught her, hit
her in the back of the head, and she stumbled. I turned the car and aimed
it at him in an attempt to block him against the freeway rail but he
jumped out [of] the way. Then, I got out of the car and helped the*

woman get into our car and the guy ran away. I couldn't just drive past that scene and simply hope she didn't get hurt. She was so terrified that she was running onto the freeway! So, we put her in the car and took her where she was going. As Black men, we are never going to gain Black women's confidence in us until we become responsible and stop brutalizing women. But, first, we have to give up this prideful ignorance where we use the excuse, "That's just the way I was taught." It's time to be taught something else.

In addition to opposing domestic violence and other forms of partner abuse, most of the men in my study had been involved in some public efforts against sexual assault. They had participated in antirape documentary films (Abdul, Rex, Jake), speak-outs, and panel discussions (Alan, Abdul, Carlos, Chad, David, Donny, Soyinka, Bruce, Paul, Rex, Ralph, Solomon, Toussaint, Victor) and published essays, poetry, and plays (Cabral, Carlos, Edmund, Malcolm, Soyinka) stressing that Black men must be held accountable for the growing violence in African American communities.

An incident in Donny's narrative led him to conduct antirape workshops with men in a local organization called Rape and Violence End Now (RAVEN):

I drove up on a man trying to rape a woman in an alley one night behind my restaurant. I was coming back to the restaurant around midnight after a catering job.... It was a summer night, so my windows were down and as I turned into the alley I heard this woman screaming.... I stopped the car. Then I heard her scream again. So I blew my horn really, really long and loud because there were apartments attached to the alley and I was trying to wake somebody, anybody up. I was also hoping to interrupt whatever was going on in that alley. A couple of lights came on, and then she wasn't screaming anymore. I got out of the car and then I think I just sort of cautiously looked around. . . . There was just silence. Then this guy came out of one of the apartments where one of the lights came on and went to his car and got a baseball bat. We looked around the parking lot, then we saw this man and this woman with her dress all torn and he started hollering at us, "Don't come near" and we said something like, "You better stop," and we kept approaching him, so he ran off. The young man who had joined me in the search called the police before he came outside. The woman was crying and I asked her if I could sit with her. I sat with her until the police came a few minutes later. The guy who was with me showed the police where the rapist ran. I stayed with the woman. Fortunately, they caught the rapist.

Although some women are raped by strangers, as appeared to be the case in Donny's narrative, women are more likely to be raped by acquaintances, relatives, boyfriends, and husbands.[14] Moreover, while substantial numbers of African American women have been raped, many victims never tell anyone about their sexual assault experiences.[15] The feminist Black men in my study concurred that negative images of Black women, depicting them as sexually promiscuous and thus not legitimate victims, pressure Black women to remain silent when assaulted and create barriers to their obtaining justice, not only in the courts but in society in general. Cudjoe had an experience that opened his eyes to the prevalence of rape on his campus.

The "Take Back the Night March" was really big at my university, and although I never participated in the actual march, one year you were supposed to tie a purple ribbon on the assaulter's door if you knew someone who had been sexually assaulted by him. There was a woman who told me a fraternity guy had raped her so I decided to tie a ribbon on his door. Well, when I got to his fraternity house, there were so many purple ribbons that you couldn't even see the knob! Due to the lack of space left on the knob, some people had tied the ribbons in other places near the door, but it was unbelievable because there were at least a hundred purple ribbons on that frathouse door.

That incident pushed him to enroll in a course that required him to take further feminist action on campus.

Because it is mostly men who commit the violence, it is mainly men who can stop it. Working in feminist men's organizations has given Chad a forum for acting publicly against rape and domestic abuse.

I am currently a board member of an organization that works with men who batter women, and before working with this organization I worked with a group of men who organized around educating men to stop rape.... Profeminist men's organizations provide a setting where men can address their accountability to women in ways that challenge the ways we seek power over women as well as each other.... As the White Ribbon Campaign states, "Confronting men's violence requires nothing less than a commitment to full equality for women and a redefinition of what it means to be men, to discover a meaning to manhood that doesn't require blood to be spilled.[16]

The Importance of Coalition Work

In addition to an overwhelming emphasis on preventing violence against women, feminist Black men were disproportionately involved in organizations and collective protests that emphasized coalition politics. Their individual feminist Black identities help them move beyond their comfort zones to interact with activists in other movements who also claim multiple, intersecting identities and related interests. Feminist Black men understand the importance of organized efforts in the communities where they live. They take multiple approaches to social change, with a range of public activities informed and strengthened by their intersectional political perspectives. Most important, their public activism addresses intersections between feminist movements and other social movements as they expose the relationships among identity, institutions, and the political economy, then paint a picture of the society they envision in which all forms of injustice would be remediable. In addition, their narratives demonstrate the multiple sites in which Black feminist intersectional politics take place.[17]

PAUL: *My involvement in the Congress for Racial Equality, the nuclear freeze movement, and most recently the homeless, particularly homeless women, is related to my overall concern about people who have been marginalized and disenfranchised.*

JAKE: *In my job, I speak on topics as diverse as the crisis in former Yugoslavia, African American involvement in U.S. foreign policy, the abolition of nuclear weapons, and domestic and international issues regarding rape.*

SOLOMON: *I have participated in several community groups that protested against redlining, school segregation, the so-called gentrification of neighborhoods, and other topics that affect poor Black communities. Primarily working-class poor Black women managed most of these community organizations. I have also taught anthropology courses that were cross-listed with women's studies.*

DONNY: *I've conducted workshops for Planned Parenthood and pro-feminist men's organizations such as the National Organization for Men Against Sexism. My workshops address issues regarding sexuality, racism, sexism, and homophobia/heterosexism.*

EDDIE: *For fifteen years, I have belonged to a Pan African organization that stressed socialist ideology, gender equity, and humanism. My organization has been involved with other progressive organizations like the American Indian Movement.*

EDMUND: *There are many ways to approach writing, but my writing and performances are designed to uplift and challenge.... I have written pieces about skin color issues among African Americans, men who hang out on street corners, the homeless,*

> *poverty, prostitution, crack, homophobia, war, violence against Black women, divorce, and any topic that will make us think.*

VICTOR: *I'm involved in grassroots activities regarding the public schools, particularly the school board. I've also been involved in grassroots work concerning domestic violence, incarcerated kids, AIDS education in Black churches, and at one point I taught women's self-defense classes for Women Against Rape.*

As these excerpts show, Black feminist politics can bring groups together. These men continue in the tradition of feminist women of color who have historically mobilized different constituencies to engage in political work.[18] However, building alliances and negotiating commonalities while simultaneously being sensitive to the differences can be frustrating. Toussaint reports an extremely difficult effort to create coalition when he was active in an AIDS awareness organization:

> *I was active in ACT-UP (AIDS Coalition to Unleash Power), an AIDS awareness organization known for its direct action protest activities. In ACT-UP there was the ongoing challenging to get men to deal with race, gender, and class issues. A lot of the White boys in ACT-UP were like, "This is about AIDS, not race, gender, class and all of that other stuff." So I had to stay on their case constantly because some of my big interests were women of color and AIDS and transgendered women and AIDS. For example, I belonged to the Washington, D.C. chapter of ACT-UP and in its heyday maybe there were like a hundred men and only two or three women. I was like, what's going on here? So, I went out in the community and recruited some women of color. It was an ongoing battle.*

Toussaint confirms that while people can acknowledge that cultural differences among groups are socially constructed, resulting from shared histories of oppression, nonetheless these differences create distinct social groups *within* movements.[19] In fact, identity concepts of "Whiteness," "middle-class status," and "masculinity" by White male members of ACT-UP actually precluded an analysis of inequality that took race, class, and gender into account regarding the impact of AIDS.[20] Acknowledging such historical differences does not necessarily constrain the ability to form coalitions if, despite the differences, a broad vision for social change can be adopted by the coalition.[21] The feminist Black men in my study understand that and foster such links in their activism. Toussaint was also influenced by the politics of the National Party Alliance, an independent political party that endorsed an African American woman, Lenora Fulani, as a candidate for president of the

United States. Toussaint was a delegate at the party's convention, which gathered multiissue, identity-based organizations together to address how socially constructed differences are dealt with in our society, along with the race-specific, gender-specific, and sexuality-specific ways in which economic exploitation takes place.

Soyinka's activism also reflects a Black feminist political stance that refuses to separate identity and culture from the political economy.

I've been involved for the past several years with a southern-based Black trade union organization. The organization was founded during the early 1980s and was brought into existence by the struggles of Black women who were working for K-Mart Corporation. They decided that they were fed up with the low wages and the poor working conditions. When they attempted to resist and get unionized, a larger struggle emerged where people who were working for K-Mart joined hands with people in the community and created this organization. This is one of the few working-class organizations where people address race, class, and gender problems.

Other activities that participants mentioned include conducting workshops on peace education, protesting environmental racism, engaging in cooperative economics via food co-ops, publishing women's writings and writings about women, and speaking on the public lecture circuit about Black feminist topics. Eight men (Alan, Chad, David, Ralph, Solomon, Soyinka, Toussaint, and Victor) had taught challenging interdisciplinary courses at the university level (catalogued as African American Studies, Women's Studies, Lesbian/Gay/Bisexual/and Transgendered Studies, and Labor Studies) that guided students to think critically about social justice issues. David's course provides an example.

Most of the classes that I teach are about race, but it's impossible to talk critically about race without talking about gender. So, race and gender issues mainly shape the content of the work that I do. I have to constantly think about how best to communicate these political issues to students who, for the most part, are from White middle and upper-middle-class backgrounds. For instance, I teach a class on "Race and American Fiction." I try to discuss how race, gender, and class issues are analogous in many ways such that we all need to examine to what degree we are invested in these various systems. I benefit from being male on a daily basis, so I don't say to the White students, "You are the only ones who are wrong and you are all invested in White supremacy." I stress how these systems of oppression are very complicated and that we are all implicated and have a lot of work to do. My courses use literature to examine how we can be more self-conscious about our actions.

David's activism outside the classroom but within the university is typical of the situations encountered by feminist Black men employed by academic institutions.

Outside of class, I have to routinely grapple with departmental politics, particularly as these politics relate to affirmative-action issues. My department has resisted hiring Black people and women and it's incredible, the arguments that we go through every single year. *Even colleagues who you would assume to be the most liberal don't speak out. I have to constantly remind my colleagues that we need both gender and racial diversity in our department. It's really frustrating at times. My closest friends in my academic department are White women who share similar political views about the need for racial and gender diversity.*

Alan tells how the lack of diversity at his institution, particularly as it relates to Black women, resulted in a public protest.

I have served on faculty search committees to advocate for the inclusion of women of color at my university and was a member of a particular search committee that fought hard to bring a dynamic Black lesbian feminist faculty member on board. Three years later, the university decided not to renew her contract. Her critique of the institution's politics was so incisive that she represented a threat to them. I could not sit idly and allow this to happen, so I joined the fight to retain her at the university. This faculty member and I became political comrades in a struggle that demanded action—not just academic articles about the injustices that women of color face in the academy.

The battle to keep her at the university included organized student and faculty protests. We fought hard, but were not successful in keeping her. I learned a lot about the power of university institutions. What they did to her and what they did to us was nothing less than spirit murder— my comrade's precise words, "spirit murder." I often second-guess myself and wonder could I have done more. Should I have said, "If she goes, I go"? Should I have said to other faculty members of color that we need to tell the university that we will all resign if she is not retained? Well, I don't believe the university would have been upset if all faculty of color had left. They probably would have replaced us with more accommodating faculty of color. I am one of only two Black men to work in my division at this university over the course of six years and have witnessed two Black women not have their contracts renewed.... Although the fact that the university forced her out was demoralizing, the fact that we spoke out and stood up for what was just had an impact on my personal confidence as a feminist Black man and increased my commitment to the need for social change at all levels.

The experience of Derrick Bell, Harvard University's first full-time African American law professor, offers some powerful insights into the protest process, which does not necessarily end with getting a list of demands met. Although I did not interview Bell for my study, I consider his activism characteristic of feminist Black men who were included in it. Twenty years after he was hired, Bell decided to protest Harvard Law School's refusal to hire and tenure a woman of color by taking a leave from his teaching duties. Although the law school had hired a half-dozen additional Black men with faculty appointments over the years Professor Bell had been there, he hoped his drastic action might fortify students in their efforts to diversify the faculty—and even prompt a few faculty members to apply sufficient pressure to get the school to hire a woman of color. It didn't happen. Bell's protest lasted two years, after which Harvard gave him an ultimatum: either return to his teaching duties or lose his tenured position. Given the law school's refusal to hire and tenure even one woman of color during Bell's absence, he refused to return and was summarily fired. In his book about the protest, *Confronting Authority*, Bell emphasizes the value of individual and group protest actions:

> I have learned that those in power regard every act of protest—whether against the most mundane rule or the most fundamental principle—as equally threatening. The resistance I experienced at Harvard was as determined as that I have encountered at any institution that is satisfied with the status quo and fearful of change. By challenging authority, the protestor undermines the assumption that things are either as they are supposed to be or as they must be. What is most heretical, though, is that, in every case, the protester asserts the right to have a meaningful—as opposed to a token—voice. That is what those in authority resist so desperately.[22]

Feminist Black men, like activists in general, choose political strategies and tactics that can vary across movements, identities, time, and place. Alan and Derrick Bell exemplify the range of their tactical styles. In some movements they may choose to highlight their multiple identities; in others they may strategically deemphasize them. Demands for recognition through the assertion of certain identities are intertwined with material concerns and challenge social relations that are institutionally based.[23]

Recovering From and Avoiding Pitfalls

As a man's feminist commitment deepens, he often faces dilemmas regarding how to think and act in certain situations. As one writer puts it, feminist men may need clear reminders of their "deeply entrenched habits," "familiar comforts," and "the lure of indifference" that are characteristic of male power.[24] The resultant tensions and paradoxes of male feminist consciousness produce both rewarding and difficult moments. The difficult moments are easier to negotiate when men rely on empathy and diplomacy, or what I call "empathic diplomacy." Malcolm, for example, had to learn how to ensure that his very awareness of sexist behaviors and exposure to feminist analysis in women's studies courses did not silence women in nonacademic environments who had not had the privilege of such exposure.

Working in community organizations, as opposed to solely campus organizations, has provided me with an opportunity to hear what nonacademic people think about sexism and what they consider sexist behavior. Academic people will think certain things are sexist, woman-hating oriented, or male dominant, while everyday people will tell you that they don't believe a certain thing is sexist. I had to realize and accept that a lot of women that I work with don't necessarily believe that certain things are sexist, even when I think it's sexist——like calling women bitches! As a result, I've had to figure out how to maintain a good balance as an antisexist man when I disagree with women who don't see sexism when I do. For instance, I've learned to say, "Maybe you could think about it this way" and sometimes I have to think about whether I should say anything at all because I'm a man. So, I just sort of handle it as I go along. Sometimes I say the right thing and sometimes I say the wrong thing; it's definitely been a unique experience.

Feminist men (whether they like it or not) will continue to derive the benefits of being male in a patriarchal society, even though they are committed to fighting that injustice. They are bound to face ambiguous, difficult situations of male privilege in their own lives because institutions and the expectations of others continue to shape the contexts in which they act. Therefore, feminist action also means constantly resisting being seduced by patriarchal privilege in everyday life. Donny shares a situation in his activist-oriented work environment and restaurant that revealed some of his latent patriarchal tendencies.

It wasn't so long ago that I used my voice to intimidate others. The first time I ever noticed that raising my voice silenced women was at a meeting at work. I just needed to get my way, so, I raised my voice. I realized later how it affected the women. I don't think I thought it was a form of violence. Initially, I thought I was just trying to be heard. Now, I connect it to that part of sexism that has instilled fear in women that all men can be violent and can hurt them. Most women in the world who know me, know that I would never touch, hit, slap, or push any woman.

However, I've used my voice—I've noticed it recently, but I'm sure I've done it before—to hook into that fear that they have so that I can get my way. That is violent, that is wrong, and if I don't ever do that again, I'd be happy.

Toussaint, too, shows a level of awareness and sensitivity that results in a firm feminist commitment to putting women at ease:

I believe I have "conferred macho privilege" simply because of my height and my build and the physical presence that I have due to the combination. Others project machismo onto me, whether they are straight or queer. Even if I'm walking down the street and I'm wearing a queer T-shirt or a queer badge, people don't mess with me. I think it has something to do with my build and how people tend to be intimidated by tall, big men. It's something I'm really, really, sensitive about. The other day in a faculty meeting with almost all women and three men, I had to leave early. So I stood up and was talking, and then I decided to sit down. I noticed how I was just towering over these women who were basically all short women. It was too imposing, so I felt I should sit down.

None of the men in my study suggested that they should be given any special privileges because they are feminist activists. However, I did notice that a few felt almost as if they needed to punish themselves for being men and for having access to power unfairly. Unless they are making unfair use of that power, I believe this kind of guilt can undermine their sense of agency and limit their political effectiveness, in the long run. Alan discusses his struggle with sorting through these distinctions.

When I became a feminist, one of the ways that I channeled my feminism was through my efforts not to have anything to do with men. A Black male friend once told me that I was acting more like a feminist than most of the feminist women that he knew. I came to a point where I had to recognize that a prominent feature of my feminism was how I used it in attempts to hide or erase myself as a man. I have come to the understanding that as a feminist man, I don't have to be ashamed of who I am biologically. I had to accept that no matter how much I align myself with feminist women across racial, economic, and sexual boundaries, I am not a woman and cannot really understand what it means to be embodied in the female self. My contribution to the feminist movement is being in the trenches, doing the work that I need to do as a man, in order to advance the feminist project of wholeness for women and men.

Every man in the study was able to admit his weaknesses, along with his ongoing efforts to overcome them. Those confessions often constituted the most painful and embarrassing moments of the interviews. However, it should surprise no one to find sexist attitudes and behaviors among feminist men. Change is not a single event; rather, it is ongoing.

Once the self has been defined in a certain way (i.e., sexist, elitist, religious, etc.), that identity, according to personality researchers, is rarely completely undone.[25] Thus, although meaningful links to sexist attitudes and behaviors are fundamentally altered during the change process, they are not completely eliminated. On the average, feminist men may be less sexist than nonfeminist men, but they are not devoid of sexist attitudes and practices. What distinguishes them from nonfeminist men is not an illusory "nonsexist" state of being but an action-based commitment to the lifelong process of changing their sexist practices.

David Kahane's description of coping with inevitable highs and lows, in the course of men's development, is particularly relevant: "The key is to find ways to live responsibly with the contradictions described by male feminism and even to flourish in their presence, rather than trying to flee them or giving in to those parts of ourselves that crave a greater simplicity."[26] He sees the necessary conditions for a sustainable form of feminist practice among men as (1) a willingness to conceive of oneself as ethically complex and incomplete, (2) an openness to criticism and a propensity to self-criticism, and (3) engagement in activist friendships and community.[27] Soyinka illustrates the point with an example from a contemporary African film.

I really hope that there's a way to help other Black males to understand how important it is for us to find the emotional space to both encourage and challenge one another in our efforts to support women and feminist perspectives regarding justice. As frightening as that may be for some of us, I see it as a form of social activism and intervention that we desperately need to pursue. It will afford us an opportunity to better understand how we have been socialized to really work against women and even our own best interests. One of the things I have learned—and I guess I should say I'm still learning—is that it's important to be antisexist, not just because we don't want to hurt Black women or any other women but because we don't want to be beasts. In the movie Sankofa *by the Ethiopian filmmaker Haille Gerima, there is a scene where a brother who has been trained to be an overseer of the slaves is talking to a slave woman. He's trying to get her to be his woman. She cares a lot about him, but in no uncertain terms she just tells him that she's not going to be the woman of any overseer. He's wondering what does he have to do and how does he have to ask her to be his woman. Then she says this marvelous line, as she looks him in the eyes, "The real question is, are you going to be a man or are you going to be a beast?" And for me, that's what being antisexist is all about. I don't want to be a beast.*

Summary

Feminist Black men's narratives suggest that their public acts can be avenues toward broad social change, and that their feminist awareness is enhanced by such activist experiences. Through public actions, these feminist men connect their individual problems or situations to institutional factors, then link the personal and the political in agitating for transformative action. Some have been active in profeminist men's groups. However, most are involved in profeminist activities within various Black social movements and in their workplace environments, particularly the academic world. Whatever the particular site or organization, these men tend to direct their efforts toward violence prevention and coalition politics. Their activism demonstrates the ability of Black feminist politics to create connections with and among different groups and issues, thereby fostering coalition work within and across movements for social change.

Black feminist men also grapple with shifting power imbalances in their daily lives, including their activism, and must remain vigilant in terms of how those imbalances can undermine their effectiveness. Their public activities illustrate a wide range of strategies for using feminist principles to challenge injustices. The narratives themselves are extensions of their activist work—though talking about feminism can never be a substitute for putting it into practice.

CONCLUSION

Can Black Men Really *Be Feminists?*

The Black men who contributed to this book overwhelmingly concur that feminism provides benefits in their lives that make them better people. The way they behave now, in private and in public, suggests that they really *are* feminists. Most of us can gain insights into alternative ways of being through their stories of challenge and change.

As we saw from the narratives of participants in this study, popular notions of masculinity set men against one another and against women, which inevitably leads to conflict and, all too often, violence. Almost any man can identify with the emotionally, spiritually, and even physically crippling effects of that kind of masculinity. Indeed, a system based on male domination is problematic, divisive, and self-destructive for those who seek social justice on behalf of African Americans, and for the good of society as a whole. The experiences these men recount are not entirely confined to African Americans—they occur to men in any patriarchal society, regardless of race, sexuality, or class.

In this book, I focused specifically on how African American men's varying relationships to privilege complicate their experiences of subordination, conformity, and resistance to oppressive, interlocking systems based on gender, race, economics, and culture. The degrees of patriarchal privilege among Black men serve as a microcosm of other hierarchies of power among different subgroups of men so as to reinforce the White-dominated, patriarchal, capitalist structures under which everyone in the United States lives. Black men's collusion with this system inadvertently compounds their suffering because whatever patriarchal dividend they derive from the subordination of Black women, women in general, and other subordinated men is a trade-off for their own subordination to White men.

192

How men learn to confront patriarchy and become feminists can be understood through the narratives of those who are living the experience. They can respond to patriarchy in a number of ways: acceptance, adaptation, avoidance, withdrawal, not noticing/denial, or straight-up confrontation.[1] Their feminist development appears to go through phases of progression, regression, and suppression, revealing the inherently fragile, contradictory, and context-bound aspects of their resistance and compliance. Thus, their narratives are snapshots of a particular time in their life histories. Consistent with findings from personality and narrative psychology, the stories function for each man as an act of self-discovery, reconciliation with the past, and hope for the future; they help men make sense of their lives and guide their actual behaviors and practices in the present and future. My research clearly showed that feminist Black men's narratives are not "happily ever after" stories. Their feminist identities are complex and may fluctuate with the individual's situation, social location, and expectations.

As a feminist psychologist and as a Black woman, I disliked some of the things these men did before and during the toughest periods of their feminist development, yet I found myself regarding them with compassion and respect. Their narratives give voice to alternative and oppositional ways of being men, repeatedly inviting readers to challenge their own assumptions and level of comfort with the status quo. Their stories allow us to understand how men perceive change in their lives. My findings suggest that redefining masculinity according to feminist principles means moving from self-absorption and distancing to empathy and acceptance of diversity, and from *dominance over* to *sharing responsibility with* those weaker than themselves.

In fact, feminist Black men's experiences place them in a unique position to take the lead among men during this time of gender reexamination and social awakening. Their narratives confirm that for men to counter patriarchal influences: (a) an intersectional perspective assists them in linking their fate to that of women and doing coalition work with other activists involved in social justice movements; (b) feminist or feminist-oriented women are necessary allies who are essential in men's support networks and challenge them to keep growing; (c) special attention must be given to the links among patriarchy, homophobia, and heterosexism in developing their feminist attitudes and practices, (d) vigilant self-reflection and other feminist values such as emotional openness, compassion, empathy, antiviolence, and humility must be practiced; and (e) to be seriously feminist and consistent in their practice, they must engage in both private and public acts.

Black Feminist Intersectional Politics

The notion of intersections or "intersectionality," which emphasizes how multiple and simultaneous forms of oppression in society interlock, work together, and transform one another in people's lives, is central to Black feminist theory. Black feminist thought has historically emphasized the intersection of race, class, and gender, highlighting how African American women *and* other social groups are positioned within unjust power relations. It is a mistake to think that African American men's issues can be resolved without addressing the institutional mechanisms that continue to undermine attempts at individual reform. Feminist Black men's experiences illustrate why we need to understand how combined mechanisms of institutional power mesh with personal expressions of power. Most important, the diverse practices of Black feminist activists show that "identity politics" need not be narrow, insular, divisive, essentialist, "merely" cultural (as opposed to class-related) or single-issue movements.

Gender, race, sexuality, and socioeconomic class are interpreted in this research as social structures, as well as socially constructed categories of identity. They are embedded in the individual, interactional, and institutional dimensions of our society. What happens to the individual is not merely the result of individual processes. That is, social structures or institutions shape individuals, and individuals simultaneously shape institutions through their social interactions.

For instance, although the average Black man does not have the same power as the average White man, Black men are still privileged as males in other significant ways because our society is male-dominated. Even when a Black man refuses to exercise male power within African American communities and shuns the crumbs of economic or social privilege he may be offered outside those communities, because he is male he will still retain some privilege, whether he wants it or not. He will still be a part of a subgroup of men who are valued more highly in society than the average Black woman. This is what social scientists mean by institutional versus individual dynamics. A Black man may refuse to exploit the women he knows; he may share housework, childcare, and the emotional work necessary for healthy egalitarian relationships with his partner; he may reject every aspect of what may be considered distasteful macho behavior and posturing. Yet, if he makes more money than his female coworker (and statistics suggest that he does), or is preferred over an equally qualified woman, or is seen as more credible and listened to because he is a man; if the textbook he reads in African American history class ascribes most African American achieve-

ment to men; if he can routinely walk past strangers without being whis-
tled at or propositioned, and without fearing rape; if he doesn't have to
cope with trying to get and pay for an abortion, or need never worry
about the ill effects of oral contraceptives on his body—he is still part of
a privileged group.

By sustaining patriarchal values and practices within the workplace,
churches, Black social movements, and at home, Black men can become
alienated from Black women and other Black men, thereby weakening
African American communities. Although Black men may experience
temporary satisfaction and short-term gain by dominating women, children, and anyone with less money or social standing, they hamper the
advancement of our communities in particular, and social change in general, when they mimic power relations that reinforce power *over* rather
than sharing power *with* women and other men. It is important to talk
specifically about the costs of patriarchy to men if they are ever going to
understand the benefits of feminism. Acknowledging those costs allows
them to understand their stake in creating social change. Each man must
ask, how can I change the system, as well the crippling effects of sexism,
in my everyday life?

The Influence of Feminist Women

One of my study's most robust findings is that however a man may
challenge patriarchy and other oppressive systems interlocking with it,
he needs feminist women friends to guide him.

Feminist men commonly described in their narratives the importance of their friendships with feminist women. Feminist friendship
gives men a safe place to be human (and thus vulnerable). Feminist
women frequently challenge them to live with emotional integrity,
which includes acknowledging and expressing their feelings appropriately as well as sharing equally in the emotional work of close relationships. Declaring themselves feminists does not magically inoculate men
from using sexist language or exercising male privilege. The friendships
also serve as testing grounds for alternative, nontraditional ways of being
"masculine." Relationships with a feminist woman—romantic, platonic,
or professional—pushed the participants in my study further in adult
life, by requiring them to confront and change their own sexist behavior,
conscious or not.

Because friendship requires mutual trust, friendship with feminist
women taught Black men in this study to perceive their fate as truly
linked to that of women. The feminist women in their lives have an

interest in their development; they are political allies who can offer constructive criticism and opportunities for informal and formal mentoring. Negotiating contradictions is an important part of this process. When Black men perceive their challenging experiences, especially defiance or rejection on the part of feminist women, as redeeming and ultimately positive, their commitment to feminism often deepens. Although the developmental process can be frustrating and irritating as well as ego-deflating and unflattering, feminism does not make them less of a man but more. Feminism, paradoxically, makes men whole, rather than breaking them down or emasculating them.

Patriarchy, Homophobia, Heterosexism

Heterosexist and homophobic practices reinforce stereotypes that define who is a "legitimate" or "real" man or woman, in order to keep people in their place in oppressive hierarchies. Unquestionably, being a feminist man requires taking a stand that challenges such practices. Each man in the study had to unlearn patriarchal and heterosexist assumptions, and each continues to unlearn them. Therefore, feminist men must come to grips with their homophobia—as well as the homophobia of others—if they hope to sustain their feminist commitment and challenge heterosexism systemically.

As each man's definition of masculinity changed from popular notions to radically feminist ones, his friendships with women *and* men changed. Specifically, in order to have healthy friendships with other men—including their fathers—feminist Black men had to challenge a taboo on tenderness and disdain for anything that might appear feminine or "soft." Traditional masculinity requires men to distance themselves from any behavior that suggests homosexuality; Black men, both gay and straight, who learned to ignore gay-baiting and to allow emotionally close friendships with men into their lives grew toward a feminist kind of empowerment that did not depend on domination and violence.

Instead of considering gender variance pathological and transgendered people "sick," it is the values of institutionalized heterosexism that are problematic for feminists. I found that the gay, bisexual, and transgendered men in my study seemed more adept at transforming their friendships with men than the straight men, regardless of the sexuality of their male friends. Heterosexual feminist men have to learn how to be "straight but not narrow," that is, not to care if people perceive them as gay and to accept people who are. They must be willing to expand their definitions of gender and sexuality, understanding that reevaluating those definitions promotes social justice for all.

Feminist Values in Human Development

This study aims to contribute to a sociologically oriented psychology that addresses the interplay between individual and institutional factors in identity development. Feminist values and practices that facilitate the development process of a fully human adult include humility, emotional expressiveness, empathy, and nonviolent conflict resolution. Humility is indispensable in the adult change process because, with it, one becomes teachable. It is difficult to listen to others and to learn something new if one feels one already has all the answers. Being teachable facilitates a certain openness in budding feminist men that allows them to redeem themselves and, simultaneously, convinces others that they *can* be redeemed.

Men have been taught to distance themselves emotionally from others—including their own sons—in order not to appear vulnerable or weak. Yet withholding expressions of love and emotional intimacy are forms of neglect, and the price of socializing boys this way is disconnection from themselves and other people. When, however, the fathers were nurturing in their parenting, sons could develop close relationships with them and, by extension, with other men. Unequivocally, paternal nurturing and respect for justice within the family are factors that contribute to feminist development in the lives of these Black men. In particular, feminist Black men's childcare views and practices often differ from those by which they themselves were raised. They have in common the belief that they, as men, are equally responsible for nurturing their children emotionally. They try to bring up their children supportively and fairly in ways that counter patriarchal and heterosexist beliefs; they also avoid using physical violence to discipline them.

Although social scientists are still in the early stages of understanding, empirically what constitutes a healthy attitude toward people claiming variations of gender and sexual identities, I have found that empathy, putting oneself in the place of others, is a major component. Our fate, as humans, is linked with that of others across gender, sexuality, and socioeconomic class lines. Developing empathy as an emotional practice increases the likelihood that men will connect their lives with what happens to women and other marginalized, oppressed groups in society. That facilitates compassion, which allows people to live with increased integrity and enhances sensitivity to social justice in private and in public.

Private and Public Action

Feminist men must acknowledge their reality as males in a patriarchal society by being accountable to the public world. They must recognize the need for organized collective resistance, along with working on their private lives. The connection must be made between their individual problems and the inhumanity of institutional systems that reinforce those problems. This study demonstrated how Black men's contradictory experiences of power—which include both privilege and pain—can be used to challenge other Black men's abusive use of whatever power they have as a subgroup of men.

Feminist Black men in this study were involved in a range of public activist efforts, from opposing violence against women, promoting nonsexist education, and antiracist efforts to environmentalism, human rights, and foreign policy issues. Those who had a college education, and especially those exposed to feminist literature through women's studies courses, may have had some advantage in understanding feminist theory, but many took years to bridge the gap between theory and practice. Regardless of how eloquently they wrote or talked about feminism, how they acted and how their actions affected those around them were the best indicators of the depth of their commitment.

Feminist activism takes place primarily in relationship with others, and making feminist understanding operative in one's public, political life can open up new possibilities of honest, valuable connection in Black men's personal lives as well. Both private and public acts become creative forms of resistance to the binary, divisive crippling concepts of masculinity that guarantee economic difficulties and personal failures. Despite institutional constraints, African American men can engage in collaborative efforts with women and with other activists that actually go beyond definitions of race or gender, presenting new models of personhood that are applicable to all.

Implications, Recommendations, and Limitations

Experiences these feminist Black men have endured teach many lessons about the dynamics of race, gender, sexuality, and class oppression in the United States. The study found noteworthy differences among participants in terms of their feminist sensibilities, the manner in which they came into feminism, and even the narrative style of their stories. Still, a number of striking similarities emerge. While most of the men in my study came from the Black middle class, roughly half did not grow up in middle-class homes, and not all who did were insulated by their socioeconomic status from the effects of individual or systemic racism and sexism. All chose to reject the notions of masculinity that prevail in the larger society; many understood that to challenge an oppressive society, one must challenge all forms of oppression. These commonalities provide a compelling rationale for redefining masculinity in feminist ways.

Collectively, the narratives afford important insights into the quality and range of Black feminist practices. Together they give us a more complex appreciation not only of feminism but also of the efforts of individual feminist men. Their narratives demystify the processes by which African American feminist men move from theory into practice. Black feminist men apply strategies of resistance that might easily be applied to readers' own lives.

A multipronged approach to widespread social change goes beyond creating material opportunities for individual African American boys and men; it aims to undermine the interlocking institutional effects of patriarchy, racial discrimination, and market-driven economic policies. I offer the following recommendations, based on the strategies of feminist Black men.

1. Join women in feminist movement—as active agents and supporters, not merely behind the scenes—rather than create a separate men's movement. Since patriarchy is itself the original men's movement, the struggle to overthrow it must involve men as well as women.

2. Promote and teach feminist family values: humility, emotional openness, empathy, nurturing, dialogue, accountability, mutuality, power sharing, and nonviolence in and outside the home.

3. Support gender-neutral activities and a women's studies curriculum earlier in the educational process, including preschool, elementary grades, and high school, rather than starting at the college level when relationship habits and social prejudices have already formed.

4. Develop further a discipline of Black feminist masculinities studies that researches, teaches, and cultivates images of Black men beyond "dangerous," "endangered," and "patriarchal." Instead of refashioning and repackaging

White-dominated patriarchy for Black men, analyze the experiences of Black men under patriarchy, so as to challenge its assumptions and practices for *all* men.

5. Engage in coalition politics that bring a Black feminist focus to multiissue organizing in such areas as labor unions, election campaigns, community services, and public safety.

6. Develop community mentoring and awareness campaigns that emphasize Black feminist values, practices, and politics through churches, clubs, prison programs, youth groups, and the performing arts.

7. Encourage Black public figures (politicians, rap artists and musicians, movie stars, sports stars) to address intersectional issues in their speeches, artistry, and public information announcements.

8. Continue pressuring mainstream feminist organizations and their members to incorporate an intersectional analysis in their work and to cite the works of Black feminists and other women of color who laid the foundation for that analysis and applied it in practice.

9. Accept diverse gender identities and sexualities, and promote the civil and human rights of the people who claim them, as an essential practice of ethical social justice.

Before concluding, I must honestly acknowledge the limitations of my study. Though the men in it were deliberately chosen because they are atypical of contemporary male African Americans, the exclusivity of the sample, particularly their high education level, cannot be ignored. I have not collected the experiences of less educated, working-class Black men who may have adopted a feminist approach to masculinity. The university context exposes men to feminist courses, feminist friendships, and feminist mentoring in ways that other contexts do not. Hence, it is important for feminist education to start earlier than the college level as a counterweight to prevailing models of masculinity, relationship, family, and community behavior. The sample of men I chose to interview is also small, limiting the generalizability of some of my findings. However, the reader can have confidence that my findings are consistent with previous feminist, personality, and social movement research that incorporated larger samples.

Limitations notwithstanding, given the absence of *any* empirical research on Black feminist men, the value of this project is the in-depth analysis that it provides as a springboard for subsequent studies exploring the range of positive, African American feminist masculinities. I could not have done it without several postdoctoral fellowships and grants (see Acknowledgments). More funding is needed for social science research that goes beyond documenting the devastating effects of interlocking oppressive systems on Black men; we also need to document and publicly applaud those who manage to defy the odds.

Through the narratives of the Black men who contributed to this book, we come to understand, as they did, that a feminist is not just someone you are automatically; it is a type of person one must continuously become. Their practices help to define what it means to be a feminist and an ethical human being. Their contributions to the feminist fight for social justice will ultimately improve the lives of all.

Appendix A

Methodological Intersections
and Considerations

In this study of feminist Black men, I have used qualitative research strategies; regarding the quantitative findings underlying the study, I direct the reader to other sources.[1] A rigid reliance on the use of quantitative methods within a positivist framework would have seriously limited the relevance, usefulness, and theoretical sophistication of my research, given the questions I am asking. One goal of this research is to demonstrate how narrative methods and personality theories can be combined with sociological and feminist perspectives in ways that increase our understanding of processes of personal and social transformation. For practical reasons, I incorporated a semistructured interview format for data collection. Interview data were analyzed in order to explore interrelated (motivational, cognitive, emotional, and interpersonal) processes that occur in a person's life story and either facilitate or inhibit perceptions of change. Interviews also allowed me to gather details about the range of public and private political actions feminist Black men had taken, as well as the feelings and subjective meanings they attributed to those actions. Those processes are difficult to capture in questionnaire data.

Given the semistructured nature of the interview and the latitude the participants were given to rephrase, reinterpret, and actively redefine questions in light of their perceived experiences, their responses often covered a broader range of topics than the ones specific questions were designed to elicit. Therefore, the actual questions and the men's responses to them do not offer a neatly predetermined, one-to-one correspondence. For that reason, I used a combination of grounded theory and narrative analysis to analyze the data. A grounded theory approach entails using "a systematic set of procedures to develop an inductively derived theory" about the responses.[2] Researchers systematically read the interview transcripts and code them, using descriptive terms that are drawn from the text. Coding is guided by the researcher's interests in the subject matter, allowing identification of categories within and across interview data, which then enables the researcher to develop theoretical concepts. This approach allows me to explore how narrative information adds to our understanding of the lives of feminist Black men and to demonstrate the degree to which the individual cases have general social significance. However, that strategy carries both an advantage and a disadvantage. Although categorizing the interview data allows development of general, theoretical concepts, this process also fragments and compartmentalizes the information by rearranging it into separate categories, thus removing some of the context.[3]

Narrative analysis, in contrast, is a contextualizing process for evaluating chunks of text that include a coherent story with a beginning, middle, and end.[4] This strategy also entails an advantage and a disadvantage. Although narrative analysis enables researchers to examine the text in its original context, the result is often highly individualized accounts from which it can be difficult to develop general theories.[5] Some researchers have found a way to combine grounded theoretical and narrative analytical approaches in order to negotiate the strengths and weaknesses of both.[6] By integrating the two approaches, categorization and contextualization serve as complementary processes for interpreting interview data.

In addition to coding interview texts, I also identify and analyze particular narratives that exemplified key aspects of and events regarding feminist identity development among African American men. The condensed narratives highlight the voices and subjective life experiences of Black men whose feminist lifestyles have generally been ignored, and even denied, by the media and the social sciences. Given the absence of any social science research on feminist Black men, the study is less concerned with empirical generalization at this stage and more concerned with theoretical inferences from the data. Also, because the purposes of this investigation were exploratory narrative analytical description and grounded theory construction, rather than positivistic theory testing, it was not appropriate to include life histories of a comparative group of

nonfeminist or antifeminist men. Nor was it necessary to verify or trian-
gulate the men's stories by checking with their significant others or additional characters mentioned in their narratives because the emphasis was
on how the men's own subjective viewpoints help them make sense of
their lives.[7] Although this particular methodological approach limits the
generalizability of the study's findings, the value of the project is not
dependent solely on its generalizability but, rather, on its conceptual creativity and corresponding critical analyses, compared to findings from
other literatures in personality psychology, critical sociology, African
American studies, and gender studies.

Research Procedures

Recruitment. Black men who consider themselves advocates of feminism
do not belong to any formal organization with that title. Therefore, to
recruit men for this project, I sent out many flyers announcing my interest in surveying Black men who describe themselves as "antisexist,"
"profeminist," and/or "feminist." I targeted (1) national and locally
based profeminist men's organizations (e.g., the National Organization
for Men Against Sexism, the Oakland Men's Project, and D.C. Men
Against Rape), (2) Black organizations that espouse feminist-oriented
perspectives (e.g., the Black Radical Congress, Black Workers for
Justice, and the Organization for Black Struggle), and (3) individual
Black feminist men recommended to me by Black feminist women participating in a concurrent study. I also sent an e-mail version of the flyer
to thirty profeminist men's Web sites, ten progressive Black organizations that had Web sites, a Black feminist listserv, and a Black gay and
lesbian listserv.[8]

Seventy-seven men requested questionnaire packets, and fifty of
those returned completed packets. Questionnaires asked participants
about their social values, cultural and gender attitudes, sexual preference
and orientation, global self-esteem, activist experiences, political self-
efficacy, age, family status (partners, children), educational background,
and income classification. Findings from the questionnaire data have
been published elsewhere.[9]

Half of the men (25) were invited to participate in an in-depth life
history interview. To be interviewed, each man had to have participated
in a public form of feminist activism and been recommended by an
African American feminist woman. The two criteria made it possible to
know that each man had engaged in observable forms of behavior that
Black feminist women could judge as being appropriately feminist.
Having a Black feminist woman characterize a particular man as an

advocate for feminism increased the trustworthiness of the data because at least two people (the man himself and a feminist woman) could agree that the man was antisexist, profeminist, or feminist. Having a feminist woman, rather than a woman who does not self-identify as a feminist, judge his behavior also increased the trustworthiness of the data because feminist women are more likely than nonfeminist women to have critical, in depth understanding of what constitutes feminist attitudes and behavior. As one Black woman stated when recommending a study participant via e-mail, "he is not pro-feminist simply because he washes the dishes and 'baby-sits' his kids...he is pro-feminist because he consistently puts his reputation on the line by engaging in public acts that dismantle institutionalized male power and private acts that show he knows how to treat people." I also intentionally avoided including participants who were well known at the national level. High-profile Black men live exceptional lives; I was looking for a more common, everyday experience of the Black man who supports feminism.

Initially, I contacted all twenty-five men informally by telephone, verifying their self-perceptions as antisexist, profeminist, or feminist. Then I arranged for them to have individual interviews with an African American male psychologist who had participated in antisexist focus groups for antirape activists, related to a previous study. I chose a Black man with clinical interviewing skills in order to encourage the participants to speak freely about their experiences, without inhibiting their language and imagery. Halfway through the study, however, one man requested that I interview him myself because he felt more comfortable being interviewed by a Black feminist woman. His request prompted me to offer men a choice of a male or female interviewer thereafter. Eight of the ten men given that choice had no preference regarding the sex of the interviewer and were scheduled with the male interviewer. However, I interviewed one of the eight because the male interviewer was unable to do it. I also interviewed one of the two who requested a female interviewer. Finally, I interviewed the one transgendered man because I had already established a healthy rapport with him in previous social and professional interactions.[10] I was unable to accommodate a fourth man because of scheduling constraints.[11] In order to encourage full self-disclosure, I ensured confidentiality by changing the subjects' names and the names of people mentioned in their narratives, even though nearly all the men granted permission to use their real names.[12]

Face-to-face, semistructured life narrative interviews were the method of inquiry for this phase of the project. The male interviewer and I traveled to the participant's location or paid for the participant to fly to ours. Interview questions were open-ended, targeting twenty-five topics that covered experiences from childhood through adulthood. These experiences included (a) relationships with family, peers, and intimate partners; (b) formal and informal educational experiences, (c) work history and related experiences, (d) spirituality and religious background, and (e) attitudes and activist experiences concerning reproductive freedom, gender roles, sexuality, sports, and violence against women (see Appendix B for complete category list). The interview categories were based on (1) findings from two focus groups with Black feminist men who did not participate in this study but who had participated in a previous study that I conducted with African American anti-rape activists, (2) autobiographical writings by men active in the feminist movement, and (3) the two previous pieces of published research on feminist men.[13]

Participants were encouraged to reinterpret, rephrase, and redefine questions and topics in the light of their life experiences. Thus, prepared questions and topics were adapted according to the evolving themes of inquiry. The interviewer tried to discover which questions or issues were important to the participant and allow the participant's answers to shape the direction of the questions. Participants took an active role in the interview.

The average interview was conducted in one session, lasting approximately four hours. The shortest interview was three and a half hours, and the longest ten hours. Each participant was paid $50. We were able to schedule and interview twenty of the twenty-five men invited (see Table 2.1 for a list of participants).[14]

Post-interview follow-ups and coding procedures. I transcribed all of the audiotapes and conducted post-interview follow-ups over the telephone with all the men in order to clarify interview content. In their post-interview follow-ups, many participants described the interview experience as "therapeutic," "cathartic," and "validating." However, some men told me that parts of the interview (e.g., family background, relationships with women, experiences with violence as perpetrator or victim) were emotionally exhausting and triggered feelings of fear, anger, and sadness. Others reported that certain aspects of the interview (e.g., attitudes toward marriage, reproductive freedom, gender roles, sexual diversity) were politically engaging and stimulated ongoing reflection. One participant commented that the interview helped him clarify some things he needed to discuss with his son. Another said the interview stirred things up in him that he considered discussing with a therapist. Nine of the men's audiotaped voices expressed deep sorrow and anger at certain points in the interview, particularly during the painful recall of events that had significantly shaped their feminist outlook.

The male interviewer and I, who both had clinical training and experience, attempted to create an atmosphere of acceptance and positive regard before, during, and after the interview. We made ourselves available to interviewees after the interview. I made a follow-up call and sent a follow-up letter to each interviewee, thanking him for his participation and asking whether he had any questions or afterthoughts about the interview. Each man was sent a printed copy of his transcript and audiocassette copies of his interview.

After the audiotapes were transcribed and post-interview follow-up calls had been made, the evaluation of the interview responses occurred in four major phases: (1) developing of a coding system; (2) training coders, assessing interrater reliability among coders, and revising the coding system; (3) coding the interviews; and (4) assessing simple response frequencies. A research assistant and I read all twenty transcripts and formulated an initial set of response categories from those that emerged from the data. We added these data-driven categories to the preexisting theoretical categories we had created for each question or set of questions in the interview protocol. In this phase we wanted to let the categories emerge from the data as well as to impose some structure derived from theoretical perspectives.

After identifying an initial set of categories, we constructed a coding manual that provided precise category definitions as well as examples. Three coders were trained in the use of the coding system, and their independent assessment of a subset of the interviews was used to evaluate the quality of the initial set of response categories. I assessed agreement in classification by using Cohen's Kappa, with lower interrater reliability as an indication for revision of the coding system (kappa < 0.80).[15] Some necessary revisions involved the refinement of certain category definitions, the addition of new response categories, and the merging of some existing categories. The revision of the coding system continued until acceptable interrater reliability was reached (kappa > 0.80).

After we had constructed a reliable coding system, two new coders independently coded all the interviews. This process allowed a full-sample check on the reliability of the coding system. I settled any coding disagreements myself. After all interviews were coded, I assessed the simple response frequencies. The quantitative results of the content analysis are published elsewhere, but some of the findings, when relevant, are dispersed throughout the chapters.[16]

Editing procedures. Because the interview transcripts ranged from 100 to 250 double-spaced pages for each man, I have had to use excerpts from the interviews presented. The passages I chose to include and omit reflect what I thought important to the purpose of the book. These decisions were filtered through my theoretical lens. Accordingly, the narrative excerpts presented here do not include all topics discussed in the interviews. The topics included reflect the themes related to the book's emphasis, rather than all the components of a feminist man's life that may be important to him.

I have included material that characterizes each man as an individual, as well as material that highlights his similarities with the other men. Some of the narrative excerpts were chosen to facilitate my accompanying analysis of how dominant societal structures interact with various practices of masculinity. Sometimes, narrative sequences are rearranged in chronological order to highlight critical events that were turning points, or related to the turning points, in each man's feminist development.

Some qualitative researchers, such as discourse analysts, have compelling reasons for capturing and reporting every phrase spoken in interviews by both interviewer and interviewee. However, my analytical emphasis was on themes and *what* was said, rather than the exact form of *how* it was said. I have edited narratives lightly for readability, unless the person's usage communicated something significant about a particular topic or point. For example, it was not in line with the purpose of my research to include (1) a person's "um-hums," "you knows," sighs, pauses, or redundant statements; (2) the interviewer's questions or comments ("What motivated you to take a women's studies course?"); or (3) any procedural points ("We can take a break here or discuss a different subtopic"). Like previous qualitative researchers who employ this "smoothing process" when presenting interview material, I viewed these details as distractions that would unnecessarily burden readers.[17] One can edit for readability and simultaneously maintain the interview's authenticity by leaving the interviewee's style and richness of speech ("voice") intact. Therefore, apart from the aforementioned changes, the narrative excerpts presented here are faithful to the original interviews in content and wording. The men themselves might not have chosen all of the passages I selected, but I honored any promise not to include whatever information they had declared off the record before, during, and after the interviews. Qualitative researchers are often criticized for paraphrasing narratives too much and, consequently, for not providing enough textual evidence for the themes they discuss, so I made every effort to be sensitive to this risk.

Appendix B

Interview Categories

Questions covering participants' life experiences were based on the following topics:

1. Personal definition of feminism and self-definition regarding preferred feminist terminology: antisexist, profeminist, or feminist label preferred.

2. Personal ideas about what factors shaped the participants' feminist outlook and practices.

3. Family background.

4. Friendships during childhood and adulthood.

5. School-related experiences (elementary and high school).

6. Higher education or other formal professional, adult education experiences.

7. Religious and/or spiritual values and practices.

8. Work-related experiences.

9. Political organization involvement or exposure to leftist politics.

10. Women's movement exposure or experiences regarding exposure to feminist ideology.

11. Other gender-related, social, or professional groups and their impact.

12. Attitudes regarding nonromantic relationships and related experiences with women.

13. Attitudes regarding romantic relationships and related experiences with women.

14. Attitudes regarding nonromantic relationships and related experiences with men.

15. Attitudes regarding romantic relationships and related experiences with men.

16. Attitudes regarding sexual identity and orientation (lesbian, gay, bisexual, and transgendered) issues.

17. Attitudes regarding gender roles and experiences.

18. Attitudes regarding reproductive rights of women and experiences in this area.

19. Attitudes regarding childrearing.

20. Attitudes regarding violence against women and related experiences.

21. Attitudes toward the sex industry.

22. Recreational activities.

23. Experiences with oppression and related social injustices.

24. Personal contradictions.

25. Feminist activism and vision for society.

APPENDIX C

Historical and Contemporary Usage of the Terms "Feminist" and "Womanist"

The term feminism has never been widely popular in society in general and Africana studies in particular. Yet, the political goals of feminism have survived—despite continuing discomfort with the term. Many scholars in Africana studies as well as women's studies are unaware that the term "womanism" was originally used by European women and appeared in the *Oxford English Dictionary* as a nineteenth-century term for "advocacy of women's rights; enthusiasm for women's achievements, abilities, and qualities, the belief in women's superiority to men; and, any positive, pro-woman stance."[1]

The term "feminism" replaced the use of womanism in the 1890s and is credited with being coined by Hubertine Auclert, the organizer of the first female suffrage society in France who combined the French word for woman, *femme*, with *-isme*, which referred to a social movement or political ideology.[2] At a time when many other "isms" originated, including socialism and communism, *feminisme* connoted that women's issues belonged to the vanguard of change. The term was always controversial, in part, because of its association with radicalism and in part because proponents themselves disagreed about the label.[3]

Today, feminist activists have modified and redefined the term to
make it compatible with their unique perspectives; hence terms like
Black feminist, socialist feminist, and ecofeminist. Also, womanism and
womanist have been revived, redefined, and popularized by Alice
Walker (Walker uses the terms "Black feminist" and "womanist" interchangeably in her writings),[4] Clenora Hudson-Weems,[5] and certain
African American theologians (e.g., Katie Cannon[6]) as a culture-specific
and poetic synonym for Black feminist, a feminist woman of color,
and/or a woman who approaches gender issues from African-centered
or particular Black nationalist perspectives. In some cases, the term
"womanist" is used by women to emphasize their heterosexual identity
(and its associated privileges in a homophobic and heterosexist society),
given the association of the term "feminist" with lesbian sexuality.

Language is dynamic and both terms demonstrate the complexities
of particular contexts and the right/self-determination of different
groups of women and men to define and link themselves to a variety of
movements that support gender equity and justice. Of note, however, is
the fact that the term "feminist" is used most commonly in the international context when referring to the global women's movement.

Thus, feminist has been used throughout this text in order to (1)
connect the activism of Black men to a larger global context, (2) challenge homophobia/heterosexism, and (3) contest the cultural appropria-
tion of the term by white middle-class feminist women by
acknowledging, reclaiming, and honoring the historical involvement of
African American women *and* men in every wave (first, second, and
third) of feminism in U.S. history.

NOTES

Preface. Can Black Men Be Feminists? From Healthy Doubt to Critical Acceptance

1. Marecek, Fine, and Kidder 2001; Tappan 2001; Tolman and Brydon-Miller 2001.

2. Tolman and Brydon-Miller 2001.

3. My thinking on this issue has also been greatly influenced by the writings of bell hooks 1984, 1989, 1990, 1992a, 1992b, 2000a.

4. Langellier and Hall 1989, 201.

Introduction. The Patriarchal Predicament

1. The use of racial terminology in this book in no way supports biological, deterministic definitions of race. I accept social constructionist perspectives regarding the historic use of racial terminology, the shifting meaning of race, and the role that politics and ideology play in shaping such meanings. Although I view race, gender, sexuality, and class as social constructs, for primarily political reasons, I use these terms to identify people in this book. However, I do not uncritically accept the checklist approach of government ("pick one and only one category") or the way in which our society narrowly forces people into certain "boxes." People may have simultaneous identities, and the intersections of these identities are inadequately captured by a single descriptor or the descriptors commonly used. I also believe, however, that for oppressed groups, some forms of identity politics have their time, place, and utility. Given these competing realities, I have included narratives that underscore the arbitrary and permeable nature of these constructs, and I respect how the men in the study use these terms. For instance, I include men who identify as "Black" in addition to other racial and ethnic categories (such as West Indian, Latino, or Native American) and consider themselves as belonging to more than one ethnic group. Thus, "African American" in this study defines a man who accepts that he is of African

descent, is willing to refer to himself as Black, and who was raised in the United States or who has lived in the United States for at least fifteen consecutive years.

2. Ducat 2004; Gavanas 2004; Ingram 2004; Malin 2005; Moore 2001; Pope, Phillips, and Olivardia 2000; Robinson 2000; Segell 2000; Whannel 2001.

3. The term "girly/girlie men" was popularized initially by a *Saturday Night Live* sketch about two bodybuilders who used the term to deride men who were not as bulked up as they were (even though their "bulk" was due to padding underneath sweatshirts and sweatpants). The term took on new life following California Governor Arnold Schwarzenegger's usage to characterize his political opponents. Schwarzenegger received criticism from various gay rights and feminist groups. See http://en.wikipedia.org/widi/Girlie_men.

4. Cited in Gardiner 2002, 14. Original quote from Coontz 1992.

5. Connell 1995; Gardiner 2002; Kaufman 1994; Segal 1999.

6. Connell 1995; Kaufman, 1994; Segal, 1990, 1999.

7. See Segal 1999 for a feminist perspective on "the masculinity crisis" and the following publications for antifeminist perspectives: O'Beirne 2006; Schlafly 2003; Sommers 2001.

8. Franklin 2001; Mincy 2006; Oliver and Shapiro 1995; Porter 2001; Washington 1996; Williams 2004.

9. Connell 1987; Lorber 2000; Martin 2004; Risman 2004.

10. Connell 1995.

11. Connell 1995.

12. Belton 1995; Boykin 2005; Cheney 2005; Connor 2003; Estes 2006; Franklin 2002; Gates 1997; Nandi 2002; Summers 2004.

13. Collins 1998; hooks 1992b; Lemons 1998.

14. Some men who are against sexism prefer the term "antisexist." Others prefer the term "profeminist" because they want to affirm a positive identity that reflects what they stand for, as opposed to defining themselves exclusively by what they are against. Men who prefer to be called "feminist" view the term "profeminist" as still distancing them from the strongest possible support for feminism. Some activists use all three terms interchangeably. I have used all three terms to describe men who support feminism; however, I believe that men, especially Black men, should be encouraged to use the term feminist. I argue for its usage, as well as reviewing arguments against such usage, in White, 2001/2002. For other views on men using feminist terminology, see Brod 1998; Hopkins 1998; Kimmel 1998.

15. Byrd and Guy-Sheftall 2001.

16. Byrd and Guy-Sheftall 2001; Kimmel and Mosmiller 1992; Terborg-Penn 1997.

17. See Collins 2004 (sociology); Crenshaw 1989, 1991 (law); McClaurin 2001 (anthropology); Simien 2006 (political science); Stewart and McDermott 2004 (psychology) and the next chapter for details regarding intersectionality and its application in the humanities and social sciences.

18. Abalos 2002; Byrd and Guy-Sheftall 2001; Digby 1998; Kimmel and Mosmiller 1992; Murphy 2004; Neal 2005; Schacht and Ewing 1998.

19. Authors like Bly 1990 and Sommers 2001.

20. I agree with Weis, Fine, Weseen, and Wong 2000 that researchers publishing work in the interest of social justice must refrain from camouflaging or romanticizing the rough spots that reveal how our narrators may have been damaged by "advanced capitalism, racist social relations, violent gendered relations, and homophobic community life" (62–63). Our job is to demonstrate how people survive and thrive amid "the damage and the oppressive social/economic relations" without denying any of these phenomena as we "re-imagine what can be."

Chapter 1. Critical Black Feminist Intersections: Framing the Issues

1. *Webster's New Collegiate Dictionary* 1979, 599.

2. Combahee River Collective 1983. The actual term "intersectionality" was popularized by Black feminist legal scholar Kimberle Crenshaw 1989, 1991.

3. Cohen 1999; Cohen, Jones, and Tronto 1997; Collins 2004; Crenshaw 1991; Fine and Weis 1998; Hurtado 1996, 2003; McCall 2005; McClaurin 2001; Simien 2006; Spelman 1988; Springer 1999.

4. Stewart and McDermott 2004, 531–532.

5. Collins 1998, xiv.

6. Collins 1998, xiv.

7. For an overview of critical psychological perspectives see Fox and Prilleltensky 1997; Henriques, Hollway, Urwin, Venn, and Walkerdine 1998; Sloan 2000; Sullivan 1984; Tolman and Maiers 1991; Walkerdine 2001.

8. Although critical psychologies often overlap, for examples of Afrocentric critical psychologies see Akbar 1984; Baldwin 1992; White, Potgieter, Strube, Fisher, and Umana 1997; for feminist critical psychologies see Burman 1998; Fine 1992; Mama 1995; for Latino/Latina critical psychologies see Hurtado 2003; Martin-Baro 1994; for Marxist critical psychologies see Parker and Spears 1996; Tolman 1994; and for queer critical psychologies see Russell 2000.

9. For different critical perspectives on objectivity, subjectivity, and biases in psychology, see Akbar 1991; Banks 1991; Danziger 1990; Daston and Galison 1992; Fine and Vanderslice 1992; Gordon, Miller, and Rollock 1990; Guthrie 1997; Holzkamp 1992; Tolman 1991.

10. Fine and Vanderslice 1992, 203.

11. Fine and Vanderslice 1992, 202

12. Fine and Vanderslice 1992, 202.

13. Fine and Vanderslice 1992, 202.

14. Fine and Vanderslice 1992, 202.

15. Connell 1995; Fine and Weis 1998; Hurtado 1996, 2003; Lorber 2000; Martin 2004; Risman 2004; Segal 1990, 1999; Stewart and McDermott 2004.

16. For an overview see Christian 1994; Gardiner 2002; Kaufman 1994; Kimmel 1996; Segal 1990.

17. McAdams 1993, 1994.

18. McAdams 1994, 306.

19. McAdams 1994, 306–307.

20. McAdams 1994, 307.

21. McAdams 1994, 307.

22. Stryker 2000, 27.

23. Stryker 2000, 33–35.

24. Fivush and Haden 2003; Langellier 2001; Mishler 1999; Stryker, Owens, and White 2000.

25. Erikson 1963.

26. Langellier 2001, 30–31.

27. Mishler 1999, 16–20.

28. Heatherton and Nichols 1994; Mishler 1999; Rosenwald and Ochberg 1992.

29. Baumeister 1994; DiClemente 1994; Heatherton and Nichols 1994.

30. Heatherton and Nichols 1994, 11.

31. Baumeister 1994; DiClemente 1994; Heatherton and Nichols 1994.

32. Baumeister 1994; DiClemente 1994; Heatherton and Nichols 1994.

33. Collins 1998, see 8-10 for additional explanations.

34. Collins 1998, see 201-208 for additional explanations.

35. Collins 1998.

36. For examples of Black nationalist feminism see Cleage 1993; for Black Marxist and revolutionary Black feminism see and Hamer and Neville 1998 and

Kelley 2002; for Black liberal feminism see Davis 1988; and for Black lesbian feminism see Abdulahad, Rogers, Smith. and Waheed 1983 and Smith 1998.

37. See hooks 2000b.

38. Gardiner 2002; Kimmel, Hearn, and Connell 2005; Murphy 2004; Mutua 2006.

39 Kimmel 2002, ix

40. Gardiner 2002, 11.

41. Connell 1995; Gardiner 2002; Kaufman 1994; Kimmel 2002.

42. Gardiner 2002, 12.

43. Gardiner 2002, 1.

44. Gardiner 2002, 1.

45. Christian 1994; Kimmel 1998; Schacht and Ewing 1998; Segal 1990

46. Lorber 2000; Risman 1998; Stoltenberg 1989, 1993.

47. Brod 1998; Gardiner 2002; Kaufman 1994; Kimmel 1998.

48. For example, Ferguson 2000; Mincy 2006; Oliver 1998; Reese 2004.

49. Carbado 1999a; Collins 2004; D'Emilio 2003; Hopkinson and Moore 2006; Mutua 2006; Newton 2005; Summers 2004.

50. For documentation of Black men's historical involvement in each wave of feminism, see Byrd and Guy-Sheftall 2001; Lemons 1998; Kimmel and Mosmiller 1992; Terborg-Penn 1997. For contemporary arguments by feminists who contest the historical concept of feminist waves, see Hogeland 2001 and Springer 2002.

51. Christian 1994; Newton and Stacey 1997; Shiffman 1987.

52. Beam 1986a, 1986b; Dyson 2001; Hernton 1986; Lemons 1998; Marable 1983; Neal 2005; Powell 2000; Tate 1986.

53. Awkward 1996, 2002; Beam 1986a, 1986b; Carbado 1999b; Farajaje-Jones 1993; Hernton 1990; Lemons 1998; Marable 1983; Neal 2005; Salaam 1980, 1994a, 1994b, 1996.

54. Bell 1994.

55. Bell 1986; Gordon 1993.

56. Atlanta Committee for Black Liberation 1996; Harris 1999; Neal 2005.

57. Madhubuti 1994; Neal 2005; Salaam 1980.

58. Beam 1986a, 1986b; Carbado 1999a, 1999b; Farajaje-Jones 1993; Hemphill 1992; Neal 2005; Salaam 1994b.

59. Beam 1986a, 1986b; Farajaje-Jones 1993; Hemphill 1992.

60. Segal 1999, 159.

Chapter 2. Biographical Sketches: The Sons of Sojourner Truth

1. Painter 1993, 1172–1176.

2. Stanton 1969, 193.

3. Simien 2006, 43-44.

4. Simien 2006, 43-44.

5. Simien 2006, 44.

6. See White 2006a for survey data and results and Appendix A for how the men were chosen.

Chapter 3. Pawns and Patriarchs: Challenging Assumptions About Power

1. See Smitherman 1996 for one argument along such lines.

2. Dawson 2001; Simien 2006; White 2006a.

3. Simien 2006, 122.

4. Simien 2006, 122.

5. Simien 2006, 122.

6. Connell 1995, 79.

7. Sociologist Connell (1995, 76–77) describes power and masculinity by borrowing a theoretical framework of hegemony from Marxist thinker Antonio Gramsci's theory of how a ruling group wields power. "Hegemonic masculinity" describes the dominant ideas of manhood that hold the greatest cultural value during a particular historical period that become accepted as the norm. At the risk of oversimplifying the concept, I will use the term "dominant masculinity" rather than "hegemonic masculinity" which is more lay accessible.

8. For recent empirical data suggesting that Black men are equally, and in some cases more likely, to support Black feminist attitudes than Black women see Simien 2006.

9. Fox-Genovese and Genovese 2005.

10. See Chapman 1995.

11. Chapman 1995; Cone and Wilmore 1993.

12. Cole and Guy-Sheftall 2003; Collins 2004; Harris 1999; Simien 2006; E. F. White 2001.

13. Williams 1993.

14. Grant 1993.

15. Cannon 1995.

16. Chapman 1995; Grant 1993; Harris 1999.

17. Grant 1993, 337.

18. Grant 1993, 329.

19. Grant 1993, 328.

20. See Chapman, 1995, 135–167, for a feminist Black man's scholarly critique of sexism in the Black church.

21. Chapman 1995.

22. Harris 1999 quoted in Simien 2006.

23. Beale 1979; Brown Douglas 1993; Carroll 1982.

24. hooks 1984.

25. Frank 1985, 205.

26. Smethhurst 2005, 89.

27. Smethurst notes, "the Black Arts and Black Power movements were among the very few organizational and ideological spaces of that era in the United States, outside of the organized Left and the reemerging feminist movement, where one could effectively raise the issue of male supremacy and gender oppression—and sometimes Black Power and Black Arts groups would form committees or other institutional structures to address these concerns" (2005, 89).

28. D'Emilio 2003, 98.

29. Solomon's narrative excerpt refers to the following famous Black men. James Baldwin was an African American essayist and novelist (1924–1987) who spent much of his adult life in France as a result of racism in the United States. Langston Hughes, Alain Locke, and Countee Cullen were African American men who were Harlem renaissance writers.

30. Simien 2006.

31. Simien 2006.

32. L. Harris 1999a, 58, Iverson 1996; Salaam 1996.

33. Atlanta Committee for Black Liberation 1996; Men Stopping Violence 1996.

34. Atlanta Committee for Black Liberation 1996.

35. Atlanta Committee for Black Liberation 1996, 269.

36. Atlanta Committee for Black Liberation 1996, 268.

37. L. Harris 1999, 60–61.

38. L. Harris 1999, 61–62.

39. L. Harris 1999, 62.

40. Subtitle taken from the name of an essay in Lorde 1984, 10.

41. For an overview on how feminist discuss "middle-class politics of respectability" see Collins 2004 and E. F. White 2001.

42. Collins 2004; Roberts 1998; E. F. White 2001.

43. E. F. White 2001.

44. White, Potgieter, Strube, Fisher, and Umana 1997; E. F. White 2001; T'Shaka 1995.

45. E. F. White 2001, 43.

46. Richie 1994; Segal 1990; West 2002.

47. hooks 1984, 73.

48. hooks 1984, 207.

49. hooks 1984, 236.

50. Kimbrell 1995.

51. Mauer 2001, 49.

52. Messerschmidt 2001.

53. Trauma, as defined here, can be actively physically or passively caused through a violent *lack*—the absence of nurture and responsibilities normally expected of a caregiver (Real 1997, 107).

54. Real 1997, 36–37.

55. Luck, Bamford, and Williamson 2000; Sabo and Gordon 1995.

56. Silverstein and Auerbach 1999.

57. Patterson 1992; Silverstein and Auerbach 1999; Snarey 1993.

58. Patterson 1992; Silverstein and Auerbach 1999; Snarey 1993.

59. Silverstein and Auerbach 1999.

60. For current research on the effectiveness of these agencies, see Babcock, Green, and Robie 2004; for a list of profeminist men's organizations in the United States that work with men who batter see http://www.feminist.com/resources/links/links_men.html.

61. Abul, Cudjoe, and Ralph came from mixed homes in the sense that they began with two parents until around adolescence, then a parent died (Abdul) or the parents divorced (Cudjoe and Ralph).

62. Hamberger and Guse 2002; Morse 1995; Swan and Snow 2006.

63. For instance, Swan and Snow found that women in their study used equivalent levels of emotional/or verbal abuse (e.g., yelling and screaming, name calling) as their partners used against them. Women also committed significantly more moderate physical violence (e.g., throwing something, pushing, and/or shoving) than their partners used against them. However, women were more often the victims of serious types of abuse (e.g., sexual coercion, physical injuries, and restricting social contact). When women are clearly identified as the "primary aggressors" against their male partners by the police and the courts, these women are more likely to (a) believe that violence is an effective way of resolving conflict, (b) feel trapped due to their economic dependency on their male partners, (c) feel obligated to keep the family together due to cultural and religious beliefs, and (d) believe the use of violence is their right given the verbal abuse and other forms of humiliation they perceive as perpetrated by their male partners (2006).

64. Purvis and Ward 2006.

65. Several feminist perspectives exist on child sexual abuse. Most theories regarding child sexual abuse focus exclusively on the psychological features of individual offenders. However, feminist scholars have been able to make a link between culture and behavior by analyzing the institutional and social processes that influence what we think and what we do as gendered beings. Feminist perspectives are rarely discussed or published in mainstream psychological journals and may be unfamiliar to researchers and clinicians working within the field because such theories are useful in justifying and establishing social policies aimed at preventing sexual abuse of children; however, they offer little guidance in the treatment of individual offenders. See Purvis and Ward 2005 for a review.

66. Ehrmin 1996, 256.

67. Marshall, Hudson, Jones, and Fernandez 1995.

68. Cossins 2000, 111.

69. Cossins 2000, 126–127.

70. Cossins 2000, 129.

71. Baldwin 1985, xi.

72. hooks 1984, 76.

73. Daly 1987; hooks 1984.

Chapter 4. Turning Points: The Need and Willingness to Change

1. McAdams and Bowman 2001, 28.

2. McAdams and Bowman 2001, 28.

3. Rosenwald and Ochberg 1992.

4. McAdams and Bowman 2001, 28.

5. Baumeister 1994; McAdams and Bowman 2001.

6. McAdams and Bowman 2001, 5.

7. Ideas on redemption and contamination sequences in life narratives originated from research on highly generative and relatively nongenerative adults; see McAdams and Bowman 2001; McAdams, Diamond, de St. Aubin, and Mansfield 1997; and McAdams, Hart and Maruna 1998 for additional information on this line of research. The concept of generativity, introduced by Erik H. Erikson (1963), is characterized by an adult's concern for and commitment to promoting the well-being of later generations. Parenting, teaching, mentoring, counseling, and engaging in community service are examples of the various constructive, generative activities that adults seek in order to create legacies that will outlive them and contribute positively to society (see Kotre 1999 and McAdams and de St. Aubin 1998 for details). Previous findings suggest that highly generative adults report greater levels of participation in political campaigns and movements that agitate for social reform (see Cole and Stewart 1996; Hart, McAdams, Hirsch, and Bauer 2001; and Peterson, Smirles, and Wentworth 1997). For that reason, I expected feminist Black men's narratives to contain significantly more redemptive imagery and sequences than contaminative ones, given the generative quality of their activist behaviors and feminist commitments. My findings were confirmed and are detailed in White 2006c.

8. Maslow (1968) described a peak experience as a moment of acute identity awareness. In recent empirical research, peak experiences are primarily conceptualized as "cognitive and perceptual experiences that seem to be associated with holistic understandings of the self, one's role in an ordered universe, one's role in society, and presumably with the transformation of other dimensions of personality" (see Christopher, Manaster, Campbell, and Weinfeld 2002, 35). I expected peak narrative sequences to be recounted more frequently than contamination sequences, but significantly less frequently than redemption sequences. In White (2006c) I present the frequencies and condensed examples of redemption, contamination, and peak sequences in feminist Black men's life narratives in greater detail.

9. Related to McAdams's theoretical concept of redemption sequences in life narrative accounts is personality theorist Roy Baumeister's (1994) concept of the subjective process of change. For Baumeister, change occurs when salient negative factors undermine a person's commitment to a role, relationship, or involvement. The "crystallization of discontent" is a common theme in identity change narratives and is associated with a focal incident that triggered the change attempt. I use both concepts to enhance our understanding of the turning points in feminist Black men's lives that are characterized as "redemptive."

10. Baumeister, 1994; Heatherton and Nichols 1994.

11. Womanist is another term for a Black feminist in this context (see Appendix C for a brief history of both terms and their current usage).

12. Baumeister 1994.

13. Baumeister 1994.

14. McAdams and Bowman 2001.

15. McAdams and Bowman 2001.

16. McAdams and Bowman 2001.

17. Polygamy is illegal in the United States; Abdul and his "wives" and Nia and her "husbands" performed commitment ceremonies that were not legally sanctioned in order to honor their alternative unions.

Chapter 5. Romantic Relationships with Feminist Women

1. Christian 1984; Hernton 1986; Hopkins 1998; Schacht and Ewing 1998, 121–122; Tate 1986.

2. Martin 2004.

3. Fein and Schneider 1995, 1997; Hochschild 1994; Zimmerman, Holm, and Starrels 2001.

4. Boynton 2003.

5. Dempsey 2002, 104.

6. Fein and Schneider 1997, 8–9.

7. Boynton 2003.

8. Boynton 2003.

9. Fein and Schneider 1995; Millner 1997.

10. Elizabeth 2003.

11. All of their partners are aware of their bisexuality.

12. Elizabeth 2003.

13. Sandfield and Percy 2003.

14. Blaisure and Allen 1995; Christian 1994; Messner 1998; Snodgrass 1977.

15. Blaisure and Allen 1995, 10.

16. Blaisure and Allen 1995, 13.

17. Okin 1989; Starhawk 1987; Young 1990.

18. Miller 1992, 241, 247–248.

19. Hartsock 1983, 224; Hoagland 1988, 118.

20. Follett 1942; Hartsock 1983, 224.

21. Collins 2004; Giddings 1984; White 2001.

22. Blaisure and Allen 1995.

23. Atkinson and Boles 1984; Blaisure and Allen 1995; Haas 1980.

24. Blaisure and Allen 1995.

25. Rogers 1987, 39.

26. Burstow 1987.

27. Blaisure and Allen 1995.

28. Martin 2004 ;Risman 2004.

29. Schacht and Ewing 1998.

30. Kahane 1998.

31. I thank Black feminist sociologist Assata Zerai for a discussion that helped me think through this issue.

32. Schacht and Ewing 1998.

33. Kahane 1998.

34. Kahane 1998, 218.

35. Robinson 2003.

36. Jackson and Scott 2004.

37. Jackson and Scott 2004; Red Collective, 1978.

38. Jackson and Scott 2004, 155.

39. Rich 1980; Robinson 1997; Rosa 1994.

40. Jackson and Scott 2004.

41. Jackson and Scott 2004.

42. Chapman 1986; Stewart 2004, 153–165.

43. Jackson and Scott 2004.

44. Jackson and Scott 2004,156.

45. Jackson and Scott 2004.

46. Hale 1998.

47. Hale 1998.

48. On the one hand, FTMs have experienced oppression that other women have experienced because of having female bodies. On the other hand, unlike men who are born male, they have been told (sometimes even by feminists) that they simply delude themselves into thinking that they exist, that they are gender traitors grasping at male privilege when they leave the category "woman," and their masculinities are regulated and controlled by medical technologies and official structures. See Hale 1998 for an exhaustive review of related issues.

49. Hale 1998.

50. Blaisure and Allen 1995.

51. Bem 1998; Blaisure and Allen 1995; Risman 1998.

Chapter 6. Platonic Friendships with Feminist Women

1. In my study, what I refer to as a "cross-sex" friendship is defined as a voluntary, nonromantic relationship between a person who perceives himself as a man and a person who perceives herself as a woman, regardless of sexuality or biology. This definition differs from standard ones given in the cross-sex friendship literature because an individual's identity is *really* identification, based not on biology but, rather, on self-perception of sex or gender.

2. Werking 1997, 162.

3. Monsour 2002, 135.

4. Afifi and Faulkner 2000.

5. Messman, Canary, and Hause 2000.

6. Barbee, Gulley, and Cunningham 1990.

7. Aukett, Ritchie, and Mill 1988.

8. Monsour, Beard, Harris, and Kurzweil 1994.

9. Monsour 1988; Sapadin 1988.

10. Monsour 2002; Werking 1997.

11. Monsour 1988; Wright and Scanlon 1991.

12. Monsour 1988.

13. See Monsour 2002, 142–154, for a review.

14. Shakur 1987.

15. O'Meara 1994.

16. Martin 2004; Risman 1998, 2004.

17. Participants Alan, Carlos, Cudjoe, Ralph, Soyinka, Toussaint, and Victor.

18. Monsour 2002.

19. Rubin 1985.

20. Carbery and Buhrmester 1998; Rose 1985; Rubin 1985; Wright 1989.

21. Monsour 2002, 159.

22. See McCarthy and Zald 1977 and McAdam and Paulson 1993 for how my findings support, in part, the findings of resource mobilization theorists in sociology.

23. See the Atlanta Committee for Black Liberation 1996; Cleage 1993, 21–35; and Hamer and Neville 1998 for examples of strains of Black nationalism inclusive of feminism.

24. Clarke 1983, 207.

25. Klein 1989, 114.

26. Cole and Guy-Sheftall 2003, 219.

27. Waldron 2003, 163.

28. Hale 1998; Rubin 1998.

29. Rubin 1998.

30. Monsour 2002; Werking 1997.

31. Monsour 2002; Werking 1997.

32. Kahane 1998, 217.

Chapter 7. Men as Friends, Brothers, and Lovers

1. Battle and Bennett 2005; Battle and Lemelle 2002; Carbado 1999a, 1999b; Cohen 1999; Smith 1998; Summers 2002.

2. Hutchinson 1999; Lemelle and Battle 2004; Summers 2002; Thomas 1996.

3. Lemelle and Battle 2004; Simien 2006.

4. For additional information on the link between sexism, homophobia, and heterosexism see the following: Nardi 1992; Nielsen, Walden, and Kunkel 2000; Pharr 1988; Segal 1990.

5. Hutchins and Kaahumanu 1991, 369.

6. Pharr 1988; Segal 1990.

7. For more on gendered heteronormativity see Nielsen, Walden, and Kunkel 2000.

8. See DiClemente 1994 for the change process in attitudes and behaviors among addicts that also have implications for attitude and behavior changes among adults in general.

9. For additional information about the psychology of adult personality and identity changes see Baumeister 1994 and Heatherton and Nichols 1994.

10. Cited in Kimmel 1998, 67.

11. Kimmel 1998; Lemons 1998.

12. Clarke 1983; Lorde 1982, 1984; Parker 1978; Smith 1983, 1998.

13. Smith 1998, 112.

14. E. F. White 2001, 178.

15. Nardi 1999; Price 1999.

16. Price 1999.

17. Nardi 1999; Price 1999.

18. See Sellars 1995 for an interesting narrative about these friendships; http://www.xyonline.net/het.shtml.

19. See Herek 2004; Hill and Willoughby 2005.

20. Battle and Bennett 2005, 427.

21. Battle and Bennett 2005, 427.

22. Battle and Bennett 2005; Cohen 1999; Constantino-Simms 2001; Nero 1999; Schulte and Battle 2004; Simien 2006; E. F. White 2001.

23. Adams and Kimmel 1997; Mays, Yancey, Cochran, Weber, and Fielding 2002; Savin-Williams 1994.

24. Hawkeswood 1997; Reimonenq 2002 cited in Battle and Bennett 2005, 420.

25. See Lorde 1982 and Smith 1986.

26. The National Black Lesbian and Gay Leadership Forum, founded in 1988, became defunct in 2003. See www.unityfellowship church.org.

27. See Clarke 1983 for shocking, but classic examples. See Carbado 1999b, Hutchinson 1999, and Thomas 1996 for additional examples and Summers 2002 for a historical perspective on homophobia and Black Nationalist thought.

28. Battle and Bennett 2005; Battle and Lemelle 2002; Lemelle and Battle 2004.

29. Clarke 1983, 198, 203.

30. Battle and Bennett 2005, 422.

Chapter 8. Sweet Daddy: Nurturing Interactions with Children

1. Silverstein and Auerbach 1999; Wilcox 2004.

2. Dowd 2000; Gerson 1997; Silverstein and Auerbach 1999.

3. Cochran 1997; Dowd 2000; Roberts 1998.

4. Cochran 1997; Hamer 1997; McAdoo and McAdoo 2002.

5. Marable 1983; Segal 1990; Wilcox 2004.

6. Dowd 2000; Newton 2005; Risman 1998.

7. Dowd 2000; Risman 1998.

8. See Risman 1998 for a review.

9. Geffner, Jaffe, and Sundermann 2000; Graham-Bermann and Edleson 2001.

10. Gershoff 2002; Grogan-Kaylor 2005; Straus, Sugarman, and Giles-Sims 1997.

11. Giles-Sims and Lockhart 2005; Greven 1990; Straus and Stewart 1999; Wilcox 2004.

12. Dowd 2000; Roberts 1998.

13. Oliver and Shapiro 1995.

14. Bowman and Forman 1997; Cochran 1997.

15. Collins 2004; Marable 1983.

16. McAdoo 1993; McAdoo and McAdoo 2002; Risman 1998.

17. McAdoo 1993; Oliver and Shapiro 1995; Wilson 1996.

18. Dolgin 1993.

19. McAdoo and McAdoo 2002.

20. Wilcox 2004.

21. Dowd 2000.

22. Roberts 1998, 153.

23. Roberts 1998, 158.

24. Dowd 2000; Hamer 1997; Newton 2005; Roberts 1998.

25. Dowd 2000, 73.

26. Bailey 1990; Palkovitz 1984; Sanderson and Sanders Thompson 2002.

27. Wilcox 2004.

28. Blaisure and Allen 1995; Gerson 1997; Mack-Canty and Wright 2004; Risman 1998; Schwartz 1994.

29. Bem 1998; Blaisure and Allen 1995; Gerson 1997; Mack-Canty and Wright 2004; Risman 1998; Schwartz 1994.

30. Gerson 1997.

31. Mack-Canty and Wright 2004; Risman and Myers 1997.

32. See Giles-Sims and Lockhart 2005 for a review.

33. Giles-Sims, Straus, and Sugarman 1995; Straus and Stewart 1999.

34. Mack-Canty and Wright 2004.

35. Dowd 2000.

36. Dowd 2000; Risman 1998; Silverstein and Auerbach 1999.

37. Dowd, 2000; Risman 1998.

38. See Boyd-Franklin and Franklin 2000 and McAdoo 2002.

39. Giles-Sims and Lockhart 2005.

40. Nielsen et al. 2000.

41. Nielsen et al. 2000

42. Risman and Myers 1997.

43. Straus and Stewart 1999.

44. Giles-Sims and Lockhart 2005.

45. Baumrind 1991.

46. Bem 1998; Mack-Canty and Wright 2004.

47. Bowman and Foreman 1997; Dowd 2000.

48. Blaisure and Allen 1995; Gerson 1997; Risman 1998; Schwartz 1994.

49. Risman 1998.

50. Dowd 2000; Gerson 1997.

51. Mack-Canty and Wright 2004; Risman 1998; Silverstein and Auerbach 1999.

Chapter 9. Private Commitments, Public Actions

1. Christian 1994; Goldrick-Jones 2002; Schacht and Ewing 1998.

2. Collins 2004.

3. Bell 1994, 163.

4. The term "identity politics" is widely used; however, "it has increasingly become a derogatory synonym for feminist, anti-racist, and anti-heterosexist social movements, despite the role that identity plays in all social movements" (Fraser 1997, cited in Bernstein 2005, 48). "As a result, the term identity politics obscures more than clarifies and, if the term is used at all, its meaning should be clearly defined" (Bernstein 2005, 66).

5. Kivel 1992; Messner 1998; Parrish 1992.

6. See http://www.feminist.com/resources/links/links_men.html for profeminist men's groups.

7. Parrish 1992.

8. For information on the Black Feminist Caucus see http://www.black radicalcongress.org.

9. Atlanta Committee for Black Liberation 1996; Black Men for the Eradication of Sexism 2001; Brothers Absolutely Against Sexual Assault and Domestic Violence 1992; L. Harris 1999b. For articles documenting profeminist Black men's participation in local collective action see also Omolade 1994, 193; Powell 2000; White 2001, and White and Peretz 2007.

10. Goldrick-Jones 2002; Newton 2005; Segal 1990.

11. See White and Peretz 2007.

12. Clark, Beckett, Wells, and Dungee-Anderson 1994; Coker, McKeown, Sanderson, Davis, Valois, and Huebner 2000; Malik, Sorenson, and Aneshensel 1997.

13. Richie 1994, 2000; West 2002; E. C. White 1994.

14. Tjaden and Thoennes 2000.

15. Neville and Pugh 1997; Washington 2001; Wyatt, Notgrass, and Gordon 1995.

16. White Ribbon Campaign. Web site, http://www.whiteribbon.ca/.

17. Some Black feminist social scientists refer to this as political intersectionality. See Cole 2007 and Settles 2006.

18. Anzaldua 1987; Cole 2007; Reagon 1983; Silliman, Fried, Ross, and Gutierrez 2004.

19. Bernstein 2005, 50.

20. See Stockdill 2001. Also see Rossinow 1998 for a similar analysis of the New Left.

21. Bernstein 2005; Van Dyke 2003.

22. Bell 1994, 7–8.

23. See Bernstein 2005 for an extensive development of this argument.

24. Kahane 1998, 230.

25. Baumeister 1994.

26. Kahane 1998, 228.

27. Kahane 1998.

Conclusion. Can Black Men *Really* Be Feminists?

1. Gill 1992, 155.

Appendix A. Methodological Intersections and Considerations

1. White 2006a.

2. Straus and Corbin 1990, 24.

3. Jones 2001; Maxwell 1996.

4. McAdam 1993; Riessman 1993.

5. Jones 2001; Maxwell 1996.

6. Jones 2001; Maxwell 1996.

7. See Tolman and Brydon-Miller 2001 for examples of similar research.

8. The e-mail announcement was forwarded to several Black organizations, feminist listservs, and individual Black men. The men often mentioned these sources of information when they requested surveys. For instance, one man mentioned that he saw the announcement on a Black law student organization's listserv and wanted to participate in the survey. Many men mentioned that someone had forwarded the announcement to them. Once the announcement was on the Internet, it was difficult to know how each man found out about the survey, and I regret that I did not ask them.

9. White 2006a.

10. I knew two men in the study, Solomon and Paul, fairly well before the interview. I had also frequented the restaurant Donny owns, and we have mutual friends (see Table 2.1 for a list of participants).

11. Victor requested that I interview him the same day he saw the male interviewer. I spent time with them both to facilitate the rapport between them and spoke with him after his interview to ensure that he felt all right about it. Although he stated that he felt relatively comfortable, he shared additional personal information with me during two follow-up telephone conversations that are included in his narrative.

12. Even though most of the men were comfortable using their own names, I felt it important to consider, and ultimately protect, the anonymity and confidentiality of the women and children mentioned in the men's narratives.

13. Christian 1994; Shiffman 1987.

14. We were unable to interview five men. Two were living in another country during the scheduling of the interviews. We encountered ongoing scheduling difficulties with two men who traveled extensively and had excessive workloads, and we lost contact with one student after he graduated and moved.

15. Strube and Delitto 1994.

16. White, 2006b 2006c, 2006d.

17 Christian 1994; O'Neill 1998; Wescott 1992, 1994; Wolcott 1994.

Appendix C. Historical and Contemporary Usage of the Terms "Feminist" and "Womanist"

1. *Reader's Companion to U.S. Women's History* 1998, 639; Tuttle 1986, 107, 352.

2. Boles and Hoeveler 1996, 2.

3. Boles and Hoeveler 1996; Tuttle 1986.

4. Walker 1983.

5. Weems 1993.

6. Cannon 1995.

REFERENCES

Abalos, D. T. 2002. *The Latino Male: A Radical Redefinition*. Boulder: Lynne Rienner.

Abdulahad, T., G. Rogers, B. Smith, and J. Waheed. 1983. "Black Lesbian Feminist Organizing: A Conversation." In *Home Girls: A Black Feminist Anthology*, ed., B. Smith, 293–319. New York: Kitchen Table.

Adams, C., and D. Kimmel. 1997. "Exploring the Lives of Older Black Gay Men." In *Ethnic and Cultural Diversity among Lesbians and Gay Men: Psychological Perspectives on Lesbian and Gay Issues*, ed., B. Greene, 132–151. Thousand Oaks, CA: Sage.

Afifi, W. A., and S. L. Faulkner. 2000. "On Being 'Just Friends': The Frequency and Impact of Sexual Activity in Cross-Sex Friendships." *Journal of Social and Personal Relationships* 17 (2): 205–222.

Akbar, N. 1984. "Africentric Social Sciences for Human Liberation." *Journal of Black Studies* 14 (4): 395–414.

Akbar, N. 1991. "Paradigms of African American Research." In *Black Psychology*, ed., R. L. Jones, 709–725. Berkeley: Cobb and Henry.

Anzaldua, G. 1987. *Borderlands—La Frontera: The New Mestiza*. San Francisco: Spinsters/Aunt Lute.

Atkinson, M. P., and J. Boles. 1984. "WASP (Wives as Senior Partners)." *Journal of Marriage and the Family* 46: 861–870.

Atlanta Committee for Black Liberation. 1996. "A Call to End the Oppression of Women and to Advance the Black Liberation Movement: A Position Paper on theMillion Man March." In *Fertile Ground: Memories and Visions*, eds., K. Salaam and K. Brown, 267–282. New Orleans: Runnagate.

Aukett, R., J. Ritchie, and K. Mill. 1988. "Gender Differences in Friendship Patterns." *Sex Roles* 19: 57–66.

Awkward, M. 1996. "A Black Man's Place(s) in Black Feminist Criticism." In *Representing Black Men*, eds., M. Blount and G. E. Cunningham, 3–26. New York: Routledge.

Awkward, M. 2002. "Black Male Trouble: The Challenge of Rethinking Masculine Differences." In *Masculinity Studies and Feminist Theory: New Directions*, ed., J. K. Gardiner, 290–304. New York: Columbia University Press.

Babcock, J. C., C. E. Green, and C. Robie. 2004. *Clinical Psychology Review* 28(8): 1023–1053.

Bailey, W. T. 1990. "Fathers' Involvement in Their Children's Health Care." *Journal of Marriage and the Family* 54: 699–707.

Baldwin, J. 1985. "Introduction: The Price of the Ticket." In J. Baldwin, *The Price of the Ticket: Collected Nonfiction, 1948–1985*, ix–xx. New York: St. Martin's.

Baldwin, J. A. 1992. "The Role of Black Psychologists in Black Liberation." In *African American Psychology: Theory, Research, and Practice*, eds., A. K. H. Burlew, W. C. Banks, H. P. McAdoo, and D. Azibo, 48–57. Newbury Park, CA: Sage.

Banks, W. C. 1991. "Theory and Method in the Growth of African American Psychology." In *Advances in African American Psychology*, ed., R. L. Jones, 3–8. Hampton, VA: Cobb & Henry.

Barbee, A. P., M. R. Gulley, and M. R. Cunningham. 1990. "Support Seeking in Personal Relationships." *Journal of Social and Personal Relationships* 7 (4): 531–540.

Battle, J. J., and N. D. Bennett. 2005. "Striving for Place: Lesbian, Gay, Bisexual, and Transgender (LGBT) People." In *A Companion to African American History*, ed., A. Hornsby, Jr., 412–445. Malden, MA: Blackwell.

Battle, J. J., and Lemelle, A. J. 2002. "Gender Differences in African American Attitudes Toward Gay Males." *Western Journal of Black Studies* 26(3): 134–139.

Baumeister, R. 1994. "The Crystallization of Discontent in the Process of Major Life Change." In *Can Personality Change?*, eds., T. Heatherton and J. Weinberger, 281–297. Washington, DC: American Psychological Association.

Baumrind, D. 1991. "The Influence of Parenting Style on Adolescent Competence and Substance." *Journal of Early Adolescence* 11: 56–95.

Beale, F. 1970. "Double Jeopardy: To Be Black and Female." In *The Black Woman*, ed., T. Cade, 90–100. New York: Signet.

Beam, J. 1986a. "No cheek to turn." *Changing Men* 17 (Winter): 9–10.

Beam, J. 1986b. "Brother to Brother: Words from the Heart." In his *A Black Gay Anthology: In the Life*, 230–242. Boston: Alyson.

Bell, D. 1994. *Confronting Authority*. Boston: Beacon.

Bell, T. 1986. "Black Men in the White Men's Movement." *Changing Men* 17 (Winter):11–12, 44.

Belton, D., ed. 1995. *Speak My Name: Black Men on Masculinity and the American Dream*. Boston: Beacon.

Bem, S. 1998. "Feminist Child-Rearing Revisited." In her *An Unconventional Family*, 178–205. New Haven: Yale University Press.

Bernstein, M. 2005. "Identity Politics." *Annual Review of Sociology* 31: 47–74.

Black Men for the Eradication of Sexism. 2001."Mission Statement of Black Men for the Eradication of Sexism: Morehouse College, 1994." In *Traps: African American Men on Gender and Sexuality*, eds., R. Byrd and B. Guy-Sheftall, 200–204. Bloomington: Indiana University Press.

Black Radical Congress. 1998. "Principles of Unity." Retrieved April 8, 2007, from http://www.blackradicalcongress.org/unity.html.

Blaisure, K. R., and K. R. Allen. 1995. "Feminists and the Ideology and Practice of Marital Equity." *Journal of Marriage and the Family* 57: 5–19.

Bly, R. 1990. *Iron John: A Book About Men*. New York: Perseus.

Boles, J. K., and D. L. Hoeveler. 1996. *Historical Dictionary of Feminism*. Lanham, MD: Scarecrow Press.

Bowman, P. J., and T. A. Forman. 1997. " Instrumental and Expressive FamilyRoles among African American Fathers." In *Family Life in Black America*, eds., R. Taylor, J. Jackson, and L. Chatters, 15–40. Thousand Oaks, CA: Sage.

Boyd-Franklin, N., and A. J. Franklin. (with Toussaint, P.). 2000. *Boys into Men: Raising our African American Teenage Sons*. New York: Dutton.

Boykin, K. 2005. *Beyond the Down Low: Sex, Lies, and Denial in Black America*. New York: Carroll and Graf.

Boynton, P. 2003. "Abiding by the Rules: Instructing Women in Relationships." *Feminism and Psychology* 13 (2): 237–245.

Brod, H. 1998. "To be a Man, or Not to be a Man—That Is the Feminist Question." In *Men Doing Feminism*, ed., T. Digby, 197–212. New York: Routledge.

Brothers Absolutely Against Sexual Assault and Domestic Violence. 1992. "Sisters, You Are Not Alone." *Sistahs Organizin' in Unity for Real Change (SOURCE) Pamphlet.* University of Michigan African American Student Organization.

Brown Douglas, K. 1993. "Womanist Theology: What Is Its Relationship to Black Theology?" In *Black Theology: A Documentary History, 1980–1992,* Vol. 2, eds., J. Cone and G. Wilmore, xx–295. New York: Orbis.

Burman, E., ed. 1998. *Deconstructing Feminist Psychology.* London: Sage.

Burstow, B. 1987. "Humanistic Psychotherapy and the Issue of Equality." *Journal of Humanistic Psychology* 27 (1): 9–25.

Byrd, R. P., and B. Guy-Sheftall, eds. 2001. *Traps: African American Men on Gender and Sexuality.* Bloomington: Indiana University Press.

Cannon, K. G. 1995. *Katie's Canon: Womanism and the Soul of the Black Community.* New York: Continuum.

Carbado, D. 1999a. "Epilogue: Straight Out of the Closet: Men, Feminism, and Male Heterosexual Privilege." In *Black Men on Race, Gender, and Sexuality,* ed.,D. Carbado, 417–447. New York: New York University Press.

Carbado, D. 1999b. "Black Rights, Gay Rights, Civil Rights." In *Black Men on Race, Gender, and Sexuality,* ed., D. Carbado, 283–302. New York: New York University Press.

Carbery, J., and D. Buhrmester. 1998. "Friendship and Need Fulfillment During Three Phases of Young Adulthood." *Journal of Social and Personal Relationships* 15 (3): 393–409.

Carroll, C. M. 1982. "Three's a Crowd: The Dilemma of the Black Woman in Higher Education." In *All the Women Are White, All the Blacks Are Men, But Some of Us Are Brave: Black Women's Studies,* eds., G. Hull, P. Scott, and B. Smith, 115-128. Old Westbury, NY: Feminist Press.

Chapman, A. 1986. *Man-Sharing: Dilemma or Choice?* New York: William Morrow.

Chapman, M. L. 1995. *Christianity on Trial: African-American Religious Thought Before and After Black Power.* Maryknoll: Orbis.

Cheney, C. L. 2005. *Brothers Gonna Work It Out: Sexual Politics in the Golden Age of Rap Nationalism.* New York: New York University Press.

Christian, H. 1994. *The Making of Anti-Sexist Men.* New York: Routledge.

Christopher, J. C., G. Manaster, R. Campbell, and M. Weinfeld. 2002. "Peak Experiences, Social Interest and Moral Reasoning: An Exploratory Study." *Journal of Individual Psychology* 58: 35–51.

Clark, M. L., J. Beckett, M. Wells, and D. Dungee-Anderson. 1994. "Courtship Violence among African American College Students." *Journal of Black Psychology* 20: 264–281.

Clarke, C. 1983. "The Failure to Transform: Homophobia in the Black Community." In *Home Girls: A Black Feminist Anthology*, ed., B. Smith, 197–208. New York: Kitchen Table.

Cleage. P. 1993. "Basic Training: The Beginnings of Wisdom." In her *Deals with the Devil and Other Reasons to Riot*, 21–35. New York: Ballantine.

Cochran, D. L. 1997. "African American Fathers: A Decade Review of the Literature." *Families in Society* 78: 340–350.

Cohen, C. 1999. *The Boundaries of Blackness: AIDS and the Breakdown of Black Politics*. Chicago: University of Chicago Press.

Cohen, C. J., K. B. Jones, and J. C. Tronto, eds. 1997. *Women Transforming Politics: An Alternative Reader*. New York: New York University Press.

Coker, A. L., R. McKeown, M. Sanderson, K. Davis, R. Valois, and E. Huebner. 2000. "Severe Dating Violence and Quality of Life among South Carolina High School Students." *American Journal of Preventive Medicine* 19: 220–227.

Cole, E. 2007. "Coalitions as a Model for Intersectionality: From Practice to Theory." Unpublished manuscript.

Cole, E., and A. J. Stewart. 1996. "Meanings of Political Participation Among Black and White Women: Political Identity and Social Responsibility." *Journal ofPersonality and Social Psychology* 71: 130–140.

Cole, J. B., and B. Guy-Sheftall. 2003. *Gender Talk: The Struggle for Women's Equality in African American Communities*. New York: Ballantine.

Collins, P. H. 1998. *Fighting Words: Black Women and the Search for Justice*. Minneapolis: University of Minnesota.

Collins, P. H. 2004. *Black Sexual Politics: African Americans, Gender, and the New Racism*. New York: Routledge.

Combahee River Collective. 1983. "The Combahee River Collective Statement." In *Home Girls: A Black Feminist Anthology*, ed., B. Smith, 272–282. New York: Kitchen Table.

Cone, J., and G. Wilmore. 1993. *Black Theology: A Documentary History*, Vol. 2., eds., Maryknoll, NY: Orbis.

Connell, R. W. 1987. *Gender and Power: Society, the Person, and Sexual Politics*. Standford: Standford University Press.

Connell, R. W. 1995. *Masculinities*. Cambridge: Polity.

Connor M. K. 2003. *What Is Cool? Understanding Black Manhood in America*. St. Paul: Agate.

Constantino-Simms, D., ed. 2001. *The Greatest Taboo: Homosexuality in Black Communities*. New York: Alyson.

Coontz, S. 1992. *The Way We Never Were: American Families and the Nostalgia Trap*. New York: Basic.

Cossins, A. 2000. *Masculinities, Sexualities, and Child Sexual Abuse*. The Hague: Kluwer Law International.

Crenshaw K. W. 1989. "Demarginalizing the Intersection of Race and Sex: A Black Feminist Critique of Antidiscrimination Doctrine, Feminist Theory, and Antiracist Politics." *University of Chicago Legal Forum* xx: 139–167.

Crenshaw, K. W. 1991. "Mapping the Margins: Intersectionality, Identity Politics, and Violence Against Women of Color." *Standford Law Review* 43(6): 1241–1279.

Daly, M. 1987. *Webster's First New Intergalactic Wickedary of the English Language*. New York: HarperCollins.

Danziger, K. 1990. *Constructing the Subject: Historical Origins of Psychological Research*. New York: Cambridge University Press.

Daston, L., and P. Galison. 1992. "The Image of Objectivity." *Representations* 40: 81–128.

Davis, B. 1988. "To Seize the Moment: A Retrospective on the National Black Feminist Organization." *SAGE* 5 (2): 43–47.

Dawson, M. C. 2001. *Black Visions: The Roots of Contemporary African-American Political Ideologies*. Chicago: University of Chicago Press.

D'Emilio, J. 2003. *Lost Prophet: The Life and Times of Bayard Rustin*. New York: Free Press.

Dempsey, K. 2002. "Who Gets the Best Deal from Marriage: Women or Men?" *Journal of Sociology* 38 (2): 91–110.

DiClemente, C. 1994. "If Behaviors Change, Can Personality be Far Behind?" In *Can Personality Change?*, eds., T. Heatherton and J. Weinberger, 175–198. Washington, DC: American Psychological Association.

Digby, T., ed. 1998. *Men Doing Feminism*. New York: Routledge.

Dolgin, J. L. 1993. "Just a Gene: Judicial Assumptions about Parenthood." *University of California at Los Angeles Law Review* 40: 637.

Dowd, N. E. 2000. *Redefining Fatherhood*. New York: New York University Press.

Ducat, S. J. 2004. *The Wimp Factor: Gender Gaps, Holy Wars, and the Politics of Anxious Masculinity*. Boston: Beacon.

Dyson, M. E. 2001. "When You Divide Body and Soul, Problems Multiply: The Black Church and Sex." In *Traps: African American Men on Gender and Sexuality*, eds., R. Byrd and B. Guy-Sheftall, 308–326. Bloomington: Indiana University Press.

Ehrmin, J. T. 1996. "No More Mother Blaming: A Feminist Nursing Perspective on the Mother's Role in Father–Daughter Incest." *Archives of Psychiatric Nursing* 10(4): 252–260.

Elizabeth, V. 2003. "To Marry, or Not to Marry: That Is The Question." *Feminism and Psychology* 13 (4): 426–431.

Erikson, E. H. 1963. *Childhood and Society*, 2nd ed. New York: Norton.

Estes, S. S. 2006. *I Am a Man! Race, Manhood, and the Civil Rights Movement*. Chapel Hill: University of North Carolina Press.

Farajaje-Jones, E. 1993. "Breaking Silence: Toward an In-the-Life Theology. In *Black Theology: A Documentary History*, Vol. 2., eds., J. Cone and G. Wilmore,139–159. Maryknoll, NY: Orbis.

Fein, E., and S. Schneider. 1995. *The Rules: Time Tested Secrets for Capturing the Heart of Mr. Right*. London: Thorsons.

Fein, E., and S. Schneider. 1997. *The Rules 2: More Rules to Live and Love By*. London: Thorsons.

Ferguson, A. 2000. *Bad Boys: Public Schools in the Making of Black Masculinity.*Ann Arbor: University of Michigan Press.

Fine, M. 1992. *Disruptive Voices: The Possibilities of Feminist Research*. Ann Arbor: University of Michigan Press.

Fine, M., and V. Vanderslice. 1992. "Qualitative Activist Research: Reflections on Methods and Politics." In *Methodological Issues in Applied Social Psychology*, eds., F. Bryant, J. Edwards, and R. S. Tindale, 199–218. New York: Plenum.

Fine, M., and L. Weis. 1998. *The Unknown City: Lives of Poor and Working-Class Young Adults*. Boston: Beacon.

Fivush, R., and C. A. Haden, ed. 2003. *Autobiographical Memory and the Construction of a Narrative Self: Developmental and Cultural Perspectives*. Mahwah, NJ: Lawrence Erlbaum.

Follett, M. P. 1942. *Power in Dynamic Administration: The Collected Papers of Mary Parker Follett*, ed., H. C. Metcalf and L. Urwick. New York: Harper.

Fox, D., and I. Prilleltensky, eds. 1997. *Critical Psychology: An Introduction*. Thousand Oaks, CA: Sage.

Fox-Genovese, E., and E. Genovese. 2005. *The Mind of the Master Class: History and Faith in the Southern Slaveholders' Worldview*. New York: Cambridge University Press.

Frank, G. 1985. "Becoming the Other: Empathy and Biographical Interpretation." *Biography* 8(3): 189–210.

Franklin, A. J. 2002. *From Brotherhood to Manhood: How Black Men Rescue TheirRelationships and Dreams from the Invisibility Syndrome.* New York: Wiley.

Franklin, D. 2001. *What's Love Got to Do with It? Healing the Rift Between Black Men and Women.* New York: Simon and Schuster.

Freedman, E. 2002. *No Turning Back: The History of Feminism and the Future of Women.* New York: Ballantine.

Gardiner, J. K. 2002. "Introduction." In her *Masculinity Studies and Feminist Theory: New Directions,* 1–29. New York: Columbia University Press.

Gates, H. L. 1997. *Thirteen Ways of Looking at a Black Man.* New York: Random House.

Gavanas, A. 2004. *Fatherhood Politics in the United States: Masculinity, Sexuality, Race, and Marriage.* Chicago: University of Illinois Press.

Geffner, R., P. Jaffe, and M. Sundermann, M., eds. 2000. *Children Exposed to Domestic Violence: Current Issues in Research, Intervention, Prevention, and Policy Development.* Binghamton, NY: Haworth.

Gershoff, E. T. 2002. "Corporal Punishment by Parents and Associated Child Behaviors and Experiences: A Meta-Analytic and Theoretical Review." *Psychological Bulletin* 128: 539–579.

Gerson, K. 1997. "An Institutional Perspective on Generative Fathering: Creating Social Supports for Parenting Equality." In *Generative Fathering: Beyond Deficit Perspectives,* eds., A. Hawkins and D. Dollahite, 36–51. Thousand Oaks, CA: Sage.

Giddings, P. 1984. *When and Where I Enter: The Impact of Black Women on Race and Sex in America.* New York: Bantam.

Giles-Sims, J., and C. Lockhart. 2005. "Culturally Shaped Patterns of Disciplining Children." *Journal of Family Issues* 26: 196–218.

Giles-Sims, J., M. Straus, and D. Sugarman. 1995. "Child, Maternal, and Family Characteristics Associated with Spanking." *Family Relations* 4: 170–177.

Gill, H. 1992. "Men's Predicament: Male Supremacy." In *Women Respond to the Men's Movement,* ed., K. Hagan, 151–157. San Francisco: HarperCollins.

Goldrick-Jones, A. 2002. *Men Who Believe in Feminism.* Westport, CT: Praeger.

Gordon, M. D. 1993. "Why Is this Men's Movement So White?" *Changing Men* 26: 15–17.

Gordon, E., F. Miller, and D. Rollock. 1990. "Coping with Communicentric Bias in Knowledge Production in the Social Sciences." *Educational Researcher* 19: 4–19.

Graham-Bermann, S. A., and J. L. Edleson, eds., 2001. *Domestic Violence in the Lives of Children: The Future of Research, Intervention, and Social Policy.* Washington, DC: American Psychological Association.

Grant, J. 1993. "Black Theology and the Black Woman. In *Black Theology: A Documentary History, Volume One: 1966–1979*, eds., J. Cone and G. Wilmore, 323–338. Maryknoll, NY: Orbis.

Greven, P. 1990. *Spare the Child: The Religious Roots of Physical Punishment and the Psychological Impact of Physical Abuse.* New York: Knopf.

Grogan-Kaylor, A. 2005. "Corporal Punishment and the Growth Trajectory of Children's Antisocial Behavior." *Child Maltreatment* 10: 283–292.

Guthrie, R. V. 1997. *Even the Rat Was White: A Historical View of Psychology.* New York: Allyn & Bacon.

Haas, L. 1980. "Role-sharing Couples: A Study of Egalitarian Marriages." *Family Relations* 29: 289–296.

Hale, C. J. 1998. "Tracing a Ghostly Memory in My Throat: Reflections on Ftm Feminist Voice and Agency." In *Men Doing Feminism*, ed., T. Digby, 99-129. New York: Routledge.

Hamberger, L. K., and C. E. Guse. 2002. "Men and Women's Use of Intimate Partner Violence in Clinical Samples." *Violence Against Women* 8: 1301–1331.

Hamer, J. F. 1997. "The Fathers of 'Fatherless' Black Children." *Families in Society* 78: 564–578.

Hamer, J., and H. Neville. 1998. "Revolutionary Black Feminism: Toward a Theory of Unity and Liberation." *The Black Scholar* 28 (3/4): 22–29.

Harris, F. C. 1999. *Something Within: Religion in African American Political Activism.* New York: Oxford University Press.

Harris, L. 1999a. "My Two Mothers, America, and the Million Man March." In *Black Men on Race, Gender, and Sexuality*, ed., D. Carbado, 54–67. New York: New York University Press.

Harris, L. 1999b. "The Challenge and Possibility for Black Males to Embrace Feminism." In *Black Men on Race, Gender, and Sexuality*, ed., D. Carbado, 383–386. New York: New York University Press.

Hart, H. M., D. P. McAdams, B. J. Hirsch, and J. Bauer. 2001. "Generativity and Social Involvement Among African-American and Among White Adults." *Journal of Research in Personality* 35: 208–230.

Hartsock, N. 1983. *Money, Sex, and Power: Toward a Feminist Historical Materialism.* Boston: Northeastern University Press.

Hawkeswood, W. 1997. *One of the Children: Gay Black Men in Harlem*. Berkeley: University of California Press.

Heatherton, T., and P. Nichols. 1994. "Conceptual Issues in Assessing Whether Personality Can Change." In *Can Personality Change?*, eds., T. Heatherton and J. Weinberger, 3–18. Washington, DC: American Psychological Association.

Hemphill, E. 1992. *Ceremonies: Prose and Poetry*. New York: Plume.

Henriques, J., W. Hollway, C. Urwin, C. Venn, and V. Walkerdine, eds. 1998. *Changing the Subject: Psychology, Social Regulation and Subjectivity*. London: Routledge.

Herek, G. 2004. "Beyond 'Homophobia': Thinking About Sexual Prejudice and Stigma in the Twenty-First Century." *Sexuality Research and Social Policy* 1(2): 6–24.

Hernton, C. 1986. "On Becoming a Male Anti-Sexist." *The American Voice* 5: 74-101.

Hernton, C. 1990. *The Sexual Mountain and Black Women Writers: Adventures in Sex, Literature, and Real Life*. New York: Anchor.

Hill, D. B., and B. L. Willoughby. 2005. "The Development and Validation of the Genderism and Transphobia Scale." *Sex Roles* 53 (7/8): 531–544.

Hoagland, S. L. 1988. *Lesbian Ethics: Toward a New Value*. Palo Alto: Institute for Lesbian Studies.

Hochschild, A.R. 1994. "The Commercial Spirit of Intimate Life and the Abduction of Feminism: Signs from Women's Advice Books." *Theory, Culture and Society* 11 (2): 1–24.

Hogeland, L. M. 2001. "Against Generational Thinking, or, Some Things That 'Third Wave' Feminism Isn't." *Women's Studies in Communication* 24: 107–121.

Holzkamp, K. 1992. "On Doing Psychology Critically." *Theory and Psychology* 2: 193–204.

hooks, b. 1984. "Men: Comrades in Struggle." In her *Feminist Theory: From Margin to Center*, 67–81. Boston: South End.

hooks, b. 1989. "Feminist Focus on Men: A Comment." In her *Talking Back: Thinking Feminist, Thinking Black*, 127–133. Boston: South End.

hooks, b. 1990. "Representations: Feminism and Black Masculinity." In her *Yearning: Race, Gender, and Cultural Politics*, 65–77. Boston: South End.

hooks, b. 1992a. "Reconstructing Black Masculinity." In her *Black Looks: Race and Representation*, 87–113. Boston: South End.

hooks, b. 1992b. "Men in Feminist Struggle: The Necessary Movement." In *Women Respond to the Men's Movement*, ed., K. L. Hagan, 111–117. San Francisco: Pandora.

hooks, b. 2000a. "Feminist Masculinity." In her *Feminism Is for Everybody: Passionate Politics*, 67–71. Boston: South End.

hooks, b. 2000b. "Visionary Feminism." In her *Feminism Is for Everybody: Passionate Politics*, 10–118. Boston: South End.

Hopkins, P. D. 1998. "How Feminism Made a Man Out of Me: The Proper Subject of Feminism and the Problem of Men." In *Men Doing Feminism*, ed., T. Digby, 33–56. New York: Routledge.

Hopkinson, N., and N. Y. Moore. 2006. *Deconstructing Tyrone: A New Look at Black Masculinity in the Hip-Hop Generation*. San Francisco: Clies.

Hudson-Weems, C. 1993. *Africana Womanism: Reclaiming Ourselves*. Troy, MI: Bedford Publishers.

Hurtado, A. 1996. *The Color of Privilege: Three Blasphemies on Race and Feminism*. Ann Arbor: University of Michigan Press.

Hurtado, A. 2003. *Voicing Chicana Feminisms: Young Women Speak Out on Sexuality and Identity*. New York: New York University Press.

Hutchins, L., and L. Kaahumanu. 1991. *Bi Any Other Name: Bisexual People Speak Out*. Los Angeles: Alyson.

Hutchinson, E. O. 1999. "My Gay Problem, Your Black Problem." In *Black Men on Race, Gender, and Sexuality*, ed., D. Carbado, 303–305. New York: New York University Press.

Ignatiev, N., and Garvey, J. 1996. *Race Traitor*. New York: Routledge.

Ingram, R. B. 2004. *A Black Man's Dilemma: Endangered or Endeared?* Hallandale Beach, FL: Aglob.

Iverson, T. 1996. "A Time to End Privilege." In *Million Man March/Day of Absence: A Commemorative Anthology*, eds., H. Madhubuti and M. Karenga, 93–94. Chicago: Third World.

Jackson, S., and S. Scott. 2004. "The Personal Is Still Political: Heterosexuality, Feminism and Monogamy." *Feminism and Psychology* 14 (1): 151–157.

Jones, S. J. 20001. "Embodying Working-Class Subjectivity and Narrating Self: WeWere the Hired Help." In *From Subjects to Subjectivities: A Handbook of Interpretive Methods*, eds., D. Tolman and M. Brydon-Miller, 3–11. New York: New York University Press.

Kahane, D. 1998. "Male Feminism as Oxymoron." In *Men Doing Feminism*, ed., T. Digby, 213–235. New York: Routledge.

Kaufman, M. 1994. "Men, Feminism, and Men's Contradictory Experiences of Power." In *Theorizing Masculinities*, eds., H. Brod and M. Kaufman, 142–163. Thousand Oaks, CA: Sage.

Kelley, R. D. G. 2002. "This Battlefield Called Life: Black Feminist Dreams." In his *Freedom Dreams: The Black Radical Imagination*, 135–156. Boston: Beacon.

Kimbrell, A. 1995. *The Masculine Mystique: The Politics of Masculinity*. New York: Ballantine.

Kimmel, M. S. 1996. *Manhood in America: A Cultural History*. New York: Free Press.

Kimmel, M. S. 1998. "Who's Afraid of Men Doing Feminism?" In *Men Doing Feminism*, ed., T. Digby, 57–68. New York: Routledge.

Kimmel, M. S. 2002. "Foreword." In *Masculinity Studies and Feminist Theory: New Directions*, ed., J. K. Gardiner, ix–xi. New York: Columbia University Press.

Kimmel, M. S., J. Hearn, and R. W. Connell, eds. 2005. *Handbook on Men and Masculinities*. Thousand Oaks, CA: Sage.

Kimmel, M. S., and T. Mosmiller, eds. 1992. *Against the Tide: Profeminist Men in the United States, 1776–1990*. Boston: Beacon.

Kivel, P. 1992. *Men's Work: How to Stop the Violence that Tears Our Lives Apart*. New York: Ballantine.

Klein, R. D. 1989. "The 'Men Problem' in Women's Studies: The Expert, the Ignoramus, and the Poor Dear." In *Radical Voices: A Decade of Feminist Resistance from Women's Studies International Forum*, eds., R. Klein and D. Steinberg, 106–120. Oxford: Pergamon.

Kotre, J. 1999. *Make It Count*. New York: Free Press.

Langellier, K. M. 2001. "You're Marked: Breast Cancer, Tattoo, and the Narrative Performance of Identity." In *Narrative and Identity: Studies in Autobiography, Self and Culture*, D. Carbaugh and J. Brockmeier, 145–184. Philadelphia: John Benjamin.

Langellier, K. M., and D. L Hall. 1989. "Interviewing Women: A Phenomenological Approach to Feminist Communication Research." In *Doing Research on Women's Communication: Perspectives on Theory and Method*, eds., K. Carter and C. Spitzak, 193–220. Norwood, NJ: Ablex.

Lemelle, A. J., and J. J. Battle. 2004. "Black Masculinity Matters in Attitudes Toward Gays Males." *Journal of Homosexuality* 47(1): 39–51.

Lemons, G. 1998. To be Black, Male, and Feminist. In *Feminism and Men*, eds., S. P. Schacht and D. W. Ewing, 43–66. New York: New York University Press.

Lorber, J. 2000. "Using Gender to Undo Gender: A Feminist Degendering Movement." *Feminist Theory* 1 (1): 79–95.

Lorde, A. 1982. *Zami, A New Spelling of My Name*. New York: Crossing Press.

Lorde, A. 1984. *Sister Outsider: Essays and Speeches*. New York: Crossing Press.

Luck, M., M. Bamford, and P. Williamson. 2000. *Men's Health: Perspectives, Diversity, and Paradox.* Oxford/Malden, MA: Blackwell Science.

Mack-Canty, C., and S. Wright. 2004. "Family Values as Practiced by Feminist Parents: Bridging Third-Wave Feminism and Family Pluralism." *Journal of Family Issues* 25, 851–880.

Madhubuti, H. 1994. "Rape, the Male Crime: On Becoming Anti-Rapist." In his *Claiming Earth: Race, Rage, Rape, Redemption,* 111–126. Chicago: Third World.

Malik, S., S. Sorenson, and C. Aneshensel. 1997. "Community and Dating Violence among Adolescents: Perpetration and Victimization." *Journal of Adolescent Health* 21: 291–302.

Malin, B. J. 2005. *American Masculinity Under Clinton: Popular Media and the Nineties 'Crisis of Masculinity.'* New York: Peter Lang.

Mama, A. 1995. *Beyond the Masks: Race, Gender and Subjectivity.* New York: Routledge.

Marable, M. 1983. "Groundings with My Sisters: Patriarchy and the Exploitation of Black Women." In his *How Capitalism Underdeveloped Black America,* 69–103. Boston: South End.

Marecek, J., M. Fine, and L. Kidder. 2001. "Working Between Two Worlds: Qualitative Methods and Psychology." In *From Subjects to Subjectivities: A Handbook of Interpretive Methods,* eds., D. Tolman and M. Brydon-Miller, 29–41. New York: New York University Press.

Marshall, W. L., S. Hudson, R. Jones, and Y. Fernandez. 1995. "Empathy in Sex Offenders." *Clinical Psychology Review* 13: 99–113.

Martin, P. Y. 2004. "Gender as A Social Institution." *Social Forces* 82 (4): 1249–1273.

Martin-Baro, I. 1994. *Writings for a Liberation Psychology.* Cambridge: Harvard University Press.

Maslow, A. 1968. *Toward a Psychology of Being,* 2nd ed. New York: Van Nostrand.

Mauer, M. 2001. "Crime, Politics, and Community Since the 1990s." In *Prison Masculinities,* eds., D. Sabo, T. Kupers, and W. London, 46–53. Philadelphia: Temple University Press.

Maxwell, J. A. 1996. *Qualitative Research Design: An Interactive Approach.* Thousand Oaks, CA: Sage.

Mays, V. M., A. Yancey, S. Cochran, M. Weber, and J. Fielding. 2002. "Heterogeneity of Health Disparities among Black, Hispanic, and Asian American Women: Unrecognized Influences of Sexual Orientation." *American Journal of Public Health* 92(4): 632–639.

McAdams, D., and R. Paulson. 1993. "Specifying the Relationship Between Social Ties and Activism." *American Journal of Sociology* 99: 640–667.

McAdams, D. P. 1993. *The Stories We Live By: Personal Myths and the Making of the Self.* New York: Guilford.

McAdams, D. P. 1994. "Can Personality Change? Levels of Stability and Growth in Personality Across the Life Span." In *Can Personality Change?*, eds., T. Heatherton and J. Weinberger, 299–313. Washington, DC: American Psychological Association.

McAdams, D. P., and P. J. Bowman. 2001. "Narrating Life's Turning Points: Redemption and Contamination." In *Turns in the Road*, eds., D. McAdams, R. Josselson, and A. Lieblich, 3–34. Washington, DC: American Psychological Association.

McAdams, D. P., and E. de St. Aubin. 1998. *Generativity and Adult Development: How and Why We Care for the Next Generation.* Washington, DC: American Psychological Association.

McAdams, D. P., A. Diamond, E. de St. Aubin, and E. Mansfield. 1997. "Stories of Commitment: The Psychosocial Construction of Generative Lives." *Journal of Personality and Social Psychology* 72: 678–694.

McAdams, D. P., H. Hart, and S. Maruna. 1998. "The Anatomy of Generativity." In *Generativity and Adult Development: How and Why We Care for the Next Generation*, eds., D. McAdams and E. de St. Aubin, 7–43. Washington, DC: American Psychological Association.

McAdoo, J. 1993. "The Role of African American Fathers: An Ecological Perspective." *Families in Society* 74: 28–35.

McAdoo, H. P. 2002. "African American Parenting. In *Handbook of Prenting: Vol. 4. Social Conditions and Applied Parenting* 2nd ed., ed., M. Bornstein, 47–58. Mahwah, NJ: Lawrence Erlbaum.

McAdoo, H. P., and J. L. McAdoo. 2002. " The Dynamics of African American Fathers' Family Roles." In *Black Children: Social, Educational, and Parental Environments*, ed., H. P. McAdoo, 2nd ed., 3–11. Thousand Oaks, CA: Sage.

McCall, L. 2005. "The Complexity of Intersectionality." *Signs* 30(3): 1771–1800.

McCarthy, J. D., and M. N. Zald. 1977. "Resource Mobilization and Social Movements." *American Journal of Sociology* 82: 1212–1242.

McClaurin, I., ed. 2001. *Black Feminist Anthropology: Theory, Politics, Praxis, and Poetics.* New Brunswick, NJ: Rutgers University Press.

Men Stopping Violence. 1996. "An Open Letter to Minister Farrakhan." Unpublished document.

Messerschmidt, J. W. 2001. "Masculinities, Crime, and Prison." In *Prison Masculinities*, eds., D. Sabo, T. Kupers, and W. London, 46–53. Philadelphia: Temple University Press.

Messman, S. J., D. J. Canary, and K. S. Hause, K. S. 2000. "Motives to Remain Platonic, Equity, and the Use of Maintenance Strategies in Opposite-SexFriendships." *Journal of Social and Personal Relationships* 17 (1): 67–94.

Messner, M.A. 1998. "Radical Feminist and Socialist Feminist Men's Movements in the United States." In *Feminism and Men: Reconstructing Gender Relations*, eds., S. Schacht and D. Ewing, 67–85. New York: Routledge.

Miller, J. B. 1982. *Women and Power*. No. 1. Wellesley, MA: Wellesley's Centers for Women.

Millner, D. 1997. *The Sistahs' Rules: Secrets for Meeting, Getting, and Keeping a Good Black Man—Not to Be Confused with The Rules*. New York: Quill.

Mincy, R. 2006. *Black Males Left Behind*. Washington, DC: Urban Institute.

Mishler, E. G. 1999. *Storylines: Craftartists' Narratives of Identity*. Cambridge: Harvard University Press.

Monsour, M. 1988. Cross-Sex Friendships in a Changing Society: A Comparative Analysis of Cross-Sex Friendships, Same-Sex Friendships, and Romantic Relationships. Unpublished doctoral dissertation. University of Illinois, Champaign.

Monsour, M. 2002. *Women and Men as Friends: Relationships Across the Life Span in the 21st Century*. Mahwah, NJ: Lawrence Erlbaum."

Monsour, M., C. Beard, B. Harris, and N. Kurzweil. 1994. "Challenges Confronting Cross-Sex Friendships: 'Much Ado about Nothing?' *Sex Roles* 31 (1/2): 55–77.

Moore, M. 2001. *Stupid White Men: And Other Sorry Excuses for the State of the Nation!* New York: Regan.

Morse, B. J. 1995. "Beyond the Conflict Tactics Scale: Assessing Gender Differences in Partner Violence." *Violence and Victims* 10: 251–272.

Murphy, P. F., ed. 2004. *Feminism and Masculinities*. New York: Oxford University Press.

Mutua, A. D., ed. 2006. *Progressive Black Masculinities*. New York: Routledge.

Neal, M. A. 2005. *New Black Man*. New York: Routledge.

Nandi, M. 2002. "Re/Constructing Black Masculinity in Prison." *Journal of Men's Studies* 11 (1): 91–107.

Nardi, P. 1992. *Men's Friendships*. Thousand Oaks, CA: Sage.

Nardi, P. 1999. *Gay Men's Friendships: Invincible Communities.* Chicago: University of Chicago Press.

Nero, C. I. 1999. "Signifying on the Black Church." In *Black Men on Race, Gender, and Sexuality*, ed., D. Carbado, 276–282. New York: New York University Press.

Neville, H., and A. O. Pugh. 1997. "Gender and Culture-Specific Factors InfluencingAfrican American Women's Reporting Patterns and Perceived Social Support Following Sexual Assault: An Exploratory Investigation." *Violence Against Women* 3: 361–381.

Newton, J. 2005. "Fathers of Themselves." In *From Panthers to Promise Keepers: Rethinking the Men's Movement*, 157–183. Lanham, MD: Rowman & Littlefield.

Newton, J., and J. Stacey. 1997. "The Men We Left Behind Us: Narratives Around and about Feminism from White, Leftwing, Academic Men." In *From Sociology to Cultural Studies: New Perspectives*, ed., E. Long, 426–451. Malden, MA: Blackwell.

Nielsen, J. M., G. Walden, and C. A. Kunkel. 2000. "Gendered Heteronormativity: Empirical Illustrations in Everyday Life." *Sociological Quarterly* 41(2): 283–296.

O'Beirne, K. 2006. *Women Who Make the World Worse: And How Their Radical Feminist Assault Is Ruining Our Schools, Families, Military, and Sports.* New York: Penguin.

Okin, S. M. 1989. *Justice, Gender and the Family.* New York: Basic Books.

Oliver, M. L., and Shapiro, T. M. 1995. *Black Wealth/White Wealth: A New Perspective on Racial Inequality.* New York: Routledge.

Oliver, W. 1998. *The Violent Social World of Black Men.* New York: Jossey-Bass.

O'Meara, D. 1994. "Cross-Sex Friendship Opportunity Challenge: Uncharted Terrain for Exploration." *Personal Relationship Issues* 2 (1): 4–7.

Omolade, B. 1994. *The Rising Song of African American Women.* New York: Routledge.

O'Neill, P. 1998. *Negotiating Consent in Psychotherapy.* 36–39. New York: New York University Press.

Painter, N. I. 1993. "Sojourner Truth." In *Black Women in America: An Historical Encyclopedia*, Vol. 2, ed. D. Clark-Hine, 1172–1176. Bloomington: Indiana University Press.

Palkovitz, R. 1984. "Parental Attitudes and Fathers' Interactions with Their 5-month Old Infants." *Developmental Psychology* 20: 1054–1060.

Parker, P. 1978. *Movement in Black: The Collected Poetry of Pat Parker.* Ithaca, NY: Firebrand.

Parker, I., and R. Spears. 1996. *Psychology and Society: Radical Theory and Practice.* London: Pluto.

Parrish, G. 1992. "Male Supremacy and the Men's Pro-Feminist Movement. See http://www.nostatusquo,com/ACLU/ohBROTHER/retrogeov2.html. Retrieved April 14, 2007.

Patterson, C. J. 1992. "Children of Lesbian and Gay Parents." *Child Development* 63 (5): 1025–1039.

Peterson, B. E., K. A. Smirles, and P. A. Wentworth. 1997. "Generativity and Authoritarianism: Implications for Personality, Political Involvement, and Parenting." *Journal of Personality and Social Psychology* 72: 1202–1216.

Pharr, S. 1988. *Homophobia: A Weapon of Sexism.* Little Rock, AR: Chardon.

Pollack, W. 1999. *Real Boys: Rescuing Our Sons from the Myths of Boyhood.* New York: Owl.

Pope, H. G., K. A. Phillips, and R. Olivardia. 2000. *The Adonis Complex: The Secret Crisis of Male Body Obsession.* New York: Free Press.

Porter, M. 2001. *The Conspiracy to Destroy Black Women.* Chicago: African American Images.

Powell, K. 2000. "Confessions of a Recovering Misogynist." *Ms.* (April/May) 10: 72–77.

Price, J. 1999. *Navigating Differences: Friendships between Gay and Straight Men.* New York: Haworth.

Purvis, M. and T. Ward. 2006. "The Role of Culture in Understanding Child Sexual Offending: Examining Feminist Perspectives." *Aggression and Violent Behavior* 11: 298–312.

Ramsey, G. 1996. *Transsexuals: Candid Answers to Private Questions.* Freedom, CA: Crossing.

Reader's Companion to U.S. Women's History. 1998. Editors: W. P. Mankiller,G. Mink, B. Smith, M. Navarro, and G. Steinem. New York: Houghton-Mifflin.

Reagon, B. J. 1983. "Coalition Politics: Turning the Century." In *Home Girls: A Black Feminist Anthology,* ed., B. Smith, 356–368. New York: Kitchen Table.

Real, T. 1997. *I Don't Want to Talk About It: Overcoming the Secret Legacy of Male Depression.* New York: Simon and Schuster.

Red Collective. 1978. *The Politics of Sexuality in Capitalism.* London: Red Collective/Publications Distribution Cooperative.

Reese, R. 2004. *American Paradox: Young Black Men.* Durham, NC: Carolina Academic Press.

Rich, A. 1980. "Compulsory Heterosexuality and Lesbian Existence." *Signs* 5(4): 631–660.

Richie, B. E. 1994. *Compelled to Crime: The Gender Entrapment of Battered Black Women.* New York: Routledge.

Richie, B. E. 2000. "A Black Feminist Reflection on the Antiviolence Movement." *Signs* 25(4): 1133–1137.

Riessman, C. K. 1993. *Narrative Analysis.* Newbury Park, CA: Sage.

Risman, B. J. 1998. *Gender Vertigo: American Families in Transition.* New Haven: Yale University Press.

Risman, B. J. 2004. "Gender as a Social Structure: Theory Wrestling with Activism." *Gender and Society* 18 (4): 429–450.

Risman, B. J., and K. Myers 1997. "As the Twig Is Bent: Children Reared in Feminist Households." *Qualitative Sociology* 20: 229–252.

Roberts, D. E. 1998. "The Absent Black Father." In *Lost Fathers: The Politics of Fatherlessness in America*, ed., C. Daniels, 145–161. New York: St. Martin's Press.

Robinson, S. 2000. *Marked Men: White Masculinity in Crisis.* New York: Columbia University Press.

Robinson, V. 1997. "My Baby Just Cares for Me: Feminism, Heterosexuality, and Non-Monogamy." *Journal of Gender Studies* 6 (2): 143–158.

Robinson, V. 2003. "Problematic Proposals: Marriage and Cohabitation." *Feminism and Psychology* 13 (4): 437–441.

Rogers, C. R. 1987. "Comments on the Issue of Equality in Psychotherapy." *Journal of Humanistic Psychology* 27 (1): 38–40.

Rosa, B. 1994. "Anti-Monogamy: Radical Challenge to Compulsory Heterosexuality." In *Stirring It: Challenges for Feminism*, eds., G. Griffin, M. Hester, S. Rai, and S. Roseneil, 107–120. London: Taylor and Francis.

Rose, S. 1985. "Same- and Cross-Sex Friendships and the Psychology of Homosociality." *Sex Roles* 12: 63–74.

Rosenwald, G. C., and R. L. Ochberg. 1992. "Introduction: Life Stories, Cultural Politics, and Self-Understanding." In *Storied Lives: The Cultural Politics of Self-Understanding*, eds., G. Rosenwald and R. Ochberg, 1–18. New Haven: Yale University Press.

Rossinow, D. 1998. *The Politics of Authenticity: Liberalism, Christianity, and the New Left in America.* New York: Columbia University Press.

Rubin, L. B. 1985. *Just Friends: The Role of Friendship in Our Lives*. New York: Harper and Row.

Rubin, H. S. 1998. "Reading Like a (Transsexual) Man." In *Men Doing Feminism*, ed., T. Digby, 305–324. New York: Routledge.

Russell, G. 2000. *Voted Out: The Psychological Consequences of Anti-Gay Politics*. New York: New York University Press.

Sabo, D., and D. F. Gordon. 1995. *Men's Health and Illness: Gender, Power, and the Body*. Thousand Oaks, CA: Sage.

Salaam, K. 1980. "The Struggle to Smash Sexism is a Struggle to Develop Women."In his *Our Women Keep Our Skies from Falling*, 41–52. New Orleans: Nkombo.

Salaam, K. 1994a. "Impotence Need Not be Permanent: The Decline of Black Men Writing." In his *What Is Life? Reclaiming the Black Blues Self*, 131–148. Chicago: Third World.

Salaam, K. 1994b. "Why I Read Out/Look." In his *What Is Life? Reclaiming the Black Blues Self*, 153–164. Chicago: Third World.

Salaam, K. 1996. "A Million Is Just a Beginning." In *Million Man March/Day of Absence: A Commemorative Anthology*, eds., H. Madhubuti and M. Karenga, 110–111. Chicago: Third World.

Sanderson, S., and V. L. Sanders Thompson. 2002. "Factors Associated with Perceived Paternal Involvement in Childrearing." *Sex Roles* 46(3/4): 99–111.

Sandfield, A. and C. Percy. 2003. "Accounting for Single Status: Heterosexism and Ageism in Heterosexual Women's Talk about Marriage." *Feminism and Psychology* 13(4): 475–488.

Sapadin, L. A. 1988. "Friendship and Gender: Perspectives of Professional Men and Women." *Journal of Social and Personal Relationships* 5: 387–403.

Savin-Williams, R. C. 1994. "Verbal and Physical Abuse as Stressors in the Lives of Lesbian, Gay Male, and Bisexual Youths: Associations with School Problems, Running Away, Substance Abuse, Prostitution, and Suicide." *Journal of Consulting Clinical Psychology* 62: 261–269.

Schacht, S. P., and D. W. Ewing. 1998. "The Many Paths of Feminism: Can Men Travel Any of Them?" In *Feminism and Men: Reconstructing Gender Relations*, eds., S. P. Schacht and D. W. Ewing, 119–145. New York: New York University Press.

Schlafly, P. 2003. *Feminist Fantasies*. Dallas: Spence.

Schulte, L. J., and J. Battle. 2004. "The Relative Importance of Ethnicity and Religion in Predicting Attitudes Towards Gays and Lesbians." *Journal of Homosexuality* 47(2): 127–141.

Schwartz, P. 1994. *Peer Marriage: How Love Between Equals Really Works*. New York: Free Press.

Segal, L. 1990. *Slow Motion: Changing Masculinities, Changing Men*. New Brunswick, NJ: Rutgers University Press.

Segal, L. 1999. "Gender Anxieties at the Limits of Psychology." In her *Why Feminism?*, 149–173. New York: Columbia University Press.

Segell, M. 2000. *Standup Guy: Manhood After Feminism*. New York: Villard.

Sellars, N. 1995. "Coming Out Het." http://www.xyonline.net/het.shtml. Retrieved April 14, 2007.

Settles, I. H. 2006. "Use of an Intersectional Framework to Understand Black Women's Racial and Gender Identities." *Sex Roles* 54: 589–601.

Shakur, A. 1987. *Assata: An Autobiography*. Chicago: Lawrence Hill.

Shiffman, M. 1987. "The Men's Movement: An Exploratory Empirical Investigation." In *Changing Men: New Directions in Research on Men and Masculinity*, ed., M. Kimmel, 295–314. Newbury Park, CA: Sage.

Silliman, J., M. Fried, L. Ross, and E. Gutierrez. 2004. *Undivided Rights: Women of Color Organize for Reproductive Justice*. Boston: South End.

Silverstein, L. B., and C. R. Auerbach. 1999. "Deconstructing the Essential Father." *American Psychologist* 54: 397–407.

Simien, E. M. 2006. *Black Feminist Voices in Politics*. New York: SUNY.

Sloan, T. W., ed. 2000. *Critical Psychology: Voices for Change*. New York: St. Martin.

Smethhurst, J. E. 2005. *The Black Arts Movement: Literary Nationalism in the 1960s and 1970s*. Chapel Hill: University of North Carolina Press.

Smith, B. ed., 1983. *Home Girls: A Black Feminist Anthology*. New York: Kitchen Table.

Smith, B. 1998. *The Truth That Never Hurts: Writings on Race, Gender, and Freedom*.New Brunswick, NJ: Rutgers University Press.

Smith, C. M. 1986. "Bruce Nugent: Bohemian of the Harlem Renaissance." In *In the Life: A Black Gay Anthology*, ed., J. Beam, 209–220. Boston: Alyson.

Smitherman, G. 1996. "A Womanist Look at the Million Man March." In *Million Man March/Day of Absence: A Commemorative Anthology*, eds., H. Madhubuti and M. Karenga, 104. Chicago: Third World.

Snarey, J. 1993. *How Fathers Care for the Next Generation*. Cambridge: Harvard University Press.

Snodgrass, J. 1977. *A Book of Readings for Men Against Sexism*. Albion, CA: Times Change Press.

Sommers, C. H. 2001. *The War Against Boys: How Misguided Feminism Is Harming Our Young Men*. New York: Touchstone.

Spelman, E. V. 1988. *Inessential Woman: Problems of Exclusion in Feminist Thought*. Boston: Beacon.

Springer, K. 1999. "Four Mission Statements." In *Still Lifting, Still Climbing: African American Women's Contemporary Activism*, ed., K. Springer, 37–46. New York: New York University Press.

Springer, K. 2001. "Third Wave Black Feminism?" *Signs* 27: 1059–1082.

Stanton, E. C. 1969. *History of Woman Suffrage*, Vol 2. New York: Arno.

Starhawk. 1987. *Truth or Dare: Encounters with Power, Authority, and Mystery*. San Francisco: Harper and Row.

Stewart, A. J., and C. McDermott. 2004. "Gender in Psychology." *Annual Review of Psychology* 55: 519–544.

Stewart, J. B. 2004. "Perspectives on Black Families from Contemporary Soul Music: The Case of Millie Jackson." In his *Flight in Search of Vision*, 153–165. Trenton, NJ: Africa World.

Stockdill, B. C. 2001. "Forging a Multidimensional Oppositional Consciousness: Lessons from Community-Based AIDS Activism." In *Oppositional Consciousness: The Subjective Roots of Social Protest*, eds., J. Mansbridge and A. Morris, 204–237. Chicago: University of Chicago Press.

Stoltenberg, J. 1989. *Refusing to be a Man: Essays on Sex and Justice*. Portland, OR: Breitenbush.

Stoltenberg, J. 1993. *The End of Manhood: A Book for Men of Conscience*. New York: Dutton.

Straus, A., and J. Corbin. 1990. *Basics of Qualitative Analysis*. Newbury Park, CA: Sage.

Straus, M., and J. Stewart. 1999. "Corporal Punishment by American Parents: National Data on Prevalence, Chronicity, Severity, and Duration, in Relation to Child and Family Characteristics." *Clinical Child and Family Psychology Review* 2: 55–70.

Straus, M., Sugarman, D., and J. Giles-Sims. 1997. "Spanking by Parents and Subsequent Antisocial Behavior of Children." *Archives of Pediatrics & Adolescent Medicine* 151: 761–767.

Strube, M. J., and A. Delitto. 1994. "Reliability and Measurement Theory." In *Gait Aanalysis: Theory and Applications*, eds., R. L. Clark and C. A. Oatis, 88–111. New York: Mosby.

Stryker, Sheldon. 2000. "Identity Competition: Key to Differential Social Movement Participation?" In *Self, Identity, and Social*

Movements, eds., S. Stryker, T. Owens, and R. White, 21–40. Minneapolis: University of Minnesota Press.

Stryker, S., T. Owens, and R. W. White, eds. 2000. *Self, Identity, and Social Movements*. Minneapolis: University of Minnesota Press.

Sullivan, E. V. 1984. *A Critical Psychology*. New York: Plenum.

Summers, M. 2002. "This Immoral Practice: The Prehistory of Homophobia in Black Nationalist Thought." In *Gender Nonconformity, Race, and Sexuality: Charting the Connections*, ed., T. Lester. 21–43. Madison: University of Wisconsin Press.

Summers, M. 2004. *Manliness and Its Discontents: The Black Middle Class and the Transformation of Masculinity, 1900–1930*. Chapel Hill: University of North Carolina Press.

Swan, S. C., and D. L. Snow. 2006. "The Development of a Theory of Women's Use of Violence in Intimate Relationships." *Violence Against Women* 12(1): 1026–1045.

Swigart, J. 1991. *The Myth of the Bad Mother: The Emotional Realities of Mothering*. New York: Doubleday.

T'Shaka. O. 1995. *Return to the Afrikan Mother Principle of Male and Female Equality*. Oakland: Pan Afrikan Publishers.

Tappan, M. B. 2001. "Interpretive Psychology: Stories, Circles, and Understanding Lived Experience." In *From Subjects to Subjectivities: A Handbook of Interpretive Methods*, eds., D. Tolman and M. Brydon-Miller, 45–56. New York: New York University Press.

Tate, G. 1986. "Say, Brother." *Changing Men* 17: 6.

Terborg-Penn, R. 1997. "Black Male Perspectives on the Nineteenth-Century Woman."In *The Afro-American Woman: Struggles and Images*, eds., S. Harley and R. Terborg-Penn, 28–42. Baltimore: Black Classic.

Thomas, K. 1996. "Ain't Nothin' Like the Real Thing: Black Masculinity, Gay Sexuality, and the Jargon of Authenticity." In *Representing Black Men*, eds., M. Blount and G. P. Cunningham, 55–69. New York: Routledge.

Tjaden, P., and N. Thoennes. 2000. *Full Report of the Prevalence, Incidence, and Consequences of Violence Against Women: Findings from the National Violence Against Women Survey* (NCJ 183781). Washington, DC: Department of Justice, National Institute of Justice.

Tolman, C. W., ed. 1991. *Positivism in Psychology: Historical and Contemporary Problems*. New York: Springer-Verlag.

Tolman, C. W. 1994. *Psychology, Society, and Subjectivity: An Introduction to German Critical Psychology*. New York: Routledge.

Tolman, C. W., and W. Maiers, eds. 1991. *Critical Psychology: Contributions to an Historical Science of the Subject.* Cambridge: Cambridge University Press.

Tolman, D. L., and M. Brydon-Miller. 2001. "Interpretive and Participatory Research Methods: Moving toward Subjectivities." In their *From Subjects to Subjectivities: A Handbook of Interpretive Methods,* 3–11. New York: New York University Press.

Tuttle, L. 1986. *Encyclopedia of Feminism.* New York: Facts on File.

Van Dyke, N. 2003. "Crossing Movement Boundaries: Factors that Facilitate Coalition Protest by American College Students, 1930–1990." *Social Problems* 50(2): 226–250.

Waldron, V. R. 2003. "Relationship Maintenance in Organizational Settings." In *Maintaining Relationships Through Communication: Relational, Contextual, and Cultural Variations,* eds., D. Canary and M. Dainton, 163–184. Mahwah, NJ: Lawrence Erlbaum.

Walker, A. 1983. *In Search of Our Mothers' Gardens: Womanist Prose.* New York: Harcourt, Brace, and Jovanovich.

Walkerdine, V., ed. 2001. "The Meaning of Critical Psychology in the Twenty-First Century" [Special Issue]. *The International Journal of Critical Psychology 1:* 9–15.

Washington, E. 1996. *Uncivil War: The Struggle Between Black Men and Women.* Chicago: Noble.

Washington, P. A. 2001. "Disclosure Patterns of Black Female Sexual Assault Survivors." *Violence Against Women* 7: 1254–1283.

Webster's New Collegiate Dictionary. 1979. 599. Springfield, MA: G. & C. Merriam-Webster.

Weems, C. H. 1993. *Africana Womanism: Reclaiming Ourselves.* Troy, MI: Bedford.

Weis, L., M. Fine, S. Weseen, and M. Wong. 2000. "Qualitative Research, Representations, and Social Responsibilities." In *Speed Bumps: A Student-Friendly Guide to Qualitative Research,* eds., L. Weis and M. Fine, 32–66. New York: Columbia University Teachers College Press.

Werking, K. 1997. *We're Just Good Friends: Women and Men in Nonromantic Relationships.* New York: Guilford.

Wescott, M. 1992. "The Discursive Expression of Human Freedom." *American Behavioral Scientist* 36: 73–87.

Wescott, M. 1994. "Freedom and Civilization: When More Is Less." *Canadian Psychology* 35: 159–166.

West, C. M. 2002. *Violence in the Lives of Black Women: Battered, Black and Blue.* New York: Haworth.

Whannel, G. 2001. *Media Sport Stars: Masculinities and Moralities*. New York: Routledge.

White, A. M. 2001. "I Am Because We Are: Combined Race and Gender Political Consciousness Among African American Women and Men Anti-Rape Activists." *Women's Studies International Forum* 24: 11–24.

White, A. M. 2001/2002. "Ain't I a Feminists? Black Men as Advocates of Feminism." *Womanist Theory and Research* 3/4: 28–34.

White, A. M. 2006a. "Racial and Gender Attitudes as Predictors of Feminist Activism among Self-Identified African American Feminists?" *Journal of Black Psychology* 32(4): 1–24.

White, A. M. 2006b. "You've Got a Friend: African American Men's Cross-Sex Feminist Friendships and Their Influence on Perceptions of Masculinity and Women." *Journal of Social and Personal Relationships* 23(4): 523–542.

White, A. M. 2006c. "African American Feminist Masculinities: Personal Narratives of Redemption, Contamination, and Peak Turning Points." *Journal of Humanistic Psychology* 46(3): 255–280.

White, A. M. 2006d. "African American Feminist Fathers' Narratives of Parenting." *Journal of Black Psychology* 32(1): 43–71.

White, A. M., and T. Peretz. 2007. "Two Profeminist Organizations and Their African American Founders." Unpublished manuscript.

White, A. M., C. Potgieter, M. Strube, S. Fisher, and E. Umana. 1997. "An African-Centered, Black Feminist Approach to Understanding Attitudes that Counter Social Dominance." *Journal of Black Psychology* 23: 82–86.

White, E. C. 1994. *Chain, Chain, Change: For Black Women in Abusive Relationship*. Seattle: Seal.

White, E. F. 2001. *Dark Continent of Our Bodies: Black Feminism and the Politics of Respectability*. Philadelphia: Temple University Press.

White Ribbon Campaign. 1991. "Breaking Men's Silence to End Men's Violence." Website. http://www.whiteribbon.ca/. Retrieved April 14, 2007.

Wilcox, W. B. 2004. *Soft Patriarchs, New Men: How Christianity Shapes Father and Husbands*. Chicago: University of Chicago Press.

Williams, D. S. 1993. *Sisters in the Wilderness: The Challenge of Womanist God-Talk*. Maryknoll, NY: Orbis.

Williams, R. Y. 2004. *The Politics of Public Housing: Black Women's Struggles Against Urban Inequality*. New York: Oxford University Press.

Wilson, W. J. 1996. *When Work Disappears: The World of the New Urban Poor.* New York: Knopf.

Wolcott, H. 1994. *Transforming Qualitative Data.* 61–67. Thousand Oaks, CA: Sage.

Wright, P. H. 1989. "Gender Differences in Adults' Same- and Cross-Gender Friendships." In *Older Adult Friendships*, eds., R. Adams and R. Blieszner, 197–221. Newbury Park, CA: Sage.

Wright, P. H., and Scanlon, M. B. 1991. "Gender Role Orientations and Friendship: Some Attenuation, but Gender Differences Abound." *Sex Roles* 24 (9/10): 551–561.

Wyatt, G. E., C. M. Notgrass, and G. Gordon. 1995. "The Effects of African American Women's Sexual Revictimization: Strategies for Prevention." In *Sexual Assault and Abuse: Sociocultural Context of Prevention*, ed., C. F. Swift. 111–134. Binghampton, NY: Haworth.

Young, I. M. 1990. *Justice and the Politics of Difference.* Princeton: Princeton University Press.

Zimmerman, T. S., K. E. Holm, and M. E. Starrels. 2001. "A Feminist Analysis of Self-Help Bestsellers for Improving Relationships: A Decade Review." *Journal of Marital and Family Therapy* 27 (2): 165–75.

INDEX

resource mobilization theory, 226n22
restraining orders, 75–76
Rex (study subject), 14, 16t
  biographical sketch of, 26–27
  friendships of, 124–25, 149–50
  on his family, 54–55
  NOMAS and, 176–77
  political activism of, 181
  turning points for, 68t, 76
Richie, Beth, 179
Roberts, Dorothy, 158–59
Rogers, Carl, 95
Rules, The (book), 85–86, 90
Rustin, Bayard, 42

Sankofa (film), 190
Schwarzenegger, Arnold, 214n3
Scott, S., 107
sexism. *See* patriarchal power
sexual abuse. *See* childhood sexual
  abuse
Shakur, Assata, 114
Shange, Ntozake, 132
Simien, Evelyn, 13, 218n8
Sistahs' Rules, The (book), 86
Smethurst, J. E., 219n27
Smith, Barbara, 123, 139
SNCC. *See* Student Nonviolent
  Coordinating Committee
Snow, D. L., 221n63
social theory. *See* critical psychology
sociobiology, 156
Solomon (study subject), 16t, 232n10
  biographical sketch of, 27–28
  on civil rights movement, 42–43,
    154
  on domestic violence, 56–59
  political activism of, 181, 183
  relationships of, 86, 107–9, 130–31,
    148–49
  turning points for, 65t–66t, 76,
    80–81
Soyinka (study subject), 16t
  biographical sketch of, 28
  on child rearing, 172
  on domestic violence, 49–50

friendships of, 121–22, 136–38
homophobia and, 136–37, 153–54
on Million Man March, 44
NOMAS and, 176–77
political activism of, 181, 190
turning points for, 63t, 71–74, 76
Stewart, J., 166
stigmatized identity, 140, 150, 159–60
Straus, M., 166
Student Nonviolent Coordinating
  Committee (SNCC), 24, 41–42, 79,
    88
  See also civil rights movement
substance abuse, 114, 142, 151
  behavioral change and, 227n8
  domestic violence and, 50–51
  Nation of Islam and, 47
suffrage movement, 12–13, 26, 211
suicide, 151
Swan, S. C., 221n63

Take Back the Night March, 182
terminology, feminist, 13–14, 17,
  211–12, 214n14
Thailand, 131
Thomas, Clarence, 43
Tillery, Linda, 129
Titus (Bible book), 35
Toussaint (study subject), 16t, 39
  biographical sketch of, 28–29
  on child rearing, 165, 168, 170–71
  on civil rights movement, 42–43
  on domestic violence, 52
  on faculty recruitment, 37–38
  on Million Man March, 45
  political activism of, 180, 181,
    184–85, 189
  relationships of, 105–7, 109, 119–20,
    140
  on religious institutions, 36–37
  turning points for, 66t, 76, 119
transgendered people, 27–28, 42,
  108–9, 130–31, 148–49, 225n48
"transphobia," 149
trauma, childhood, 30, 50, 58–59,
  220n53